Please remember that this is a library book,
and that it belongs only temporarily to each
person who uses it. Be considerate. Do
not write in this, or any, library book.

Transformative
Getaways

JOHN BENSON

· · · · · · · ·

Transformative Getaways

FOR SPIRITUAL GROWTH,
SELF-DISCOVERY, AND
HOLISTIC HEALING

· · ·

An Owl Book

HENRY HOLT AND COMPANY

NEW YORK

Henry Holt and Company, Inc.
Publishers since 1866
115 West 18th Street
New York, New York 10011

Henry Holt® is a registered trademark
of Henry Holt and Company, Inc.

Library of Congress Cataloging-in-Publication Data
Benson, John.
Transformative getaways: for spiritual growth, self-discovery,
and holistic healing / John Benson.—1st Owl Book ed.
p.   cm.
"An Owl book."
Includes bibliographical references and index.
1. Retreats—United States—Directories.   I. Title
BL628.B443   1996   95-43027
910'.2'02—dc20   CIP
ISBN 0-8050-4479-5

Henry Holt books are available for special promotions
and premiums. For details contact: Director, Special Markets.

First Owl Book Edition—1996

Designed by Victoria Hartman

Printed in the United States of America
All first editions are printed on acid-free paper. ∞
1   3   5   7   9   10   8   6   4   2

Contents

Foreword

We live in a time when the stress and urgency of everyday life is building. We are exhausted trying to keep up with the pace and responsibilities of modern life. We are experiencing a breakdown in the fabric of society, a loss of community. We feel progressively isolated from nature, trapped by the pressures of our increasingly technological environment. We yearn deeply for those experiences that nurture the soul, that provide healing for body and mind, that elevate our spirits. *Transformative Getaways* is a guide to those places and journeys that are dedicated to offering these experiences.

They're called getaways or retreats, but in truth they are a return or coming home to our real self, to the place within. In a society that separates us from nature, the organizations profiled in this book provide the opportunity to bring together both inner and outer nature.

We all need time in our lives to switch our natural rhythms, to find environs conducive to healing and inner peace. The word *vacation* comes from the Latin *vacare*, which means "to empty." The antidote to our daily busyness is not a vacation filled with "doing," but rather, one providing experiences that open us to "being"—the exploration of the true self.

Each place or journey will provide a unique experience, yet they all hold a common purpose. These are gathering places for those of us who share the desire to leave behind the more superficial realm of daily existence in search of connection with who we really are on a deeper level.

How wonderful to come together with people of like mind and spirit, to honor our bonds with nature, to allow time and space to rejuvenate and nurture our inner selves, and to expand our horizons through learning or adventure. These places offer us the opportunity to tune in to what we each truly need in our lives. This connection with our own humanity further deepens our connection to all of humanity.

Our ancestors lived in small villages in natural environments, so unlike our typical modern setting. Their sense of community lasted an entire lifetime; they knew each other from birth to death, while today we frequently don't even know our neighbors. My experience with groups on journeys and at workshops has convinced me that we can recapture our ancestors' sense of community. It will be different, for we live in a time of constant change, but if we open ourselves to the feeling shared at these centers, we find a community of the heart and spirit that is deeply healing to us all.

Stephan Rechtschaffen, M.D.
Founder, Omega Institute of Holistic Studies,
and author of *Time Shifting: A Guide to
Creating More Time for Your Life*

Acknowledgments

The author is grateful for the assistance of the many people with whom he spoke at the 322 organizations profiled and listed in this book. Virtually without exception, they were tremendously helpful. Fred Rose and Kathy Zemann at the Omega Institute of Holistic Studies were especially helpful in providing referrals to other centers throughout North America.

During this book's conception and creation, a number of people provided creative ideas, feedback and information, and valuable moral and technical support. These friends and associates include Roberta Beckman, Jean-Françoise Benoist, Greg Cambridge, Myra Clark, Jen Forker, Yosh Gloger, Pam Holt, Bill McMillan, Chi Shao, and Heidi Yorkshire.

Special thanks to Henry Holt editor-at-large Bryan Oettel—for recognizing the potential of this book, for patiently convincing me to relinquish self-publication, and for easing the birth of this edition with his good humor and sound editorial advice. Thanks also to literary agent Elizabeth Wales for negotiating the book contract.

Transformative Getaways

The journey to God is merely
the reawakening of the knowledge
of where you are always,
and what you are forever.

A Course in Miracles

Man does not weave the web of life.
He is merely a strand in it.
Whatever he does to the web,
He does to himself.

Chief Seattle

Be a lamp unto yourself.

Shakyamuni Buddha

Who Can Benefit from This Book

This book is for anyone who wishes to get away for a time from the routine of work and family life; to immerse him- or herself in the practices of self-healing and personal and spiritual growth; and to emerge from this experience with life-transforming energy, skills, and wisdom. More specifically, this book may be of help if

- you feel the urge to connect with like-minded souls, to walk once again down familiar spiritual pathways, or to explore new paths

- you suspect you might benefit from learning or practicing a particular healing, centering, or spiritual discipline under the guidance of an experienced teacher

- you would like to delve deeper into the psychological or recovery work to which you are already committed

- you are feeling trapped by negative patterns of thinking, feeling, or behaving

- you are at a major turning point such as getting married, changing careers, or losing a spouse

- you yearn to open up to the shared perspectives, griefs, and joys of your own gender or sexual preference group

- you have recently experienced severe physical or emotional trauma.

This book may also be helpful to teachers and healers who are seeking opportunities, venues, or ideas for their own "host organization."

Exploring This Book

Transformative Getaways profiles 260 host organizations offering more than 3,000 guided adventures, vacations, and retreats ranging in length from weekend getaways to sojourns lasting several months. Included are prayer and meditation retreats, personal growth programs, holistic vacation spas and family camps, emotional and physical recovery programs, healing journeys and pilgrimages, and wilderness and ocean programs such as vision quests and dolphin swims.

A few organizations address virtually all levels of mind/body well-being. Many have a predominantly centering, psychotherapeutic, or spiritual orientation. And some focus primarily on physical health concerns: special diets, recuperation, or general fitness. But all place significant emphasis on healing in a context broader than the physical body alone.

In addition, sixty-five organizations are described briefly at the back of the book. Each has a clear self-transformative focus but, for one reason or another, did not meet the criteria for a profile in this edition.

GENERAL FORMAT

Profiles of organizations are presented in the book's four main chapters: "Single-Site Getaways," "Multisite Getaways," "Journeys to Distant Places," and "Wilderness and Ocean Programs." In these chapters, the organizations are grouped by geographic location, with organization names appearing in alphabetical order within each geographic category. The locations of the single-site organizations are also pinpointed on thirteen regional maps.

For easy access, the indexes appear at the front the book. Four indexes are provided:

- *Alphabetical Index.* A coded profile for each organization (numbered and listed in alphabetical order). It is keyed to the other three indexes by numbers and letters.

- *Program Type Index.* Twenty general categories of transformative processes or experiences facilitated by host organizations.

- *Special Needs and Interests Index.* Fifteen types of people, needs, or interests that are addressed by host organizations.

- *Spiritual/Religious Orientation Index.* Fifteen types of spiritual or religious orientation embraced by a number of host organizations.

At the back of the book you will find the criteria for inclusion of organizations, a list of additional organizations, and a guide to other useful directories.

FORMAT OF THE PROFILES

Each profile includes a description followed by line entries. The description covers the nature of the host organization's programs and services, physical facilities and leisure activities, and staff or visiting teachers. Line entries are for details such as address, phone number and fax number (if there is one), season of operation, summary of program type(s), and program rates.

Profiles of single-site getaways also provide details on lodging, meals, and (in many cases) services available (unless identified as "free" or "courtesy") at additional cost. And profiles in the other chapters include a line noting the regions in which programs are conducted.

Quoted rates usually cover the cost of the entire program: lodging, meals, board, tuition, and airfare (in the case of trips). Otherwise, separate rates are given for tuition, lodging, and meals. Some profiles in the chapter "Journeys to Distant Places" specify separate airfare rates or note that such rates are not included in the package.

The "$" symbol indicates U.S. dollars in all cases except for organizations based in Canada, in which case "$" means Canadian dollars unless stated as "$ U.S."

Other abbreviations: "A/C" for air conditioning; "B&B" for "bed-and-breakfast" (a level of service or a type of inn); "BYO" for "bring your own"; "RV" for "recreational vehicle."

MAKING PLANS

Readers interested in a particular program should call or write the host organization at least several weeks in advance. Since most programs place a limit on the number of participants, reservations are a good idea.

Calling or writing in advance is almost always required in the case of prayer and meditation centers, where unannounced visitors might disrupt the serene environment of a retreat-in-progress. Advance notice may also be required by small centers, where the staff cannot simultaneously tend to the needs of drop-in visitors and workshop participants. So please respect the note "No visits without prior arrangements" (or similar language) when it appears after the phone number of an organization.

Indexes

*F*our indexes are included here. Because of the brevity of expression allowed by codes, the Alphabetical Index can often provide a more complete picture of an organization's programs, activities, and services than is possible in the written profile. The other three indexes allow the reader to identify profiled organizations that address specific interests, needs, and orientations.

Alphabetical Index

In this index, each organization name is followed by numbers, capital letters, and lowercase letters. Each number is the code number for a category in the Program Type Index. Each capital letter is the code letter for a category in the Special Needs and Interests Index. And each lowercase letter is the code letter for a category in the Spiritual/Religious Orientation Index.

In each line, the name of the organization is preceded by a number used to identify the organization in the other three indexes. And each line ends with a number indicating the page on which the organization is described.

Program Type Index

This index lists and defines twenty general categories of programs.
Each definition is followed by numbers corresponding to the numbered
listings in the Alphabetical Index, so readers can see which therapies
and activities the various organizations have to offer.

1. **Body cleansing:** colonics, fasting, and spa treatments.
   4, 11, 25, 26, 33, 42, 57, 83, 85, 105, 113, 137, 152, 156, 187, 188, 191,
   193, 201, 209, 218, 241, 246

2. **Bodywork:** includes acupressure, aromatherapy, bioenergetics,
   chiropractic, craniotherapy, do-in (self-massage), hakomi, massage, polarity, rolfing, and shiatsu.

2, 4, 6, 8, 11, 15, 16, 19, 23, 25, 26, 33, 36, 50, 55, 56, 60, 70, 77, 78, 79, 80, 81, 82, 83, 84, 88, 91, 94, 108, 109, 113, 114, 116, 117, 118, 120, 123, 124, 125, 127, 129, 130, 131, 133, 134, 135, 144, 146, 149, 152, 153, 161, 163, 164, 166, 168, 169, 170, 177, 178, 185, 188, 191, 193, 201, 202, 204, 206, 209, 212, 221, 237, 239, 247, 248, 254, 256, 257, 258

3. **Breathwork:** therapies such as breathwork, diaphragmatic breathing, Holotropic Breathwork, Integrative Breathwork, and rebirthing.
16, 33, 35, 50, 54, 59, 63, 79, 84, 91, 114, 124, 138, 154, 160, 168, 171, 177, 206, 209, 218, 221, 229, 245, 247, 254

4. **Ceremony:** traditional, loosely structured, or spontaneously created ritual conducive to transpersonal or self-transcendent experience.
1, 5, 6, 10, 12, 22, 23, 32, 33, 34, 37, 38, 39, 41, 45, 47, 51, 52, 53, 56, 58, 59, 63, 73, 76, 79, 81, 86, 91, 94, 96, 101, 104, 106, 112, 126, 127, 140, 142, 144, 150, 151, 154, 155, 157, 159, 161, 162, 170, 176, 181, 182, 183, 184, 186, 196, 197, 207, 208, 221, 229, 233, 243, 244, 252, 253, 254

5. **Counseling:** spiritual direction and psychotherapeutic counseling, intuitive counseling (e.g., astrology, numerology, palm and tarot readings), and channeled guidance from disembodied spirits.
19, 20, 23, 25, 26, 27, 29, 30, 33, 34, 36, 38, 39, 47, 49, 50, 55, 61, 63, 64, 68, 74, 76, 80, 81, 82, 94, 115, 116, 121, 130, 132, 134, 143, 148, 163, 164, 170, 175, 177, 178, 179, 181, 185, 190, 192, 197, 202, 207, 226, 239, 240, 252

6. **Diet modification:** cooking classes, living foods (the Dr. Ann Wigmore regimen), macrobiotics, and nutritional counseling.
11, 15, 19, 25, 26, 55, 56, 59, 64, 68, 78, 80, 85, 87, 88, 91, 113, 115, 123, 124, 125, 128, 129, 134, 135, 137, 152, 153, 156, 161, 166, 172, 185, 187, 191, 198, 204, 209, 214, 215, 216, 229, 237, 239, 241, 243, 245, 246, 248, 250, 258, 260

7. **Group process work:** includes cooperative endeavor and teamwork (e.g., encampments), dyads, group discussion and sharing, psychodrama, and trust-building exercises.
1, 2, 3, 4, 6, 13, 19, 21, 22, 27, 29, 30, 34, 36, 38, 39, 43, 50, 51, 53, 57, 58, 62, 63, 65, 66, 81, 82, 83, 89, 92, 99, 105, 106, 108, 114, 116, 118, 119, 126, 132, 138, 142, 145, 146, 151, 154, 157, 159, 162, 164, 165, 167, 170, 171, 172, 173, 175, 176, 177, 186, 190, 192, 194, 196, 197, 199, 201, 208, 221, 223, 241, 245, 246, 250, 253, 254

8. **Hatha yoga:** asanas (postures) and pranayama (yogic breathing) in various styles such as Iyengar, kundalini, and Kripalu.
   8, 14, 15, 16, 23, 24, 25, 26, 28, 33, 36, 38, 40, 42, 50, 56, 57, 59, 60, 62, 63, 68, 69, 70, 80, 83, 84, 87, 88, 91, 93, 94, 96, 104, 105, 109, 113, 115, 118, 120, 121, 124, 125, 126, 127, 128, 129, 130, 131, 135, 137, 144, 146, 149, 152, 153, 156, 161, 163, 164, 168, 187, 188, 191, 193, 198, 201, 203, 204, 205, 206, 209, 211, 212, 213, 214, 215, 217, 220, 225, 226, 227, 229, 235, 236, 237, 238, 246, 247, 248, 255, 256, 257, 258, 259

9. **Inner process work:** includes biofeedback, brainwave training, dreamwork, emotional release and self-esteem work, Enneagram, gestalt, hypnosis, journal writing, past-life recall, and shamanic journeying.
   1, 2, 3, 4, 5, 6, 11, 13, 17, 23, 25, 26, 27, 28, 29, 30, 36, 39, 41, 43, 47, 50, 51, 52, 56, 57, 58, 59, 62, 63, 67, 74, 75, 76, 77, 79, 82, 83, 84, 87, 89, 91, 96, 99, 103, 104, 105, 106, 108, 113, 114, 116, 118, 119, 120, 121, 125, 129, 130, 132, 133, 137, 139, 142, 143, 146, 147, 148, 149, 151, 154, 156, 157, 159, 160, 161, 163, 164, 165, 166, 167, 170, 171, 172, 173, 177, 181, 183, 187, 191, 192, 196, 197, 198, 201, 202, 206, 207, 208, 221, 223, 228, 233, 238, 245, 253, 254, 255

10. **Meditation/relaxation:** includes focusing, guided visualization, inner listening, mantra meditation, mindfulness meditation, music meditation, interspecies and devic attunement.
    1, 2, 3, 4, 5, 6, 7, 8, 11, 13, 14, 15, 16, 17, 18, 19, 21, 23, 29, 30, 31, 33, 35, 36, 40, 43, 44, 46, 49, 50, 51, 54, 56, 57, 59, 60, 61, 68, 70, 75, 76, 79, 82, 84, 85, 86, 87, 88, 89, 91, 93, 94, 95, 96, 97, 102, 103, 104, 105, 106, 108, 109, 110, 111, 113, 114, 116, 117, 119, 120, 121, 122, 123, 125, 127, 128, 129, 130, 132, 136, 137, 138, 143, 144, 145, 146, 147, 149, 152, 153, 154, 155, 156, 158, 160, 161, 163, 164, 168, 171, 172, 173, 175, 176, 177, 180, 182, 183, 185, 187, 188, 189, 191, 192, 193, 195, 196, 197, 199, 201, 202, 204, 205, 207, 209, 210, 211, 212, 213, 214, 215, 216, 217, 219, 220, 222, 223, 224, 225, 226, 228, 229, 233, 234, 235, 236, 237, 238, 241, 242, 244, 245, 247, 248, 249, 254, 258, 259, 260

11. **Movement:** primarily aikido, Alexander Technique, chi gung, dance, Feldenkrais, and tai chi.
    2, 4, 5, 6, 8, 17, 22, 23, 29, 37, 38, 39, 47, 53, 56, 57, 61, 62, 67, 68, 70, 76, 83, 84, 88, 91, 94, 96, 109, 111, 117, 118, 120, 122, 124, 125, 126, 127, 132, 138, 144, 146, 149, 151, 152, 154, 158, 159, 161, 162, 163, 164,

168, 172, 174, 181, 183, 185, 186, 188, 192, 195, 196, 198, 199, 201, 211, 221, 230, 231, 232, 234, 241, 245, 249, 250, 255, 259, 260

12. **Natural medicine:** noninvasive, nondrug healing techniques such as acupuncture, aromatherapy, electromagnetic balancing, flower and gem essences, herbs, homeopathy, iridology, naturopathy, and sound therapy.
4, 16, 25, 26, 33, 34, 47, 50, 51, 76, 84, 85, 88, 100, 105, 123, 127, 134, 137, 150, 153, 161, 185, 187, 189, 202, 204, 239, 241, 247, 252

13. **Nature therapy:** includes relaxed activities in nature such as bird-watching, gardening, hikes and nature walks, soaks in mineral springs, swimming with dolphins, wildlife tracking and viewing.
2, 12, 19, 22, 24, 42, 48, 49, 51, 52, 53, 55, 57, 58, 63, 64, 75, 77, 86, 91, 92, 100, 104, 107, 109, 115, 124, 125, 150, 152, 157, 166, 168, 172, 179, 186, 189, 193, 198, 204, 211, 216, 221, 228, 234, 235, 239, 241, 246, 260

14. **Power places:** abodes of living saints; ancient monoliths, pyramids, and temples; sacred mountains, lakes, and Earth vortex locations; sites of religious apparitions.
1, 9, 20, 29, 41, 42, 44, 48, 52, 63, 70, 71, 72, 95, 97, 100, 104, 107, 112, 140, 150, 155, 179, 182, 184, 199, 200, 240, 244, 247

15. **Prayer:** all types of prayer including petitionary, intercessionary, contemplative/centering, and devotional/chanting.
2, 3, 4, 5, 7, 8, 19, 21, 28, 33, 38, 40, 43, 51, 55, 56, 60, 63, 68, 78, 82, 90, 101, 116, 119, 126, 127, 133, 134, 139, 141, 143, 147, 154, 173, 178, 180, 202, 204, 208, 215, 216, 218, 219, 220, 228, 234, 239, 249, 255, 259

16. **Psychic and energy healing:** includes aura cleansing, chakra and energy balancing, color and crystal healing, kinesiology, psychic surgery, reiki, and therapeutic touch.
3, 6, 8, 16, 20, 23, 33, 44, 50, 57, 61, 94, 100, 105, 109, 113, 115, 132, 154, 159, 179, 181, 182, 185, 202, 218, 228, 229, 240, 245, 248

17. **Self-expression:** includes art therapy, crafts (e.g., mask and drum making), drawing, music making, painting, poetry, pottery, sand-tray therapy (a "return to childhood" session, where participants build sand castles or create other art forms), singing, songwriting, and storytelling.

2, 4, 5, 6, 8, 13, 17, 23, 24, 29, 30, 37, 39, 46, 51, 53, 56, 57, 59, 62, 67, 72, 75, 79, 81, 84, 86, 91, 94, 96, 100, 106, 111, 118, 119, 125, 127, 145, 146, 151, 154, 156, 160, 161, 162, 163, 164, 168, 169, 172, 173, 174, 176, 177, 185, 191, 196, 197, 198, 201, 206, 208, 211, 214, 216, 223, 228, 233, 235, 237, 238, 245, 248, 249, 254, 255, 259, 260

18. **Selfless service:** practicing love in action by donating work, either to or through the host community.
7, 8, 14, 17, 18, 33, 40, 61, 63, 66, 90, 96, 110, 111, 121, 126, 127, 129, 136, 138, 141, 173, 180, 181, 204, 210, 214, 216, 219, 224, 228, 236, 237, 238, 252

19. **Vision quest:** several days alone in the wilderness (usually with fasting and vigil) to receive guidance (in a dream or vision) on one's purpose or direction in life.
10, 12, 22, 32, 34, 41, 45, 51, 53, 58, 67, 73, 74, 92, 100, 106, 126, 157, 162, 176, 189, 194, 199, 243, 251

20. **Wisdom literature:** reading, study, and talks on scriptures (e.g., Bible, Vedas, Buddhist Sutras, and *A Course in Miracles*) widely regarded as divine revelation.
5, 8, 14, 43, 56, 57, 65, 75, 90, 102, 105, 110, 111, 116, 123, 126, 133, 139, 147, 158, 170, 173, 178, 180, 197, 210, 211, 215, 216, 219, 222, 227, 235, 259, 260

Special Needs and Interests Index

The following index lists and defines fifteen categories of special needs and interests. Each definition is followed by numbers corresponding to the numbered listings in the Alphabetical Index, so readers can locate the organizations that best serve their particular needs and/or interests.

A. **Adults:** programs open to any individual adult.
All entries *except* 9, 24, 71, 72, 86, 142, 176, 221, 253

B. **Community sojourns:** host communities that accommodate short-term residents or work-study guests.
5, 8, 14, 33, 40, 56, 57, 60, 87, 90, 91, 96, 109, 110, 114, 120, 126, 149, 153, 158, 161, 173, 175, 180, 181, 189, 197, 201, 202, 204, 210, 211, 212, 214, 216, 217, 219, 233, 234, 235, 255, 259, 260

C. **Couples:** programs designed specifically for couples or to enhance understanding, love, and sexuality in relationships.
13, 17, 23, 27, 29, 30, 33, 39, 44, 57, 60, 64, 65, 76, 77, 82, 84, 91, 99, 105, 106, 109, 113, 115, 116, 119, 120, 121, 124, 128, 133, 143, 144, 151, 161, 163, 164, 167, 168, 179, 183, 185, 190, 192, 197, 207, 208, 226, 238, 245, 255

D. **Families:** programs with organized activities for children as well as their parents.
2, 5, 12, 17, 24, 38, 56, 57, 68, 81, 82, 90, 91, 94, 96, 99, 105, 118, 120, 124, 126, 131, 132, 135, 159, 161, 167, 170, 172, 173, 185, 197, 198, 211, 214, 216, 223, 228, 232, 236, 249, 255

E. **Gays/lesbians:** programs that facilitate self-understanding, self-acceptance, and spiritual growth among gays and lesbians.
23, 38, 40, 47, 57, 116, 159, 161, 177, 197, 208, 211, 221, 223, 260

F. **Men only:** programs that initiate or reinitiate men into the spiritual and emotional dimensions of being a man.
10, 14, 22, 23, 29, 30, 38, 57, 66, 76, 81, 82, 84, 99, 106, 109, 113, 115, 116, 120, 133, 139, 142, 157, 159, 161, 185, 194, 196, 197, 207, 208, 221, 223, 233, 238, 255

G. **Personal retreats:** individual rest, meditation, and spiritual retreats, self-directed or with adviser input.
8, 14, 18, 23, 29, 30, 33, 38, 40, 43, 46, 65, 80, 82, 84, 105, 109, 110, 111, 115, 116, 118, 119, 120, 121, 126, 127, 129, 133, 143, 144, 149, 151, 159, 160, 167, 175, 177, 180, 181, 186, 193, 196, 201, 206, 219, 220, 225, 233, 234, 237, 249

H. **Recovery:** programs for people working on emotional issues such as dysfunctional family, abuse, or addictive behavior (e.g., smoking and overeating).
6, 19, 23, 25, 26, 27, 29, 38, 40, 55, 57, 59, 78, 81, 82, 84, 87, 89, 105, 106, 114, 116, 119, 124, 133, 134, 143, 147, 149, 153, 161, 165, 170, 171, 172, 178, 185, 190, 197, 223, 233, 239, 241, 250

I. **Regeneration/healing:** programs suitable for people in postoperative recovery or with a life-threatening illness.
4, 19, 25, 26, 30, 36, 55, 78, 88, 118, 153, 178, 241, 245, 248

J. Rental facilities: centers that allow use of their facilities by outside groups for private or public workshops.
29, 30, 39, 60, 76, 77, 105, 108, 109, 115, 118, 121, 125, 144, 149, 151,
156, 159, 175, 177, 201, 206, 213, 233, 245, 249

K. Senior citizens: programs addressing the problems and concerns
common to people in the latter years of their lives.
4, 19, 21, 25, 26, 36, 38, 55, 78, 88, 118, 119, 134, 139, 153, 161, 178, 209,
211, 239, 248, 249

L. Spiritual/life transition: programs for people who are at significant turning points in their lives.
10, 12, 22, 32, 34, 45, 51, 53, 66, 69, 73, 74, 82, 92, 120, 157, 176, 177,
194, 215, 243, 251, 253

M. Teacher/professional trainings: programs that train teachers,
healers, or others in the helping professions.
10, 27, 29, 35, 39, 57, 59, 65, 81, 84, 87, 118, 120, 157, 161, 164, 165, 167,
170, 174, 175, 182, 202, 204, 208, 214, 215, 216, 217, 218, 223, 241, 245,
252, 253, 255

N. Wheelchair accessibility: host organizations that offer wheelchair
access or wheelchair-suitable quarters.
3, 4, 26, 56, 57, 82, 215, 252

O. Women only: programs for women to explore and celebrate the
spiritual and emotional dimensions of being a woman.
5, 9, 10, 12, 14, 22, 23, 25, 30, 38, 44, 46, 47, 51, 53, 56, 57, 62, 63, 66,
71, 72, 76, 82, 84, 86, 87, 91, 99, 105, 106, 109, 113, 114, 116, 119, 120,
133, 139, 144, 151, 157, 160, 161, 162, 168, 172, 176, 177, 184, 185, 196,
197, 201, 207, 208, 216, 223, 228, 229, 233, 236, 237, 241, 249, 252, 253

Spiritual/Religious Orientation Index

This index lists and defines fifteen spiritual/religious categories. Each
definition is followed by numbers corresponding to the numbered listings in the Alphabetical Index, so readers can identify organizations em-
bracing a particular spiritual or religious tradition.

In certain cases, an organization may embrace two or more spiritual/religious traditions. This accounts for some of the listings in the Alphabetical Index that have two or more lowercase letter codes. The other listings of this type indicate nonsectarian Buddhist retreat centers (noted by all three Buddhist tradition codes) or communities with a primary tradition that also encourage multitraditional worship (the "h" code).

a. **Catholic:** Roman Catholic faith with a contemplative and/or broadly ecumenical outlook.
119, 133, 139, 141, 143

b. **Christian Fundamentalist:** non-Catholic, Christian faiths emphasizing Bible study and prayer.
19, 55, 64, 78, 134, 178, 239

c. **Goddess/ecospirituality:** ancient and modern traditions (including Wicca and Deep-Ecology) honoring the interdependence of Earth, its plants, and its creatures.
9, 47, 51, 71, 72, 81, 138, 176, 184, 199, 252

d. **Hindu/yogic:** India's ancient spiritual paths of bhakti yoga (devotion), jnana yoga (self-inquiry), karma yoga (selfless service), and raja yoga (meditation).
7, 8, 16, 28, 31, 60, 87, 112, 120, 121, 129, 149, 200, 204, 212, 214, 215, 216, 217, 236, 255

e. **Judaic:** Judaic religious traditions that encourage joyous celebration, creative self-expression, and/or mystical union with the divine.
56, 145, 196

f. **Liberal Protestant:** non-Catholic, nonmetaphysical Christian faiths stressing social service and prayer.
17, 38, 43, 90, 116, 173, 245

g. **Metaphysical Christian:** faiths honoring Jesus as a teacher and exemplar of the divinity in all people.
33, 60, 65, 170, 202

h. **Multitraditional:** spiritual communities that accommodate the ritual practices of several (or even all) religions.
5, 126, 154, 196

i. **Native American/shamanic:** a largely American form of spirituality with rituals such as sweat lodge, pipe circle, medicine wheel, and vision quest.
12, 32, 41, 48, 51, 52, 58, 81, 104, 107, 136, 140, 186, 194, 228, 233, 240

j. **Sufi:** a mystically oriented spiritual path that originated in the Muslim faith.
5, 101, 234

k. **Taoist:** an ancient Chinese spirituality that emphasizes balance and harmony in all one's relations with self, others, and nature.
122, 129, 230

l. **Theosophical/ascended masters:** certain societies and new religions that believe angels and ascended spiritual masters are assisting humankind.
61, 96, 181, 198

m. **Theravada Buddhist:** a form of Buddhism (dominant in Burma, Ceylon, India, and Thailand) known for its Vipassana (insight) meditation.
14, 18, 35, 46, 95, 97, 112, 138, 222, 242

n. **Tibetan Buddhist:** a form of Buddhism emphasizing compassion, ritual practices, and visualization meditations.
14, 35, 97, 110, 111, 112, 127, 158, 212, 228

o. **Zen Buddhist:** a form of Buddhism (dominant in China, Japan, Korea, and Vietnam) known for its koans, its rigorous sitting meditation, and its aesthetics.
14, 35, 40, 75, 86, 97, 180, 210, 219, 234, 235, 259, 260

SINGLE-SITE GETAWAYS

$\mathscr{T}$his chapter profiles 182 single-site getaway providers, grouped by geographical region. Within each region, the states included are arranged alphabetically, as are the organizations found in each state.

The list below indicates the breakdown of regions and the states included in each.

UNITED STATES

Southern Pacific: *California, Hawaii*
Northwest: *Montana, Oregon, Washington*
Southwest: *Arizona, Colorado, New Mexico, Utah*
North Central: *Illinois, Iowa, Michigan, Minnesota,
South Dakota, Wisconsin*
South Central: *Missouri, Oklahoma, Texas*
New England: *Maine, Massachusetts, New Hampshire,
Rhode Island, Vermont*
New York State
Mideast: *Indiana, Maryland, Ohio, Pennsylvania,
Virginia, West Virginia*
Southeast: *Alabama, Florida, Georgia, North Carolina*

MEXICO AND THE CARIBBEAN

Mexico, Bahamas, Puerto Rico, U.S. Virgin Islands

CANADA

British Columbia, Ontario, Quebec

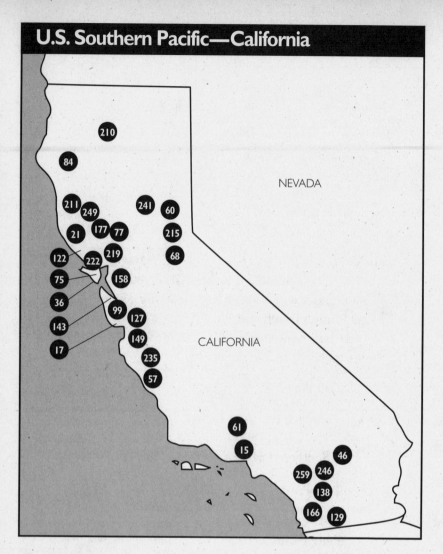

U.S. Southern Pacific—California

UNITED STATES: *Southern Pacific Region*

The Ashram   Calabasas, CA

The Ashram is a two-story house fifteen minutes north of Malibu Beach in the Santa Monica Mountains. Its grounds contain a garden, a small heated swimming pool and Jacuzzi, a sunbathing solarium, and a redwood geodesic dome for yoga and meditation sessions. The house has spacious porches, a gymnasium, and an exercise area.

The Ashram's program emphasizes rigorous exercise, diet, and inner centering. Up at 6:30 A.M. for meditation followed by a glass of grapefruit juice for breakfast, a guest can look forward to a morning of steep mountain hiking, calisthenics, and water exercise. Following lunch and a siesta, the afternoon includes a massage, a jog, exercise to music, an evening walk, and predinner yoga and meditation.

The Ashram's proprietor is Anne-Marie Bennstrom, a former Swedish cross-country ski champion. Half of her guests are returnees, and they include many Hollywood celebrities.

Address	P.O. Box 8009, Calabasas, CA 91372
Phone	(818) 222-6900
Season	Year-round.
Programs	Standard, 1-week program "to enhance your physical, mental, and spiritual well-being."
Lodging	10-person guest capacity with 2 guests per room.
Rates	$2,200 per week.
Meals	3 daily vegetarian meals, mostly green, leafy, and raw.
Services	Free van pick-up and drop-off at nearby locations.

Ben Lomond Quaker Center   Ben Lomond, CA

This eighty-acre retreat and conference facility is set among towering redwoods, fir trees, and ferns ten miles north of Santa Cruz in the Coastal Range. The property includes hiking and nature trails, two lodges, a private retreat cottage, and a Friends Meeting House with majestic vistas of the San Lorenzo River Valley. All guests are welcome to attend the daily, early morning centering/meditation meeting.

The center hosts retreats for Quakers and for the general public. The latter include couples' and women's weekends plus retreats with themes like "Spirituality and Sexuality" and "Forgiving Others, Forgiving Ourselves." The public is also invited to two weeklong events: an "Art and the Spirit" retreat in early July, with daily morning and afternoon workshops led by artists and teachers; and a reflection and renewal retreat at the end of the year.

Address	P.O. Box 686, Ben Lomond, CA 95005
Phone	(408) 336-8333
Season	Year-round.
Programs	Weekend and weeklong retreats fostering self-exploration and centering, creative self-expression, and creative fellowship.
Lodging	Accommodations for fifty+ guests in semiprivate rooms, bunk bed rooms, and an open dorm. Shared bathrooms.
Rates	Weekend retreat $110. "Art and the Spirit" week $250. Year-end retreat week $220.
Meals	3 daily vegetarian meals. Participants share in kitchen chores and final, predeparture cleanup.

Blue Mountain Center of Meditation   Dillon Beach, CA

This center conducts at least one weekend retreat each month plus weeklong retreats in the spring and fall. All retreats are held at a spacious and cozy retreat house overlooking the Pacific Ocean fifty miles due north of San Francisco. And all are based on Eknath Easwaran's Eight Point Program of meditation, mantra repetition, one-pointed attention, slowing down, training the senses, putting others first, satsang (devotional worship), and spiritual reading.

Each weekend retreat includes basic instruction in meditation; morning, noon, and evening meditations; videos of talks by Eknath Easwaran; and small group sessions for answering questions about the Eight Point Program. Weeklong retreats also include reading assignments from Sri Easwaran's books. All retreats are conducted by senior Eight Point Program students and allow time for reflection, fellowship, and walks along the beach.

Eknath Easwaran is a native of India, a prolific author, and a retired professor of English literature (University of California, Berkeley) who recommends meditation on inspirational passages from the world's great sacred literature. Sri Easwaran is also the founder of Setu, a spiritual growth program oriented toward people in the second half of life.

Address	P.O. Box 256, Tomales, CA 94971
Phone	(707) 878-2369. No visits without prior arrangements.
Season	Year-round.
Programs	Weekend and weeklong meditation and spiritual practice retreats.
Lodging	Shared accommodations for a maximum of 15 people.
Rates	Standard weekend retreat $275. Setu weekend retreat $350. Weeklong retreat $500.
Meals	3 daily vegetarian meals.

Commonweal   Bolinas, CA

A nonprofit health and environmental research institute located on a sixty-acre coastal site (at the southern entrance of Point Reyes National Seashore) one hour north of San Francisco. The property includes an MCI transmitter facility, ten buildings, and an organic garden—all surrounded by 1,000 acres of National Park Service land.

One of Commonweal's several ongoing projects is the Commonweal Cancer Help Program (CCHP), a weeklong retreat designed to encourage spiritual, emotional, and physical healing for people with cancer. The daily schedule includes two yoga and meditation sessions, a morning self-exploration and sharing session, a deep relaxation and imagery session, free time, and an evening program. Free time may be used for beach walks, massage, and sand-tray sessions, plus individual consultations with staff members (including psychotherapists, physical therapists, and yoga therapists).

Each CCHP retreat is limited to eight participants who must be under the care of an oncologist or other allopathic (conventional) physician, be able to handle Commonweal's rural environment, and be well enough to benefit from the program. Medical care is not provided during the retreat.

Address P.O. Box 316, Bolinas, CA 94924
Phone (415) 868-0970. Fax (415) 868-2230.
Season Year-round.
Programs Weeklong self-healing program for people with cancer.
Lodging Single rooms in 3 guest houses.
Rates $1,280 per person.
Meals 3 daily vegetarian meals.

Dhamma Dena Desert Retreat   Joshua Tree, CA

Dhamma Dena is a twelve-acre silent meditation retreat center in the vicinity of Joshua Tree National Monument. The high desert site is encircled by distant mountains and illumined by ever-changing desert hues. Water is trucked in and reused.

Center founder Ruth Denison leads at least three annual Vipassana meditation programs: a four-week retreat in late December/early January, plus two-week women's retreats in the spring and fall. Most other guided Dhamma Dena retreats are led by Jim Hopper, a meditation teacher from the Los Angeles area.

Self-led retreatants are welcome to join early morning stretching and meditation sessions plus evening meditations on days when guided retreats are not in progress. All retreatants, teacher-guided and self-led, are expected to help out with center chores.

Address HC-1, Box 250, Joshua Tree, CA 92252
Phone (619) 362-4815. No visits without prior arrangements.
Season Year-round.
Programs Teacher-led meditation retreats ranging from 3 days to 4 weeks. Also self-led meditation and meditation/work retreats.
Lodging Separate housing for up to 50 men and women in main house, cabins, and bunkhouses. Japanese-style outhouses. BYO sleeping bag.

Rates	Facility fee $28 per day. Guided retreatants customarily make an additional donation for the meditation teachings.
Meals	3 light vegetarian meals eaten each day.

Esalen Institute   Big Sur, CA

Looking out over the Pacific Ocean forty-five minutes south of Monterey, Esalen Institute is well known for its personal growth workshops. But the institute's greatest achievements have been in research and development dealing with human potential. For example, it was during his years as an Esalen scholar-in-residence that Stanislav Grof (founder of the International Transpersonal Association) invented Holotropic Breathwork (see page 290).

The institute's hand-in-glove approach to research and education is exemplified in *The Future of the Body*, written by Esalen cofounder Michael Murphy. The book's theories are based on insights from more than thirty years of public Esalen workshops taught by a faculty of visiting and resident artists, psychologists, psychiatrists, healing arts practitioners, spiritual teachers, and educators from many fields.

All Esalen workshops are conducted on a campus that includes a heated swimming pool and ocean view, hot spring baths where clothing is generally discarded, and casually furnished guest quarters bathed in ocean air and the sound of the surf.

Most Esalen workshops involve weekend or five- to seven-day commitments. Some are two weeks, three weeks, or longer. Twenty-six-day stays are possible from mid-September through mid-June through an ongoing residence program, which allows participants to attend any of the five-day workshops during their stay.

Participants in the work-study program work thirty-two hours per week for one, two, or three months. In the study portion of the program, they select one of two monthly sections. Each section focuses on one type of growth practice (e.g., gestalt, meditation, massage), and different sections are offered each month.

Address	Highway 1, Big Sur, CA 93920
Phone	(408) 644-8476 for a catalog. Fax (408) 667-2724 or call (408) 667-3005 for reservations.
Season	Year-round.

Programs 2-day to 3-week workshops on topics in general fields such as arts/creativity, contemplative/spiritual and religious studies, dreams, health/healing, intuitive development, martial arts/yoga/sports, relationship/communication, women's/men's studies. 26-day-residence and 1-month to 3-months work-study programs also available.

Lodging Capacity for 100+ overnight guests in shared (2 or 3 per room) and bunk bed (4–6 per room) accommodations. Also space for sleeping bags indoors. Limited wheelchair access.

Rates Weekend workshop $200–380. 5-day workshop $375–740. 7-day workshop $570–1,110. 26-day residence program $2,520–3,195. Work-study program $650–750 per month.

Meals 3 daily buffets with vegetarian option. Vegetables and greens from Esalen gardens.

Services Cranial-sacral work, Feldenkrais, rolfing, Esalen and deep-tissue massage. Preschool children's program. Friday and Sunday van service between Esalen and the Monterey Airport and Greyhound stop.

The Expanding Light at Ananda   Nevada City, CA

Ananda Village is many things: the host of a variety of yoga and meditation retreats, the headquarters of the expanding Ananda Church, and a spiritual community spread across 800 acres in the foothills of the Sierra Nevada Mountains. The village was founded in the late 1960s by the talented author/composer Swami Kriyananda, an American disciple of the late Paramahansa Yogananda (author of the classic *Autobiography of a Yogi*). Located ninety minutes northeast of Sacramento, the village's population of some 275 adults and 100 children makes it one of the largest communities in Nevada County.

Ananda offers workshops on meditation, healthy living, and yoga postures plus holiday and other special programs (e.g., couples, family, elder hostel). All are facilitated by resident staff, and most, except the popular "Spiritual Renewal Week," range from two to five days. Unstructured "Rest and Recharge Weekends" and personal retreats allow retreatants to enjoy daily yoga and meditation sessions, spiritual counseling, evening entertainment, and an occasional class or outing.

A typical weekday schedule begins at 6:30 A.M. (7 on weekends) with spiritual practices that include energizing exercises, yoga postures, and meditation. A silent breakfast is followed by class or group activities, meditation at noon, lunch at 12:30 P.M., class or group activities from 2 to 4:30, spiritual practices preceding dinner, and an evening program. Throughout the day, there is ample time to just relax—alone with nature or a good book, or in the company of other spiritually minded people.

Address   14618 Tyler Foote Road, Nevada City, CA 95959
Phone   (800) 346-5350 or (916) 292-3496. Fax (916) 292-4258.
Season   Year-round.
Programs   Weekend and 5-day programs on healthy living, meditation, and hatha yoga. 12- to 26-day yoga, meditation, and yoga teacher trainings. Also work-study and work exchange.
Lodging   Accommodations for up to 50 guests in double rooms, single-room cabins, and a bungalow—all with nearby showers. Also shaded campsites for tents (BYO) and RVs (no hookups).
Rates   Weekend retreat $84–170. 5-day program $260–475. Personal retreat $42–85 per day. Work-study $21–64 per day.
Meals   3 daily vegetarian meals.
Services   Available in Ananda Village: massage and yoga therapy, chiropractic and medical care, Jacuzzi.

Far Horizons   Sequoia National Park, CA

Located at an altitude of 7,200 feet amid the towering trees of Sequoia National Park, Far Horizons is an adult summer camp operating on a special use permit from the U.S. Department of Agriculture.

Since its founding in 1954, Far Horizons has offered programs that share the Theosophical Society's mission to investigate unexplained laws of nature and humankind's latent powers; to study comparative religion, science, and philosophy; and to promote the "Universal Brotherhood of Humanity, without distinction of race, creed, sex, caste or color." Far Horizons welcomes anyone (including children accompanied and supervised by an adult) who is willing to participate in all camp activities.

A typical camp day begins with an early outdoor breakfast. Campers then help with cleanup and (on some days) with food preparation. Program sessions run from 10 A.M. to noon. Afternoon is free for hiking, viewing Kings Canyon, swimming in Hume Lake, or just reading and resting. Another program session or group discussion follows dinner. Then there are activities around the campfire, such as singing, telling stories, performing skits, or just sharing conversation.

Address   P.O. Box 857, Kings Canyon National Park, CA 93633
Phone   (209) 565-3692
Season   June through September.
Programs Mostly 5-day workshops (ending on Sunday) reflecting the theosophical emphasis on spiritual, psychological, and physical well-being.
Lodging   Campsites, cabins, plus rooms and apartments (usually shared). No electricity (and hence no disturbing electrical fields).
Rates   Daily rates for programs, meals, and lodging: singles $30–60, couples $56–100, kids ages 12–17 $10, kids ages 6–11 $5, kids under 6 free. Also half rate for 3–4 hours of daily work during 1 program (5 days).
Meals   3 daily vegetarian meals.

French Meadows Summer Camp   Tahoe National Forest, CA

For twenty-five years, this camp has served families committed to learning and living a macrobiotic way of life. The Tahoe National Forest site lies eighty miles northeast of Sacramento at a 6,000-foot elevation on the western slope of the Sierra Nevadas. The campground is bordered by a stream, with a reservoir, suitable for swimming, a quarter mile away. The camp is sponsored by the George Oshawa Macrobiotic Foundation (GOMF), which also operates the Vega Institute (profiled later in this section).

Each day begins with activities such as meditation, yoga, cooking instruction, or a walk in the forest. Following breakfast, a chanting session is led by Vega Institute founders Herman and Cornellia Aihara. Midmorning lectures by Herman and guest teachers touch on subjects like "Controlling Food Addictions" and "Essence of Macrobiotic Psychology." Early afternoon is free for swimming, hiking, or just taking it easy. Late afternoon workshops cover macrobiotic cooking, self-massage, hatha yoga, and other techniques. The day ends around a campfire with singing and storytelling.

Address	GOMF Summer Camp, Vega Institute, 1511 Robinson Street, Oroville, CA 95965
Phone	(916) 533-7702. Fax (916) 533-7908.
Season	10 days in mid-July.
Programs	Family summer camp celebrating a macrobiotic lifestyle.
Lodging	Tent sites for up to 125 people. Nearby outhouses are the campsite's only permanent structures. BYO tent and sleeping bag.
Rates	Adults $500–600, youths (8–16) $300–350, children (3–7) $200–250. Discounts for early registration and GOMF members.
Meals	3 daily macrobiotic meals prepared over open wood fires.
Services	Children's and youths' activities offered during lectures. Also massage and dietary consultations.

Green Gulch Farm   Muir Beach, CA

A twenty-five-minute drive north of San Francisco will take you to Green Gulch Farm, a 115-acre property adjoining Golden Gate National Recreation Area and a half-mile ocean beach. The property contains a teahouse, meditation hall, guest houses, and fifteen acres of vegetable, herb, and flower gardens. The resident community tends the gardens and offers classes, workshops, and retreats.

A sister community to the San Francisco Zen Center (SFZC) and Tassajara (which is profiled later in this section), Green Gulch has been in operation since 1972. It is a place where a large spiritual community (mostly nonresident) can study Buddhist teachings, practice meditation, and experiment with organic gardening. It also serves as a learning center for the general public. Programs are led primarily by Bay area SFZC members.

People new to meditation may take a one-day "Introductory Sitting" class. Experienced meditators may participate in intensive meditation retreats (called sessions) lasting one, five, or seven days. Weekend workshops (e.g., "Applied Wisdom and Compassion") combine meditation and Zen Buddhist teachings. Personal retreats allow guests to stay as long as they wish with as much or as little contact with residents as they wish. And "Practice Retreats" (a minimum three-day commitment) involve participation in morning community activities followed by free time for the rest of the day.

People with a strong interest in the Zen lifestyle can participate in the "Guest Student" program (a three-day to six-week commitment), which includes a daily schedule of work, study, and meditation. Or they can enroll in a seven-week "Practice Period" for intensive training in Zen meditation, teachings, and ceremonies, plus daily work.

Address   1601 Shoreline Drive, Muir Beach, CA 94965
Phone   (415) 383-3134. Fax (415) 383-3128.
Season   Year-round.
Programs   Residential "Guest Student" program, weekend workshops, intensive meditation and "Practice Period" retreats. Also "Practice Retreats" and personal retreats.
Lodging   Artistically handcrafted wooden guest house with an atrium and 15 rooms, each with 2 beds. Family suite elsewhere on property.
Rates   "Guest Student" $12.50 per day. Weekend workshop $225–250. 5- to 7-day meditation retreat $125–210. "Practice Period" $15 per day. "Practice Retreat" $30–50 per day. Daily rates for personal retreats: singles $55–85, couples $90–120.
Meals   3 daily vegetarian buffets with produce from the gardens.

Harbin Hot Springs   Middletown, CA

This workshop center occupies 1,160 acres in a rugged foothill canyon located two and a half hours north of San Francisco. The property's mineral water springs fill two warm pools, a hot pool, a cold plunge, and a large chlorine-free swimming pool. There is also a dry sauna, a large redwood sundeck, and many trails through the surrounding forest and meadowland. A quiet atmosphere is maintained at the pool areas, which are open all day throughout the year (clothing is optional).

Residential workshops touch on subjects like "Sex, Love, and Intimacy," "Therapeutic Massage," and "Diving into the Self." All guests may use the pools and participate in the community activities of daily meditations, yoga classes, a weekly "unconditional dance," full- and new-moon celebrations, plus twelve-step meetings. Harbin also has full conference facilities accommodating up to 300 people.

The center is operated by a spiritual community of some 150 adults and children. Residential work opportunities are often available. Through its School of Shiatsu & Massage, Harbin also offers certification programs in various bodywork therapies, including the developed-at-Harbin Watsu (water shiatsu) massage. Many guests are happy to pay extra for a Harbin massage.

Address   P.O. Box 82, Harbin Hot Springs, CA 95461
Phone   (707) 987-2477
Season   Year-round.
Programs   Many 2- to 11-day workshops on bodywork, personal growth, and relationships. Day visitors are allowed to join in community events and use pools. BYO towels.
Lodging   Creekside camping (some wooden platforms); male and female dorms; single, double, and family rooms with shared, half, or full bath. Children cannot be accommodated in dorms or private rooms.
Rates   Weekend workshops $150–350. Meals and lodging: adults $14–45 per night, $105–1,280 per week; children $10–14 per night, $70 per week. Day visit: adults $12–17, children $10–12.
Meals   A restaurant, poolside café, and vegetarian kitchen are available for use by all guests including campers and day visitors.
Services   Various types of massage, including Esalen, deep tissue, reflexology, shiatsu, and Watsu. Also rebirthing, rebalancing, hypnotherapy, and chiropractic treatments.

Heartwood Institute   Garberville, CA

A rustic 240-acre campus and healing community set amid the rolling forests and meadows of the coastal mountains 200 miles north of San Francisco. Facilities include a picturesque log lodge with a spacious deck; a large converted barn for crafts and classes; outdoor hot tub, wood-fired sauna, and large pool; gardens and campsites tucked in the trees. Heartwood is a serene and beautiful place, rich with wildlife and sweeping visions.

Primarily for the general public, the institute hosts two- to nine-day retreats such as the annual women's weekend, "Zen and Pure Land Meditation" retreats, hatha yoga retreats, open-house weekends, along with lifestyle retreats that include dietary healing, centering, and bodywork practices. The general public may also join holistic health professionals in one- to three-week intensives on bodywork and massage, oriental healing arts, hypnotherapy, and addiction counseling.

In addition, Heartwood offers vocational training programs in transformational therapy, massage therapy, and addiction counseling. Students are encouraged to participate in daily hatha yoga and meditation sessions. Dances, talent shows, and rituals further unite the community.

Address   220 Harmony Lane, Garberville, CA 95542
Phone   (707) 923-5000. Fax (707) 923-5010.
Season   Year-round.
Programs Personal growth retreats, vocational/personal growth intensives, plus various vocational training programs in holistic health care.
Lodging   Campsites or classroom sleep space. BYO sleeping bag.
Rates   Weekend retreat $100–220. 6- to 9-day retreat $530–890. 1-week intensive: tuition $390–825, food and lodging $224–434. 2-week intensive: tuition $850–1,200, food and lodging $448–868. 3-week intensive: tuition $1,500, food and lodging $672–1,302.
Meals   3 daily, mostly vegetarian meals with herbs, fruits, and vegetables from the gardens. Guests may use the snack kitchen.
Services Bodywork and massage, breathwork, transformational therapy, hypnotherapy, and nutritional assessment.

Institute of HeartMath   Boulder Creek, CA

The Institute of HeartMath (IHM) was founded in 1991 to develop tools people can use to relieve stress and break through to greater levels of clarity, creativity, love, and intuitive insight. IHM's mind/body self-management techniques are continually being expanded and refined through research into the relationships between the heart, mental/emotional balance, cardiovascular function, and the hormonal and immune systems.

In addition to corporate consulting to "put the heart back into the people business," IHM offers ongoing self-empowerment retreats. The core offering is the "Heart Empowerment Retreat." Other retreats include "Women's Empowerment," "Men's Empowerment," "Inner Quality Management" (applying HeartMath techniques in the workplace), plus back-to-back "Empowered Parent" and "Teen Camp" retreats to accommodate family vacations. The retreat site is in the Santa Cruz Mountains, forty-five minutes west of San Jose.

IHM's founder and president is Doc Lew Childre, the inventor of FREEZE-FRAME stress intervention techniques and a successful composer of music for emotional and mental regeneration. Music plays an important role in all IHM programs, and the IHM staff includes talented singers and musicians who often provide evening entertainment.

Address   P.O. Box 1463, 14700 West Park Avenue, Boulder Creek, CA 95006
Phone   (408) 338-8700. Fax (408) 338-9861.
Season   Year-round.
Programs 2- to 3-day personal empowerment retreats (most on weekends).
Lodging   Double and triple occupancy rooms.
Rates $750–1,000.
Meals   3 daily meals, all with vegetarian options.

Kumar Frantzis Summer Retreats   Sonoma County, CA

Bruce Kumar Frantzis trained in kung fu while earning black belts in judo, jujitsu, karate, and aikido. He went on to become the first Westerner certified to teach the complete system of tai chi by the People's Republic of China, where he practiced chi gung in hospitals and clinics. Kumar also holds an advanced degree in acupuncture plus a Ph.D. in health sciences with a specialty in body/mind therapies.

Each summer, Kumar and his staff host three six-day intensive workshop retreats at Anvil Ranch, a 12,000-acre wilderness setting two hours north of San Francisco. The first two are chi gung retreats: one divided into a beginners/intermediates group and an advanced group; the other divided into a beginners/intermediates group and an intermediates group. The third retreat focuses on the ways Taoist meditation is practiced during tai chi.

Each retreat includes five hours of daily classes. In addition, every other day includes an optional one-hour prebreakfast class (in Taoist meditation during the chi gung retreats, and in push hands during the meditation retreat). When they are not in class, students can soak in the hot tub, swim or boat on a natural lake, hike in the surrounding hills, visit nearby wineries, or drive thirty minutes to gorgeous beaches.

Address   P.O. Box 99, Fairfax, CA 94978
Phone   (415) 454-5243
Season   3 weeks in July and August.
Programs 3 6-day intensive retreats—the first two on chi gung and the third on tai chi Taoist meditation.
Lodging   Dorms plus a few double rooms for couples, assigned on a first-pay basis. Campsites (BYO tent and bedding) for everyone else.
Rates $769 for each retreat. Those attending 2 retreats can stay at Anvil Ranch on intervening Saturday for $25 with light breakfast.
Meals   Gourmet meals suitable for both vegetarians and carnivores.
Services Free at each retreat: a shuttle from Santa Rosa to Anvil Ranch on the first day and a shuttle back on the final day.

Land of Medicine Buddha   Soquel, CA

Land of Medicine Buddha describes itself as "a center for healing and developing a good heart." It is one of the Western centers founded by the late lama Thubten Yeshe (now reincarnated, it is said, as a youth born in the mountains of Spain to Buddhist parents). Located seventy-five miles south of San Francisco, the center occupies fifty-five acres of forest and meadowland bordering a state park in the foothills of the Santa Cruz Mountains. The property includes trails, a sauna, soaking tubs, and a swimming pool.

This colorfully decorated refuge supports the healing of the body, mind, and environment through programs drawing on the wisdom of various cultures and traditions. Many programs draw on Tibetan Buddhist spiritual and healing practices. Others focus on various Buddhist meditative practices or the Chinese healing arts. The visiting teachers are supported by a small full-time resident staff.

The staff invite workshop participants to contribute one or two hours of work, usually in the kitchen or on the grounds. They also offer weekly chi gung classes, weekly special evening classes (often on Tibetan Buddhist wisdom and practices), plus monthly "Medicine Buddha Practice" meetings. When residential programs are not in session, travelers are welcome to use the center as a personal retreat.

Address   5800 Prescott Road, Soquel, CA 95073
Phone   (408) 462-8383. No visits without prior arrangement.
Season   Year-round.
Programs   2- to 5-day programs to liberate the healing energies of innate wisdom and compassion.
Lodging   Artistically decorated rooms, each accommodating 2 to 4 guests. Also a few private rooms.
Rates   2- or 3-day program: tuition is either a donation or a $50–150 fee, room and board $95–125. 5-day program: tuition $650, room and board $215.
Meals   3 fresh, organic vegetarian buffets served each day.
Services   Massage, acupuncture, personal counseling therapies.

Liberty Retreat   Boulevard, CA

Set in the hilly high desert country seventy miles east of San Diego, Liberty Retreat is a rustic 153-acre yogic oasis that includes a practice hall, meditation cabin and tepees, and fully equipped exercise room, plus an outdoor bathing area with steam room, Jacuzzi, and cold plunge.

The retreat's main offerings are five-day intensives organized to provide progressive training in hatha, kundalini, Tao, and meditation yogas with a foundation in the Tantra and Sufi paths. The intensives, which may be taken individually, also include Japanese hydrotherapy and various bodywork sessions. The weekend workshops serve as both practice periods for experienced practitioners and as introductions to yoga for beginners.

Liberty Retreat is run by Circle of Friends—a multitraditional spiritual community under the guidance of Murshid Isa Moumanie Kadre. Guests are welcome to stay for any length of time with the same daily program of yoga asanas, kundalini sound practice, meditation, study, and work practice that is offered during weekend workshops.

Address	Circle of Friends, P.O. Box 3189, Rancho Santa Fe, CA 92067
Phone	(800) 434-9642. Fax (619) 753-5785. Advance reservations required.
Season	Year-round.
Programs	5-day intensives and weekend workshops focusing on yogic healing.
Lodging	Simple but comfortable accommodations for 30 guests and 13 staff.
Rates	5-day intensive $375. Weekend workshop $150. Guest stay including yoga and meditation sessions and instruction $75 per day.
Meals	3 daily vegetarian meals or the option of a detox liquid diet.
Services	Shuttle sometimes provided between San Diego and retreat site.

Manzanita Village   Warner Springs, CA

Forty-five minutes west of Escondido, Manzanita Village is an eighteen-acre meditation center located in the canyons of Cleveland National Forest at a 3,300-foot elevation. Manzanita hosts four- to ten-day Vipassana meditation retreats, usually spanning holiday periods during the second half of the year. There is an annual two-month meditation retreat (which may be attended for one or both months) from November 1 through December 31. Also, from time to time, deep ecologist teacher/activist Joanna Macy leads a weekend workshop.

Most meditation retreats are led by Christopher Reed and Michele Benzamin-Masuda, both longtime students of Zen master Thich Nhat Hanh and Joanna Macy. Chris is a clinical hypnotherapist with many years of Vipassana meditation experience. Michele is a fifteen-year meditation practitioner, an artist, and a performer with black belts in aikido and iaido.

Address	P.O. Box 67, Warner Springs, CA 92086
Phone	(619) 782-3604. No visits without prior arrangement.
Season	Year-round.
Programs	4- to 10-day meditation retreats. Also personal retreats and long stays by advance arrangement.
Lodging	Men's and women's dorms in 4-room bunkhouse with kitchen and shower. Toilets in nearby outhouse. BYO sleeping bag.
Rates	Teacher-led retreats: 4–6 days $185–205, 8–10 days $275–295, 1 month $500, 2 months $850. Personal retreats: 1 night $20–30, 1 week $125, 1 month $400.
Meals	3 daily vegetarian meals.

Mercy Center   Burlingame, CA

The Sisters of Mercy operate Mercy Center as a suburban spiritual education center. Four miles south of San Francisco International Airport, the forty-acre grounds include three meditation paths designed by Father Thomas Hand, who lived for twenty-eight years in Japan and who leads weekend and nine-day meditation retreats drawing on practices from both Christian and Eastern traditions.

The center also hosts women's, men's, and twelve-step retreats; two- to nine-day workshops on such topics as dreamwork, biospirituality, and Enneagram guidance; plus private or individually directed contemplative retreats. And usually at least once each year, the center hosts a retreat (or trip to France) focusing on the uplifting music and prayer of France's Taize religious community. This gathering is especially popular with young adults between the ages of eighteen and thirty.

Address   2300 Adeline Drive, Burlingame, CA 94010
Phone   (415) 340-7474. No visits without prior arrangement.
Season   Year-round.
Programs   2- to 9-day workshops and guided retreats focusing on spiritual growth and life enrichment.
Lodging   Accommodations for 90+ men and women in private rooms.
Rates   Sample program rates (including room and board): 2–3 days $120–155, 5–7 days $280–375. Private retreat $35–38 per day.
Meals   3 daily, cafeteria-style meals.

Mount Madonna Center   Watsonville, CA

This spiritual education and retreat center is operated by a nonsectarian community of about seventy-five adults and thirty children. Located a few miles east of Santa Cruz, the center's 355 acres contain thirty buildings in redwood forest and grasslands with views looking down on Monterey Bay. On the grounds are hiking trails; a hot tub and a small lake suitable for swimming; and a gym plus volleyball, tennis, and basketball courts.

Mount Madonna's programs are led by well-known teachers, such as Ayurveda teacher Dr. Vasant Lad. Popular program topics include Ashtanga yoga and meditation. Other topics include sacred ecology, ritual healing, creative self-expression, inner child work, and/or conscious relationships. Guests may participate in daily morning yoga sessions and then spend time enjoying solitude, fellowship, and recreation. Opportunities for a long-term stay are available through work-study and part-time employment.

The center is sponsored by the 400-member Hanuman Fellowship, a diverse group united by the practice of yoga as a spiritual path. Many of the center's founders are followers of Baba Hari Dass, who has maintained continuous silence (communicating only by writing) for over forty years and is often present at Ashtanga yoga and meditation retreats.

Address   445 Summit Road, Watsonville, CA 95076
Phone   (408) 847-0406. Fax (408) 847-2683.

Season   Year-round.

Programs 2- to 7-day workshops and retreats designed to foster creativity and health in a spiritual context. Also a 5-week course on ayurveda.

Lodging   Accommodations for up to 300 guests in single, double, triple, and dorm (4- to 7-person) rooms—most with shared bathrooms. Also tent and RV sites.

Rates   Program tuition: weekend $120; 4–7 days $375–625; 5-week course $360 per week, $1,695 for full program. Daily room and board $22–65.

Meals   Cafeteria-style breakfast, dinner, and snack. Vegetarian menu with dairy options and produce from Mount Madonna's gardens.

Services Oil massage and herbal steam bath.

Nyingma Institute   Berkeley, CA

Housed in a four-story hilltop home with views of distant San Francisco Bay, the Nyingma Institute offers residential programs on Tibetan Buddhist practices as adapted for Western use by Tarthan Tulku—the institute's founder and a prolific author. The five-week summer retreat (also open for one-, two-, or three-week stays) focuses each year on the teachings in a particular Tulku book (e.g., *Mastering Successful Work*).

Other annual Nyingma offerings include the weeklong "Kum Nye Relaxation and Healing Spring Retreat," the weeklong year-end "Contemplation and Renewal Retreat," the four-month (ending in December) "Human Development Training Program," and the two-month (January and February) "Integration Program" that is intended primarily as a bridge between the four-month program and a return to life beyond this space set on the edge of the University of California's Berkeley campus.

In addition to meditation and class sessions, all retreat days include mindful work periods. Work-study (with much more work than study) is also an option. The work is mostly building maintenance and publishing chores. (The institute's Dharma Publishing Company is a major publisher of English-language Tibetan Buddhist texts and books on that body of knowledge.)

Address	1815 Highland Place, Berkeley, CA 94709
Phone	(510) 843-6812
Season	Year-round.
Programs	1- to 8-week retreats and trainings on Buddhist meditation, psychology, natural healing, and creative action.
Lodging	An overnight capacity for 20 men and women in separate rooms, each with 3 or 4 beds.
Rates	Sample retreat rates: 1 week $500–600, 5 weeks $2,000, 2 months $3,000, 4 months $6,000.
Meals	3 daily vegetarian meals.

Optimum Health Institute of San Diego   Lemon Grove, CA

On four quiet acres of verdant lawns and gardens in the hills of suburban San Diego, the Optimum Health Institute of San Diego offers instruction in holistic health along with a live foods diet. The institute's revitalizing curriculum is designed as a three-week program, but one- or two-week stays are also beneficial and permitted.

Classes are conducted Monday through Friday on such topics as mental and emotional detoxification, self-esteem, relaxation/pain control, the body, personal care, elimination and digestion, menu planning, food combination and preparation, organic gardening, and wheat grass planting. There are daily exercise sessions. In their spare time, guests may enjoy the Jacuzzi.

Address	6970 Central Avenue, Lemon Grove, CA 91945
Phone	(619) 464-3346
Season	Year-round.
Programs	Ongoing weekly optimum health program focusing on improving nutritional, physical, mental, and emotional balance.
Lodging	Private and double accommodations in 1- and 2-story buildings.
Rates	$295–550 per person per week.
Meals	3 daily live foods meals (sprouts, greens, fruits, vegetables, fruit juices, enzyme-rich Rejuvelac, and wheat grass juice).

Services   Colonics, massage, and chiropractic treatments. Also reduced-rate Orange Cab service from airport and train stations.

Pocket Ranch   Geyserville, CA

Pocket Ranch is a rolling 2,600-acre property in Alexander Valley wine country, two hours north of San Francisco. Nestled in the shadows of Geyser and Pocket Peaks, the ranch offers a sanctuary-like setting for its programs. The staff includes clinical psychologists, psychiatric nurses, counselors, and interns. The director and founder of Pocket Ranch is Barbara Findeisen, a leader in the field of pre- and perinatal psychology.

The ranch's "STAR" program is a seventeen- or twenty-one day individualized intensive process conducted in a group context within a safe and nurturing environment. Healing modalities include individual processing sessions, daily writing assignments, breathwork, emotional release work, guided imagery, sand-tray therapy, and integrative bodywork. Complementing twelve-step programs, "STAR" (Self Analysis Towards Awareness Rebirth) helps adults recover their natural emotional vibrancy, openness, and love.

The "Woodlands" program offers short-term residential treatment for adults experiencing acute distress from burnout, grief, childhood and sexual abuse issues, and spiritual emergency. "Woodlands" provides round-the-clock clinical care using both traditional and alternative healing methods so that people can turn their lives around as quickly as possible. The average length of stay is two to three weeks.

On a space-available basis, the ranch welcomes personal retreatants who (like all guests) may enjoy the hiking trails, outdoor swimming pool, hot tub, and volleyball court. Ranch facilities are also available for private workshop rentals.

Address   P.O. Box 516, Geyserville, CA 95441
Phone   (707) 857-3359. Fax (707) 857-3764.
Season   Year-round.
Programs   "STAR" program, a 17- or 21-day intensive inner journey; "Woodlands" treatment program for people in emotional or spiritual crisis.

Lodging   Accommodations for up to 40 "STAR" program guests in rustic, double occupancy cabins. "Woodlands" guests housed in a building with outdoor decks and a whirlpool bath.

Rates   "STAR": 17 days $4,800, 21 days $5,600. "Woodlands": $600 per day or $3,500 per week. Personal retreat $75–100 per night.

Meals   3 daily meals. Selections for meat eaters and vegetarians.

Services   Individual counseling, imagery, birth regression, breathwork, and bodywork/massage (Swedish, Esalen, shiatsu, and deep tissue).

Shasta Abbey   Mount Shasta, CA

Set on sixteen acres of evergreen forested land near majestic Mount Shasta, Shasta Abbey is a monastery that follows the Buddhist tradition of Serene Reflection Meditation (a hybrid of Japanese Soto Zen and Chinese Tsao-Tung). Permanent residents include thirty-five male and female monks under the spiritual guidance of the Reverend P. T. N. H. Jiyu-Kennett, a British native certified in Japan as a meditation master. The reverend's formal music education is reflected in the four-part harmony of morning and evening prayers sung in English.

Shasta Abbey also serves as a retreat center for laypeople who are interested in Zen Buddhist training. Nearly every month, the abbey hosts introductory weekends with meditation instruction and basic Buddhist teachings. Other programs open to all include weeklong summer "Basic Teaching and Practice" retreats.

A typical introductory weekend begins with a Friday afternoon orientation followed by dinner, meditation instruction, and meditation. Saturday wake-up and lights-out times are 5:55 A.M. and 9:40 P.M. During the day there are sitting meditation periods, classes, services, working meditation periods, along with times for rest and spiritual reading. After a similar Sunday morning schedule, guests depart after lunch. Social conversation is limited to teatimes, and all guests are required to adhere to the schedule.

People who have attended an introductory retreat or a "Basic Teaching and Practice" retreat may apply for regular weekend and weeklong meditation retreats. They may also apply for resident lay training, which focuses on applying meditation in daily life. An important part of the practice is bringing to all activities the compassionate awareness of meditation.

Address   P.O. Box 199, Mount Shasta, CA 96067

Phone   (916) 926-4208. Fax (916) 926-0428. Requires 1 month or more prior notice.

Season   Open to guests year-round except 3–4 weeks in late December and early January.

Programs   Weekend and weeklong retreats on meditation and Buddhist teachings. Also short- or long-term resident lay and monastic training.

Lodging   20 rooms in guest house—private except during large retreats.

Rates   Weekend retreat $60–70. Weeklong retreat $130–150. Resident training: 1 week $90, 2 weeks $160, 3 weeks $230, per month $300.

Meals   3 daily vegetarian meals (including eggs and dairy products). Meals are usually ritual affairs and eaten in silence.

Services   Spiritual counseling.

Shenoa Retreat and Learning Center   Philo, CA

Located two and a half hours north of San Francisco, Shenoa is a 160-acre retreat and learning center adjoining Hendy Woods State Park and bounded on three sides by the Navarro River. The grounds include an open-air sanctuary, a large meadow, hiking trails, a swimming hole, and a swimming pool. Guests can also enjoy tennis, volleyball, Ping-Pong, and badminton.

The center's annual program schedule generally includes holiday weekend family gatherings, yoga retreats and vacations, weeklong astrology and "Course in Miracles" camps, a weeklong "Living with Focusing" workshop, weekend and five-day sustainable living workshops, and a four-and-a-half-month "Gardening with Spirit" internship. All events reflect Shenoa's vision of a world transformed through right livelihood, harmonious relationships, and Earth stewardship.

Shenoa's Land Steward Village encompasses a limited number of fully furnished cottages available for rent when not in use by their owners, members of the center's large extended "family." Shenoa also offers personal retreats, work exchange and full-time employment opportunities, as well as rental facilities for private workshops and retreats.

Address   P.O. Box 43, Philo, CA 95466
Phone   (707) 895-3156. Fax (707) 895-3236.
Season   Open May through November, March through November for programs.
Programs   2- to 14-day workshops, retreats, and family gatherings focusing on holistic health, community building, and environmental harmony. Guests make reservations directly with the visiting teachers.
Lodging   Lodging for up to 55 people in 2- to 5-person cabins (private for couples and families) with hot showers and electricity. Also campsite space for up to 50 people near to bathrooms and showers.
Rates   Programs: 3-day family gathering, adults $90–175, children half price or free; 2- to 3-day workshop $165–235; 5- to 7-day camp or workshop $295–795. Personal retreat $31–64 per night.
Meals   3 daily gourmet vegetarian meals with produce from 1-acre organic garden. Nondairy entrées available on request.

Sivananda Ashram Yoga Farm   Grass Valley, CA

The eighty-acre Sivananda Ashram Yoga Farm lies in a valley in the northern Sierra Nevada foothills about ninety minutes from both Sacramento and Lake Tahoe. The simple farmhouse serves as an all-purpose lodge, dining hall, and practice and meeting facility. Meals are served at 10 A.M. and 6 P.M. Daily hatha yoga sessions are at 8 A.M. and 4 P.M. The day begins and ends with satsang—meditation, chanting, readings, and discussion. During the winter, activities are held indoors in the woodstove-heated farmhouse. A cedar sauna is open year-round.

Guests are encouraged to take a "Yoga Vacation" at any time and for any length of time. Most weekends have a theme such as "Juice Fast," "Five Points to Health," "Vedic Astrology," or "Introduction to Ayurvedic Healing." Theme topics are often discussed or demonstrated in midday lectures or workshops. Otherwise, the hours between 11 A.M. and 4 P.M. are for rest, reflection, or leisure activities like hiking, swimming in the pond, or visiting nearby state parks, mining museums, and shops.

Address   14651 Ballantree Lane, Grass Valley, CA 95949
Phone   (800) 469-9642 or (916) 272-9322. Fax (916) 477-6054.
Season   Year-round.
Programs   Regular daily program, with mandatory attendance of hatha yoga and meditation sessions. Classes taught by ashram staff. Also work-study program and 4-week May teachers' training camp.
Lodging   Accommodations for up to 40 in 8 guest rooms with shared showers and toilets. Tent space on grounds. Limited access for the disabled.
Rates $25–60 per night. Teachers' training camp $1,295–1,545.
Meals   2 daily buffet-style, vegetarian meals.
Services   Massage. Also a weekend shuttle to and from San Francisco.

Sonoma Mountain Zen Center   Santa Rosa, CA

This twenty-year-old center is a cluster of spare wooden buildings set on eighty hilltop acres eleven miles southeast of Santa Rosa. It is run by a small residential community under the spiritual direction of Jakusho Kwong-roshi, the Chinese-American dharma successor to the late Soto Zen master Shunryu Suzuki-roshi.

Those new to meditation and/or Zen may come on designated Saturdays to an "Introduction Zen Workshop" or a "One Day Sitting." A first-time attendee may stay for free the preceding Friday night. During the July "Ango Practice" period, more ambitious guests may come for a one-to four-week retreat with six meditation periods each day. The center also supports solo retreats by students of other Buddhist traditions, who take meals alone or with the community.

The center's formal "Guest Practice" program allows visitors to experience "everyday Zen" by living and practicing in the community for anywhere from a few days to three months. Daily practice includes morning and evening meditation (sitting and walking), chanting, three and a half hours of work practice, informal communal meals, study groups, and private interviews. Each day begins at 5:15 A.M. and ends at 9 P.M.

Serious Zen students may apply for resident training, which requires full participation in all center activities including intensive three- to five-day retreats (each with ten daily meditation periods).

Address	Genjo-ji, 6367 Sonoma Mountain Road, Santa Rosa, CA 95404
Phone	(707) 545-8105 mornings. No visits without prior arrangement.
Season	Year-round except last 2 weeks in December.
Programs	Introductory 1-day workshops and sittings, 3- to 5-day intensive retreats, guest residency opportunities ranging from a few days to 3 months, residency training program, and solo retreats.
Lodging	A 3-bedroom house with bath and kitchen plus 5 rustic cabins heated by woodstoves and electric heaters. BYO sleeping bag.
Rates	"Introduction Zen Workshop" $35. "One Day Sitting" $25. Intensive retreat $30 per day. Guest residency $20 per day. Residency training $400 per month. "Solo Meditation Retreat" $25 per day.
Meals	3 daily vegetarian meals.

Spirit Rock Meditation Center   Woodacre, CA

Spirit Rock is a nonsectarian meditation retreat center located thirty miles north of San Francisco on Miwok Indian sacred grounds purchased from the Nature Conservancy. The 400 acres of rolling hills and meadows embrace a stream, ponds, and trails, plus meditation platforms and benches with spacious views. Center facilities presently include a meditation hall and kitchen/dining hall. Three residence halls, housing up to fifty retreatants, are expected to be ready for occupancy by mid-1997. In the meantime, residential retreats are being held at other northern California facilities.

Most Spirit Rock residential retreats are led by Bay Area resident teachers such as Jack Kornfield, James Baraz, and Sylvia Boorstein. The daily schedule (from 5 A.M. to 10 P.M.) includes sitting and walking meditation, group and individual interviews with instructors, plus talks based on the ethics and traditions of Buddhist psychology. Nonresidential on-site activities include classes, visits by notable guests such as Thich Nhat Hanh, as well as single-day and weekend retreats (during the hours of 9 A.M. and 5 P.M.). Retreatants bring their own sitting cushions and (for outdoors sittings) insulating mats.

Address   P.O. Box 909, Woodacre, CA 94973
Phone   (415) 488-0164. Fax (415) 488-0170. Call before visiting.
Season   Year-round.
Programs   Nonsectarian courses and retreats (1–20 days long) usually on Vipassana (insight) and Metta (loving kindness) meditation.
Lodging   Men's and women's dorms.
Rates   4- to 10-day residential retreat $40–45 per day plus teacher donation. Nonresidential retreat $25 per day plus teacher donation.
Meals   Residential retreat offers vegetarian breakfast and lunch along with late afternoon tea. Lunches served at some nonresidential retreats.

Tassajara   Carmel Valley, CA

Tassajara is a remote, year-round Zen monastery open to guests during the summer months. Overlooking the Pacific Ocean from the heavily forested and mountainous Ventana Wilderness, the community is located two hours southeast of Carmel. The last leg of the trip to Tassajara is a fourteen-mile dirt road that climbs 5,000 feet in six miles, levels off for three miles, then descends steeply.

Originally constructed as a hot springs resort, Tassajara features a bathhouse with showers, steam rooms, creekside sundecks, large plunges and small tubs fed by hot sulphur springs. Men and women bathe in separate areas. Guests can also enjoy a swimming pool and hiking trails in the surrounding wilderness. Children are welcome, but there is no child care or children's play area.

Each year, the center hosts about a dozen retreats and workshops. Usually about half of those programs are retreats devoted to Zen or to Zen and yoga. Other popular workshops explore Zen and nature, organic gardening, and vegetarian cooking. Many program leaders are scheduled with Tassajara and its sister organizations San Francisco Zen Center and Green Gulch Farm (profiled earlier in this section).

There are also "Guest Practice" and "Work Practice" programs. For a minimum of three days, a "Guest Practice" participant joins in the morning monastic schedule of Zen meditation at 6 A.M. followed by three and a half hours of work. Participants may also meet with program teachers and attend classes and lectures. For anywhere from five days to all summer, "Work Practice" participants follow the full monastic schedule.

Address	Zen Center, 300 Page Street, San Francisco, CA 94102
Phone	(415) 431-3771. No visits without prior arrangement.
Season	May through early September.
Programs	5-day Zen retreats plus other 5-day workshops and retreats. "Guest Practice" and "Work Practice" programs. Also vacation stays.
Lodging	Rustic dorms, cabins, rooms, suites, and yurts with no phone and no electricity. Rooms and pathways lighted by kerosene lamps.
Rates	Food and lodging $67–200 per night. 5-day Zen retreat add $100. Other 5-day programs add $200. "Guest Practice" $45 per night. "Work Practice" $70 per night for first 5 days (the minimum) of the stay.
Meals	3 daily buffet-style vegetarian meals. Options of nondairy dinner and oil-free salad at lunch.
Services	Jamesburg pick-up and delivery by 4-wheel-drive "Stage."

Vega Institute   Oroville, CA

One and a half hours north of Sacramento on Highway 70, Vega Institute is located in the residential heart of Oroville. The surrounding countryside is rich with organic farms and orchards, an ideal environment for a residential study center dedicated to teaching macrobiotics as a way of life.

The institute hosts two to five programs each month. Especially popular are the two-week "Macrobiotic Lifestyle and Essentials" and "Cancer and Healing" programs. Typical one-week programs are "A Personal Peace," the annual "Women's Spirituality Week," "Cooking for One," "Family Festival," and "Feng Shui: Creating Harmony in Your Home and Workplace." There are occasional one-week retreat/conference programs, as well as three- and four-week trainings for macrobiotic counselors and cooking teachers.

While conference/retreat programs feature guest speakers, all other programs are conducted by institute directors David and Cindy Briscoe with assistance from institute founders Herman and Cornellia Aihara. David specializes in macrobiotic counseling and education; Cindy is a chef and cooking class instructor. The Aiharas have more than forty years of international experience as teachers of macrobiotics.

Address 1511 Robinson Street, Oroville, CA 95965
Phone (800) 818-8342 or (916) 533-7702. Fax (916) 533-4999.
Season Year-round.
Programs 1- and 2-week programs on macrobiotic cooking, healing, lifestyle, and counseling. Occasional 1-week retreat/conference.
Lodging 22 cotton futon beds in shared and private rooms, all near the sauna, in main building. Also a 4-person cottage. BYO linens.
Rates Program tuition (meals included): 1 day $150, 1 week $545–595, 2 weeks $995–1,095. Retreat/conference tuition (meals included) $450–525. Weekly accommodations $75–375.
Meals 2 daily macrobiotic meals with plenty of locally grown organic grains and produce.
Services Macrobiotic counseling.

We Care Health Center   Desert Hot Springs, CA

Guests at We Care Health Center can enjoy a variety of activities, from early morning walks in the desert to afternoon dips in the pool or nearby mineral springs. Usually there are clear vistas of the jagged San Jacinto Mountains etched against an azure sky. Along with this natural beauty, clean air, and exercise, guests can enjoy the friendly atmosphere fostered by center director Susana Lombardi—a certified lymphologist and massage and colon therapist.

We Care offers an all-natural liquid diet rejuvenation program. Both private and retreat accommodations are offered with eight-day, six-day, and weekend programs. The eight- and six-day programs include yoga classes (meditative light stretching), nutrition classes, cooking demonstrations, lymphatic massages, and colon hygiene.

Address   18000 Long Canyon Road, Desert Hot Springs, CA 92241

Phone   (619) 251-2261 or (800) 888-2523.

Season   Year-round.

Programs   8-day "Deluxe Revitalization," 6-day "Vegetarian Cleanse," weekend "Mini Cleanse."

Lodging   12 large and small private rooms with or without TV, telephone, maid service, and private bath.

Rates   8 days $925–1,499. 6 days $799–1,250. Weekend $249–599.

Meals   Hourly drinks, including raw vegetable juices, herbal teas, water with lemon, and detox drinks (with psyllium, bentonite, chlorophyll).

Services   Massage, foot reflexology, aromatherapy, iridology, scalp revitalization, colon hygiene, salt rubs, herbal glows, facials.

Wellspring Renewal Center   Philo, CA

This forty-five-acre center is dedicated to the renewal of the human spirit. It is located in the scenic coastal hills of Mendocino County. The farmhouse and cabins open onto rolling meadows and the refreshing headwaters of the Navarro River, suitable for summer rafting and swimming. The property includes volleyball and basketball courts, a sweat lodge, campground, and campfire pit, along with trails into the redwood forests of the neighboring state park.

Some Wellspring programs are loosely structured family weekends hosted by the resident staff. Most programs, however, are led by visiting teachers on such topics as "Sexuality and Spirituality," "Aging as a Spiritual Journey," and "Developing Our Healing Gift." In recent years, annual programs have included "Arts and Crafts Week," "Five-Day Silent Retreat," "Women's Fall Renewal Weekend," and "Winter Solstice Celebration."

Study, meditation and prayer, community meals, shared work, and recreation are all part of the Wellspring experience. Personal retreatants are welcome when programs are not in progress.

Address   P.O. Box 332, Philo, CA 95466
Phone   (707) 895-3893. No visits without prior arrangement.
Season   Year-round.
Programs Weekend, 5- and 6-day programs focusing on healing, creativity, spiritual growth, and living in harmony with nature.
Lodging   Accommodations for more than 80 guests in 2 lodges with double bedrooms and small kitchens, rustic cabins, campground tepees, and tent cabins.
Rates   Weekend program $85–130. 5- or 6-day program: adults $200–460, children $100–160. Guest stay: adults $6–25 per night, children $3–10 per night; for 3 daily meals, add $20 for adults, $12 for children.
Meals   3 daily meals, mostly vegetarian with fruit and vegetables from organic garden and neighboring farms. Freshly baked breads and desserts.

Zen Mountain Center   Mountain Center, CA

A 160-acre meditation retreat situated 5,500 feet above sea level in a steep canyon of the San Jacinto Mountains. The Pacific Coast trail cuts across a corner of the property, from where there are vistas of the Pacific Ocean. Los Angeles lies 120 miles to the southeast. Unfinished wood cabins and meditation hall enhance the center's rustic charm. Solar energy provides electricity and heats water for the bathhouse.

A small community of residents at the Zen Mountain Center (ZMC) supports personal meditation retreats, one-day group sittings, "Introduction to Zen" workshops, occasional weekend programs, and daily monastic practice (except for Monday, ZMC's day off). Popular weekend programs include "Tai Chi," "Meditation in Motion: Yoga and Zen," plus retreats for families, women, and homosexuals. All ZMC programs are led by abbots and other members of the Zen Center of Los Angeles (ZCLA). ZMC facilities may also be rented by private groups.

Each summer there is a ninety-day "ango" practice period with three intensive one-week "sesshin" meditation retreats. Each ango day begins at 3:45 A.M. and includes seven hours of sitting meditation, teacher/ student interviews, work periods, and study of a discipline such as tai chi, Alexander Technique, yoga, tea ceremony, sutra chanting, or callig- raphy. Days of the month with a 4 or a 9 are days off for rest, relaxation, and hiking. Guests may join in ango for anywhere from a few days to the entire three-month period. At other times of the year, long-term stays are possible on a resident-training basis.

Address	P.O. Box 43, Mountain Center, CA 92561
Phone	(909) 659-5272. No visits with prior arrangement.
Season	Year-round.
Programs	2- and 3-day weekend programs, intensive 1-week sesshins, summer ango, resident training, plus personal retreats.
Lodging	Dormitory housing for up to 30 in small cabins and trailers. Also summer campsites. Bathhouses and outhouses. BYO sleeping bag.
Rates	1-day "Introduction to Zen" $50. 1-day sitting $10–15. 2- and 3-day programs $150–200. 1-week sesshin $30–50 per day. Ango $450–550 per month. Resident training $500 per month. Personal retreat (including meals or kitchen use) $60 per day. Discounts for members and winter events.
Meals	3 daily vegetarian meals, generally eaten together.
Services	Car pooling between ZMC and ZCLA can generally be arranged.

The Art of Being and META Institute   Maui, HI

This organization hosts annual summer and winter vacations combin- ing self-discovery, life-enhancement, and spiritual renewal. The vaca- tion site is Akahi Farm, a private fifty-five-acre estate with a hot tub, tropical gardens, and secluded meadows situated in the north shore countryside of Maui, Hawaii. Leisure activities include body surfing,

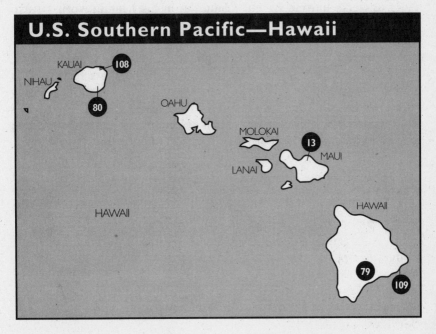

U.S. Southern Pacific—Hawaii

KAUAI
NIHAU
108
80
OAHU
MOLOKAI
13
MAUI
LANAI
HAWAII
HAWAII
79
109

snorkeling, hiking in the bamboo forests, and camping at the waterfalls of the Seven Sacred Pools.

July and August options include a two-week "High on Life" vacation, the first week of which can be taken alone. "High on Life" is the creation of META Institute directors Paul and Niyaso Carter. Paul is a psychotherapist who uses gestalt process, sacred arts, and expressive arts (e.g., drawing, movement, and chanting) in his healing work. Niyaso teaches and facilitates meditation, yoga, breathwork, movement awareness, and voice dialogue.

Other July and August options include the one-week "Body, Heart, and Soul" workshop, created by the Carters in partnership with Alan Lowen as a tantric path to higher consciousness through the awakening of sexual energy. Other segments of the four-part "Body, Heart, and Soul" training are presented on Maui each January and February and elsewhere (including Europe) at other times of the year.

Address	The Art of Being, P.O. Box 38, Paia, Maui, HI 96779
Phone	(808) 572-2234. Fax (808) 572-1435.
Season	January and February, July and August.
Programs	1-, 2-, and 3-week Hawaii holistic and tantric healing vacations.
Lodging	Single, double, and shared rooms.
Rates	Approximate rates: 1 week $1,235, 2 weeks $2,010, 3 weeks $3,100.
Meals	3 daily gourmet vegetarian meals.
Services	Massage.

Hawaiian Healing Arts & Massage   Wood Valley, HI

"If you want a vacation, take one after the workshop," says Shawn LaSalla-Kimmel, who conducts weeklong healing arts workshops at a retreat center on the Big Island of Hawaii. Shawn is a licensed massage therapist and longtime student of Hawaiian elders in the native healing arts. She is assisted at some of the workshops by her husband, Ken, a Jungian therapist who has researched the healers and mediums of South America.

All workshops include breathwork, Hawaiian rituals, and visits to sacred sites. Rituals consist of vision walks, hula basics, and ceremonial lei making. Sacred sites include Kilauea Volcano, ancient temples, and the City of Refuge. Other workshop elements covered are Hawaiian massage, visualization exercises, gestalt dreamwork, drumming, and sacred dance. Workshop participants get one hour off at lunch for beach time.

Address	Pacific Northwest Center for Hawaiian Healing Arts & Massage, 219 1st Avenue South, Suite 405, Seattle, WA 98104
Phone	(206) 447-1895
Season	February and March.
Programs	2 weeklong healing arts workshops. Occasionally a weeklong healing and transformative dream workshop.
Lodging	Men's and women's dorms.
Rates	$995–1,195 per week.
Meals	3 daily meals with vegetarian options.

Hawaiian Wellness Holiday or Metaphysical Vacation   Koloa, Kauai, HI

Dr. Grady and Roberleigh Deal host "Wellness Holiday" and "Metaphysical Vacation" programs on the Hawaiian island of Kauai. Both programs include meals and lodging for three days, one week or two weeks, along with yoga, scenic hikes, and two weekly massages or chiropractic treatments. The "Wellness" program also includes exercise classes, nutritional counseling, health lectures, and a detoxification/rejuvenation/weight loss program. Additional elements of the "Metaphysical" program are excursions to vortex centers and sacred sites, astrology and numerology readings, lectures and workshops on metaphysics.

Dr. Grady Deal is a chiropractor, psychological counselor, gourmet cook, and author of *Dr. Deal's Delicious Detox Diet and Wellness Lifestyle*. Roberleigh Deal is a hike leader, massage therapist, yoga and aquacise teacher, and author of *Numerology for Personal Transformation*. Mira Hunter, a professional yoga teacher, assists the Deals with both programs.

Address	P.O. Box 279, Koloa, Kauai, HI 96756
Phone	(808) 332-9244 or (800) 338-6977.

Season   Year-round.

Programs   3-day, 1-week, and 2-week vacations emphasizing either health and exercise ("Wellness Holiday") or personal transformation and metaphysics ("Metaphysical Vacation").

Lodging   Garden view rooms at the Sheraton Kauai Beach Resort or Waikomo Streams Condominiums. Also ocean view rooms at Nihi Kai Villas Condominiums. All accommodations in the Poipu Beach area.

Rates   3 days: singles $895–1,030, couples $1,395–1,575. 1 week: singles $1,995–2,395, couples $2,985–3,465. 2 weeks: singles $3,790–4,550, couples $5,965–6,775.

Meals   3 daily meals with several options: vegetarian, Fit for Life, macrobiotic, raw foods, juice fasting, and Dr. Deal's Delicious Detox Diet. Fish and eggs available.

Services   Courtesy airport pick-up and drop-off service. Additional massage and chiropractic sessions (beyond those included in the programs).

Kai Mana   Kilauea, Kauai, HI

Shakti Gawain, the well-known author and consciousness teacher, hosts weeklong personal growth intensives at her home in Kauai. Each program includes three or four group sessions facilitated by Shakti, three individual voice dialogue sessions (the technique developed by Drs. Hal and Sidra Stone), two massages, meditation and visualization classes, nature attunement rituals, and excursions. The number of participants in each program ranges from ten to twenty people.

Set on a cliff surrounded by ocean and mountains, Shakti's five-acre estate includes a large main house and guest cottage. In their free time, workshop participants can explore the nearby trails and beaches, enjoy a soak in the hot tub, and watch the sun set from a deck above waters where whales and dolphins often surface. When not in use for intensives, Kai Mana rooms may be rented for guest stays.

Address   Box 612, Kilauea, Kauai, HI 96754

Phone   (808) 828-1280 or (800) 837-1782. Fax (808) 828-6670.

Season   From time to time throughout the year.

Programs Weeklong intensives (led by Shakti Gawain) focusing on healing and balancing all levels of being.

Lodging Shared (for couples) and single accommodations at Shakti's home or a nearby B&B.

Rates Intensive: singles $1,600, couples $3,000. Guest stay $75–125 per night for singles or couples.

Meals Intensives include breakfast and lunch. Guests can prepare dinners in guest kitchenette facilities or dine out at local restaurants.

Services Massage, bodywork, and counseling sessions with Shakti when she is on the island.

Kalani Honua   Kalapana, HI

A twenty-acre conference and retreat center forty-five minutes by car from Hilo Airport, Kalani Honua ("Harmony of Heaven and Earth") is the only coastal lodging facility within Hawaii's largest conservation area. Bordered by tropical forest, and by cliffs overlooking the ocean, the property includes a large outdoor pool, tennis court, dry sauna, and Jacuzzi. Clothing is optional after 7 P.M. at the center's pool/spa area and at the natural steam baths, warm springs, and black sand beach a few minutes away.

There are many ways of visiting Kalani Honua. A guest can come here on private vacation, participate in a private group retreat, or attend one of the many public residential workshops, festivals, and conferences held here each year by various outside groups. Most group programs (listed in the center's schedule of events) focus on physical, energetic, creative, and celebratory forms of well-being. Anyone may also participate in ongoing classes in yoga, chi gung, hula, and contemporary dance.

The center's purpose is to support the arts, physical and emotional healing, and traditional Hawaiian culture. It gives a 50 percent discount on lodging rates to resident professional artists and sponsors free weekly talks on Hawaiian history, mythology, and crafts.

Address RR 2, Box 4500, Pahoa, HI 96778

Phone (808) 965-7828 or (800) 800-6886 (reservations). Fax (808) 965-9613.

Season   Year-round.

Programs   2- to 14-day workshops, festivals, and conferences encouraging creative expression, holistic health, and personal and spiritual growth. Also a 3-month work-study program.

Lodging   Accommodations for 75–85 overnight guests in private cottages, 2-story cedar lodges (each with kitchen, dorm space, private rooms, and suites). Also orchard campsites.

Rates   Nightly lodging: adult $15–85, each additional adult $15, children up to age 3 free, children ages 3–12 $10. 10% lodging discount on stays of at least 7 nights. 3 meals about $25 per day with half price for children. Program fees vary widely and usually include room and board.

Meals   3 daily vegetarian buffets (with fish or chicken options) with produce from the Kalani Honua herb garden and nearby farms. Lodge kitchen facilities are available for use by guests.

Services   Massage. Airport transfers. Children's programs in the summer.

UNITED STATES: *Northwest Region*

Eagle Song Camps   Ovando, MT

Native wisdom is the heart of author/teacher Brooke Medicine Eagle's camps, held each summer in western Montana. Most of the Eagle Song Camps are at Blacktail Ranch, 8,000 valley acres that include a bear shaman's cave, an ancient ceremonial medicine wheel, and a sweat lodge next to a beaver-dammed creek. The ranch bunkhouse contains a kitchen, dining hall, lounge, bathrooms, hot tub, and sauna. Meetings are held in tepees and a large yurt. Campers pitch their tents in a meadow beneath the aspen groves and high pines of the surrounding Rocky Mountains.

The two most popular and consistent annual events are the ten- and fourteen-day, women-only "Deepening of Spirit" and "Healing Vision" camps. These "vision camps" include two-day solo vision quests, ritual, drumming, dance, chanting, and meditation. There is usually also a summer vision camp open to both men and women. Sometimes in the spring, there is a seven-day "Beauty Way" arts and crafts camp for men and women at the Boulder Hot Springs Hotel in Montana's Peace Valley, an ancient sanctuary area for native tribes.

Most camps offer opportunities for horseback riding, swimming, and hiking. Guest teachers include storytellers, craftspeople, therapists, and naturopathy experts.

Address	Singing Eagle Enterprises, #1 2nd Avenue East—C401, Polson, MT 59860
Phone	(406) 883-4686. Fax (406) 883-6629.
Season	June through August.
Programs	7-, 10-, and 14-day "Earth Wisdom" healing camps, some for women only. 10- and 14-day camps include 2-day solo vision quests.
Lodging	Vision camps: BYO tent, sleeping bag, and pad and use bunkhouse bathrooms. "Beauty Way" camps: lodging at Boulder Hot Springs Hotel.

U.S. Northwest

Montana
- 51   Eagle Song Camps
- 63   Feathered Pipe Ranch
- 198 Royal Teton Ranch Summer Conference

Oregon
- 23   Breitenbush Hot Springs
- 27   Caring Rapid Counseling Center
- 151 Namaste Retreat Center

Washington
- 35   Cloud Mountain
- 90   Holden Village
- 96   Indralaya

Rates   Camps: 7 days $995, 10 days $1,025–1,075, 14 days $1,475.

Meals   Vision camps: 3 nutritious daily meals prepared by a staff under Brooke's guidance. "Beauty Way" camps: healthy hotel fare.

Feathered Pipe Ranch   Helena, MT

A fifteen-minute drive from Helena, Feathered Pipe is a 110-acre ranch with log and stone buildings. A new addition is a cedar bathhouse with huge hot tubs, a sauna, and massage rooms staffed by professional masseurs. Ranch guests can also enjoy a refreshing lake swim or an invigorating hike in the foothills of the surrounding Rocky Mountains.

Most of the dozen or so programs offered each season are about one week long. All are led by teachers who are well-known and respected in their fields. Feathered Pipe also offers vacationers evening and Saturday horseback rides and, before they head home, the option of a "Flowing with Nature" one-day river rafting trip with storyteller/naturalist Tom McBride.

The ranch strives to live up to its name—the feathered pipe symbolizes connecting with the circle of life. Another way Feathered Pipe founder and director India Supera seeks to expand that circle is by guiding pilgrimages to sacred places around the world.

Address   Box 1682, Helena, MT 59624

Phone   (406) 442-8196. Fax (406) 442-8110.

Season   May through August.

Programs 3- to 10-day programs in natural health, native and women's wisdom, astrology, and hatha yoga.

Lodging   Main Lodge has double and dorm (4 to 6 people) rooms. There are also tepees, yurts, and tents—all near bathroom facilities.

Rates   Programs: 3 days $425–445, 6–8 days $1,065–1,099, additional charge for double room with shared or private bath. Horseback ride: $50 per evening, $100 per day. 1-day river rafting adventure $100.

Meals   3 gourmet natural food meals, mostly vegetarian (occasionally fish and chicken) and organically grown whenever possible.

Services Massage.

Royal Teton Ranch Summer Conference   Corwin Springs, MT

This 600-member spiritual community spreads across 28,000 acres of alpine forests and meadows at an altitude of 6,400 feet. It is also the international headquarters of Church Universal and Triumphant, Summit University, Summit University Press, and Montessori International. The church was founded in 1974 by Elizabeth Clare Prophet to spread the teachings of the ascended masters as dictated through Prophet.

Each summer, the ranch hosts a large ten-day, family-oriented camp/conference attended primarily by church members but open to all. The daily schedule includes morning and early evening workshops on the teachings of the ascended masters, early afternoon dictations by Prophet, plus church rituals and sacraments such as baptisms and weddings. In the evenings, there are talks on the conference theme.

There is also a full schedule of morning activities and courses primarily for nonchurch members. These include hatha yoga, tai chi, canoeing, herb walks and guided hikes, inner-child workshops, macrobiotic cooking, and astrology. On the day after the conference ends, there are guided tours of Yellowstone National Park and Beartooth Pass.

Address   Summit University, Box 5000, Livingston, MT 59047

Phone   (800) 437-3366 or (406) 222-8300.

Season   11 days in late June and early July.

Programs   Conference with holistic health courses and activities, plus workshops and dictations on the teachings of the ascended masters.

Lodging   Camping in large meadows. Campers use own tents or same-sex dorm "tent houses." BYO sleeping bag. RV parking (but no hookups).

Rates   5–10 days: adults $215–245, children $70–80, just morning activities $85. 1–4 days: adults $110, children $40, just morning activities $45. Average meal costs: breakfast $3–4.50, lunch or dinner $5.50–7, soup and sandwich under $5.

Meals   Cafeteria offers macrobiotic cuisine (whole grains, vegetables, and fish) along with poultry and meat. Also campsite cooking and the nearby Ranch Kitchen restaurant.

Services   Programs for children and teens, largely recreational but with some church teachings.

Breitenbush Hot Springs   Detroit, OR

On eighty-six acres straddling the Breitenbush River two hours southeast of Portland rests Breitenbush Hot Springs, a holistic health retreat
operated by a resident community. Guest facilities include a large lodge
built in the 1930s and cabins with hydroelectric and geothermal heating.
There are a sauna, hot and cold tubs, and hot springs pools where swim-
suits are always optional. Nearby is Devil's Creek swimming hole. Trails
for hikers and cross country skiers lead out into the surrounding National Forest and Mount Jefferson Wilderness.

Breitenbush programs focus on the expressive arts, body/mind disciplines, and healing relationships (both past and present). Most programs are led by healing arts practitioners from the Pacific Northwest,
including the Breitenbush community. Particularly popular offerings
are the monthly sweat lodge ceremonies, the twice annual service
weeks, and weekend holiday and solstice celebrations.

Guests can also enjoy Breitenbush as a personal retreat. Daily community activities include prebreakfast meditations and postbreakfast
sharing circles in the sanctuary, where all spiritual traditions are respected. Weekly activities may include Breitenbush tours; sessions in
tai chi, yoga, and EDGU, a spinal revitalization technique that involves
a series of free-flowing upper-body rotations made while grounded in a
fixed stance; evening concerts, storytelling, high-tea poetry readings,
and song and drumming circles.

Address	P.O. Box 578, Detroit, OR 97342
Phone	(503) 854-3314
Season	Year-round.
Programs	2- to 8-day programs on body/mind disciplines, healing re-lationships, and expressive arts. Also personal retreats and monthly sweat lodge ceremonies.
Lodging	40 1- and 2-bedroom cabins—all with heat and electricity, some with toilet and sink. Campsites and large tents, with mattresses, on platforms near showers and rest rooms. BYO towels and bedding.
Rates	2- to 4-day workshop or celebration $100–350. 5- to 7-day program $375–830. Daily rates for personal retreat: adults $35–85, children up to age 3 free, ages 4–6 $10, ages 7–12 $15, and ages 13–16 $20. Discounts for seniors and stays over 1 week.

Meals	3 daily vegetarian meals for overnight guests. Can accommodate dairy-, egg-, and wheat-free diets. Herb teas and hot water are provided.
Services	Massage, hydrotherapy, herbal sheet wraps, aromatherapy, reiki.

Caring Rapid Counseling Center   Coos Bay, OR

Caring Rapid Counseling Center is located 150 miles north of the California border on the scenic southern Oregon coast. The center offers 3- and 5-day "Neurohealing Private Workshops" based on the spiritual and emotional healing techniques developed by self-help pioneer Ken Keyes and John Bradshaw, the well-known proponent of inner-child healing work. The workshops are designed to create "a relaxed enjoyment of life" by healing the childhood wounds at the root of negative core beliefs.

All workshops are facilitated by staff trained—and for many years directed—by Ken Keyes. Ken died in late 1995 at age seventy-four. A quadriplegic for the last fifty years of his life, Ken embraced his polio as the gift that challenged him to discover the "living love" principles he espoused in fifteen books as well as lectures, seminars, and workshops throughout America. Keyes's *Handbook to Higher Consciousness* was one of the major sparks to the birth and early years of the Western personal growth movement.

Address	1620 Thompson Road, Coos Bay, OR 97420
Phone	(503) 267-6412. Fax (503) 269-2388.
Season	Year-round.
Programs	3- and 5-day private emotional and spiritual healing workshops.
Lodging	Nearby motel rooms.
Rates	Workshops and lodging: 3-days $1,500; 5-days $2,000.
Meals	Meals available for purchase at a nearby hospital cafeteria, local restaurants, and grocery stores.
Services	Airport pick-up and drop-off, plus transportation to and from motel.

Namaste Retreat Center   Wilsonville, OR

Namaste Retreat Center rests on ninety-five wooded acres in rolling farmland thirty minutes south of Portland. The grounds and facilities include ponds, nature walks, badminton and volleyball fields, and a large indoor pool and Jacuzzi. Also on the grounds is the Living Enrichment Center, Namaste's parent organization and one of the largest New Thought churches in the United States.

Roughly once each month, Namaste hosts weekend and weeklong workshops facilitated by leading spiritual and personal growth authors and teachers (e.g., Jean Houston, Barbara Marx Hubbard, Joan Borysenko, Gay and Kathlyn Hendricks). From time to time, Namaste also hosts a ten-day experiential conference featuring a large and distinguished guest faculty. At other times, the center is open for personal retreats and group rentals.

Address 29500 SW Grahams Ferry Road, Wilsonville, OR 97070
Phone (503) 682-5683 or (800) 893-1000. Fax (503) 682-4275.
Season Year-round.
Programs Weekend and weeklong programs (most weeklong workshops having a weekend option) on spiritual and personal growth.
Lodging Accommodations for up to 158 guests in shared and single rooms, most with shared bath, in newly remodeled 4-room cabins.
Rates Programs: weekend $195–395, 5 days $495–995, 10 days $1,995–2,195. Personal retreat: $44–49 per day with 3 meals.
Meals 3 daily home-style meals accommodating vegetarians and special dietary needs.
Services Free airport shuttle. Watsu (water massage).

Cloud Mountain   Castle Rock, WA

This rustic retreat center is situated on five acres of wooded land containing several buildings, a sauna, a small lake, an organic garden and greenhouse, a fishpond, cats, chickens, and peacocks. A short walk up the road leads to views of snowcapped Mount Rainier and Mount St. Helens. Seattle is just over two hours to the north, and Portland, Oregon, is just over one hour to the south.

The center supports the work of the Northwest Dharma Association (NWDA) by hosting workshops and retreats led by monks and lay teachers from the Zen, Tibetan, and Theravada/Vipassana Buddhist traditions. Well-known teachers come from as far away as Asia and England. The center also hosts occasional workshops that combine meditation with other centering and spiritual disciplines. In all cases, retreatants help with meal preparation and cleanup.

A schedule of Cloud Mountain programs and other Northwest Dharma activities is published in NWDA's bimonthly, twenty-four-page newsletter. Subscriptions are available from NWDA at 311 West McGraw, Seattle, WA 98119; (206) 286-9060.

Address	P.O. Box 807, Castle Rock, WA 98611
Phone	(360) 274-4859. Fax (360) 274-9119. No visits without prior arrangement.
Season	Year-round.
Programs	Meditation and Buddhist teaching retreats; most are 2–10 days long.
Lodging	Lodging for up to 35 guests in dorms and private rooms. Hot-water shower houses, outhouses, and indoor flush toilets. BYO bedding, towels, and meditation cushion.
Rates	Typical food and lodging rates for meditation and Buddhist teachings retreats: weekend $70, 4 days $140, 8–10 days $275–335. Teacher contributions made at end of each retreat.
Meals	3 daily vegetarian meals with alternatives (on request) to wheat or dairy dishes. Tea, fruit, and snacks available during the day.

Holden Village   Holden, WA

An ecumenical Christian education, retreat, and renewal community located in a former miners' village deep in the Glacier Peak Wilderness Area of the Cascade Mountains. The village has no phone service, and its valley is too deep for cellular phone or TV reception. There are also no cars. The village is accessible only by a three-hour boat ride across Lake Chelan followed by an eleven-mile bus ride to the foot of Copper Mountain.

During the summer, teaching sessions are held every day (except Sunday) in the morning, late afternoon, and evening. Discussion topics cover interpersonal, religious, environmental, and social justice concerns—often presented from the perspective of a marginalized group. Other activities include afternoon nature walks, art and crafts classes, evening concerts, and forums. Evening vespers and a Sunday evening Eucharist service in the Lutheran tradition are open to all.

Believing that "the struggle of our world is learning to live in community," Holden encourages interaction through living, working, playing, learning, dining, and worshiping together. The many ways of participating in Holden Village include retreats, intensive study sojourns, work-study programs, and short- and long-term volunteer stays, as well as sabbaticals for pastors, writers, professors, artists, musicians, and others.

Address	Chelan, WA 98816
Phone	None.
Season	Year-round.
Programs	Summer daily educational sessions, 1-month intensive study sojourns, 10-week fall work-study program, plus 3- to 4-day winter retreats on specific topics of faith and life.
Lodging	2- and 4-person rooms. Maximum capacity for 255 guests, 145 volunteer staffers, and 40 teachers.
Rates	Adult nightly rates typically $32–48, with lower rates applying for longer stays. Discounts for children. Special weekly rates for families. 1-month sojourn $576. 10-week work-study $775.
Meals	3 daily family-style meals, with limited use of meat.
Services	Free round-trip shuttle from and to the dock at Lake Chelan. Also summer programs for children up to 10 years old.

Indralaya   Eastsound, WA

This Orcas Island retreat was founded in 1927 to explore the potential for self-transformation in community and cooperation with nature. The seventy-eight-acre property encompasses a pebbled beach, meadows, forests, trails, an ancient apple orchard, a large organic vegetable garden, and a cozy library. The land is shared with rabbits, deer, sea otters, and other wildlife. By car and ferry, the camp is three hours northwest of Seattle.

The modestly priced programs include silent meditation, yoga, and tai chi retreats; therapeutic touch, personal growth, and metaphysical teachings workshops; as well as family-oriented events such as weekend work parties and "Celebrating Families" weeks. All guests are welcome to join daily morning community meditations and to enjoy hiking and canoeing. Personal retreatants contribute two hours of work each day. During the summer, Indralaya also hosts a series of Saturday evening concerts performed under the stars, by a blazing fire, or in a rustic hall.

While open to all, Indralaya retains a strong commitment to the theosophical principles of its founding members. One of those members (Dora Kunz, a past president of the U.S. Theosophical Society) remains an active workshop leader.

Address	Route 1, Box 86, Eastsound, WA 98245
Phone	(360) 376-4526. No visits without prior arrangement.
Season	Mid-March through October.
Programs	2- to 7-day metaphysical, personal growth, and holistic health workshops. 2- to 8-week "Summer Fellowship Staff" openings.
Lodging	Capacity for as many as 130 overnight guests in double occupancy rooms and rustic cabins, some for smokers and some with plumbing. BYO bedding. Also tent, trailer, and RV sites.
Rates	Tuition: work party weekends free, 2- and 3-day programs and retreats $10–15, 5- to 7-day programs $30–70. Nightly program lodging (including 3 daily meals): adults $35–50, teens $25, ages 6–12 $7.50, children up to age 6 free. Daily rates for personal retreat: 1 adult $30, each additional adult

in same cabin $10. Meals: breakfast and lunch $5 each, dinner $10.

Meals   3 daily buffet-style, lacto-ovo vegetarian meals. Personal retreatants may prepare meals in their cabins.

Services   Courtesy pick-up and drop-off of guests at the Orcas ferry landing.

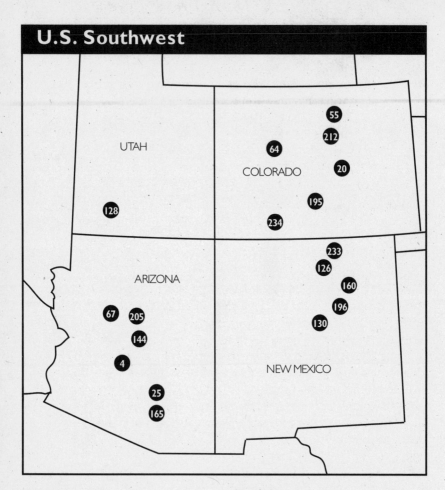

U.S. Southwest

Arizona
4   A.R.E. Medical Clinic
25   Canyon Ranch
67   Four-Fold Way Trainings
144   Merritt Center
165   Onsite
205   Sedona Spirit

Colorado
20   Blue Mountain Center
55   Eden Valley Lifestyle Center
64   Filoha Meadows
195   Rocky Mountain T'ai Chi Ch'uan
212   Shoshoni Yoga Retreat
234   Tara Mandala

New Mexico
126   Lama Foundation
130   Light Institute of Galisteo
160   Ocamora Foundation
196   Rose Mountain
233   Takoja Institute

Utah
128   The Last Resort

UNITED STATES: *Southwest Region*

A.R.E. Medical Clinic   Phoenix, AZ

This clinic offers seven- and eleven-day "Temple Beautiful" programs based on the concepts of regeneration and spiritual growth found in the Edgar Cayce readings, which are archived at the Virginia headquarters of the Association for Research & Enlightenment (A.R.E.). These experiential programs are designed for people seeking spiritual insights, ways to improve their physical health, or adventures in consciousness. The programs are directed by a registered nurse and William A. Mc-Garey, M.D., the author of *Healing Miracles* and the founder and director of this twenty-five-year-old clinic.

Each "Temple Beautiful" program begins with a physician evaluation of the participant's medical records and laboratory tests. This is followed by individual and group counseling; a daily morning exercise regimen designed to fit each individual's needs; plus formal lectures and informal sessions on topics such as meditation and prayer, guided imagery, dream interpretation, music and movement in dance, psychic insights, journal keeping, and group work.

"Temple Beautiful" includes massage, acupressure, reflexology, steam cabinet, whirlpool, and colon therapy; biofeedback instruction and monitored autogenic exercises to teach relaxation skills; as well as pain- and/or stress-reducing energy therapies such as Myopulse, Electro-Acuscope, and electromagnetic balancing with the ETA machine. The staff also works with each participant to design an ongoing program to be followed at home.

Address	4017 North 40th Street, Phoenix, AZ 85018
Phone	(602) 955-0551. Fax (602) 956-8269.
Season	Year-round.
Programs	7- and 11-day holistic health lifestyle programs not limited to people with serious or chronic health problems.
Lodging	Accommodations for up to 17 people in shared and private rooms in the clinic's spacious Oak House. Wheelchair ac-

cessible. But nonambulatory guests must come with an attendant.

Rates $4,900 for both 7- and 11-day residential programs. Attendants who accompany guests pay $2,000 and participate in all activities.

Meals   3 daily meals with emphasis on fruits and vegetables. Some guests are placed on a special diet by the clinic physician.

Services   Complimentary transportation from and to the airport.

Canyon Ranch   Tucson, AZ

An ultramodern holistic health spa located on sixty acres of desert oasis in the foothills of the Santa Catalina Mountains. Clustered around a spacious hacienda are eight outdoor tennis courts, sunlit gyms, three outdoor pools, and one indoor pool with nearby whirlpools, saunas, and steam rooms. Surrounding the complex is the scent of sagebrush, the ever-changing mountain light and shadow, and saguaro cactus pointing into the dry desert sky.

All vacations at Canyon Ranch include health and fitness assessments; presentations by fitness, nutrition, stress management, and medical experts; fitness classes, sports activities such as hiking and mountain biking, plus full use of spa and resort facilities. The ranch's premier offering is the weeklong "Life Enhancement Program" (LEP), designed to address health objectives, among them smoking cessation, weight loss, stress reduction, prevention and reversal of heart disease. Offered on a virtually continuous basis, LEP includes nutrition and diet management consultations, behavioral health classes, exercise physiology consultations, and movement therapy. Each LEP session is limited to forty participants.

From time to time, the ranch also offers weeklong special programs such as "Woman to Woman" and "Spiritual Pathways." "Woman to Woman" focuses on issues such as healthy living, sexuality and physical changes, personal growth, and maintaining a balanced life. "Spiritual Pathways" includes classes in yoga, tai chi, chi gung, meditation, and breathing, along with lectures, workshops, and discussions of spirituality and the inner life.

Like its smaller sister resort in Massachusetts (see profile of Canyon Ranch in the Berkshires later in this chapter), Canyon Ranch has been voted the world's best health spa by the readers of *Conde Nast Traveler* magazine. The magazine notes that Canyon Ranch offers "a rounded, holistic approach" with individual counseling, group workshops, plus techniques such as biofeedback and hypnotherapy. Physicians, psychologists, registered dieticians, exercise physiologists, and certified health educators make up the ranch staff, which is nearly three times as large as the number of guests.

Address   8600 East Rockcliff Road, Tucson, AZ 85715
Phone   (520) 749-9000 or (800) 742-9000. Fax (520) 749-7755.
Season   Year-round.
Programs   Holistic vacations including weeklong programs such as the "Life Enhancement Program," "Woman to Woman," and "Spiritual Pathways."
Lodging   140 rooms in suites and private condominium cottages with modern, southwestern furnishings and decor. The Life Enhancement Center has special guest quarters. Limited wheelchair access.
Rates   "Life Enhancement Program" $2,340–3,360. "Spiritual Pathways" $1,940–2,960. "Woman to Woman" $3,280–4,537. Discount on second consecutive week. Rates exclude sales tax and 18% service charge.
Meals   3 daily gourmet meals with alternative vegetarian menu.
Services   Programs include some professional health services plus some spa and sports services. Program guests may purchase other such services plus specialty services (e.g., astrology and spiritual awareness consultations, handwriting and tarot card readings).

Four-Fold Way Trainings   Paulden, AZ

Author and cultural anthropologist Angeles Arrien conducts six- and twelve-day "Four-Fold Way Trainings" at Wildflower Lodge, located 130 miles northwest of Phoenix. The lodge has a swimming pool and Jacuzzi and is surrounded by high desert national forest with nearby hiking trails and Anasazi ruins.

The Four-Fold Way is an educational experience designed to increase one's sense of harmony with nature, oneself, and others by accessing and balancing the four inner paths of the teacher, the healer, the visionary, and the leader. This experience makes use of multicultural healing practices such as singing, dancing, storytelling, silence, and (in the case of the twelve-day trainings) a three-day, two-night solo wilderness quest.

The six-day "Foundational Training" is a condensed introduction to the Four-Fold Way. Anyone with this or equivalent training (also offered elsewhere by Angela Arrien) may enroll in the twelve-day "In-Depth Trainings," each structured around a theme such as "Conflict Resolution, Mediation, and Group Skills," "Building Healthy Relationships," and "Soul Work: Dreams, Meditation, and Creativity." Each "In-Depth Training" includes a three-day, two-night solo wilderness experience.

Address	Angeles Arrien, P.O. Box 2077, Sausalito, CA 94966
Phone	(415) 331-5050. Fax (415) 331-5069.
Season	May through October.
Programs	6- and 12-day group trainings designed to empower participants to connect to their true selves, to let go of limiting behavior patterns, and to envision new goals.
Lodging	Shared (2 per room) accommodations for up to 35 guests.
Rates	6-day program $1,200. 12-day program $2,400.
Meals	3 daily, mostly vegetarian meals.

Merritt Center   Payson, AZ

Nestled in the Tonto National Forest at a 5,000-foot altitude ninety miles north of Phoenix, the Merritt Center is a place for personal renewal. On the grounds are a meditation garden, an organic garden, and a spa/Jacuzzi. Nearby are hiking trails in the Tonto National Forest.

The center's popular six-day "Senior Retreats" (for people fifty-five and older) include yoga, tai chi, and classes relating to self-renewal. Frequent "Wellness Weekends" offer yoga or tai chi and sometimes a stress prevention forum. Other weekend program topics include women's wisdom and concerns, self-empowerment and communications, dreamwork, Native American wisdom, and meditation. Most programs are facilitated by center owner Betty Merritt, who is joined on couples weekends by her husband, Al. The center may also be visited on an unprogrammed getaway basis.

Address   P.O. Box 2087, Payson, AZ 85547
Phone   (520) 474-4268. Fax (520) 474-8588. No visits without prior arrangement.
Season   Year-round.
Programs 6-day and weekend retreats on self-renewal and empowerment.
Lodging   Double occupancy rooms for up to 30 guests.
Rates   6-day retreat $275. Weekend retreat $110–150. Nightly rate per person for personal retreat: weekend $95–110, midweek $40–60.
Meals   3 daily family-style meals with no red meat and no alcohol.
Services Massage and flotation tank.

Onsite   Tucson, AZ

Nestled in the foothills of the Santa Catalina Mountains on the north side of Tucson, Onsite is a residential personal growth workshop center specializing in emotional healing for people from dysfunctional families. The facility includes a gym, an outdoor swimming pool, and a baseball field. At a separate but nearby site, Sierra Tucson (Onsite's sister organization) provides long-term residential therapy for people with severe addictions.

Onsite's major offering is the eight-day "Living Centered" program. Other, more frequent offerings are the five-day "Couples Renewal" and the five-day "Learning to Love Yourself" workshops. The latter program includes a ten-hour family reconstruction psychodrama plus summer teen and children's tracks. Other five-day workshops include "Time Out for Women" and "Time Out for Men." Each workshop is usually broken into four or five groups, each with eight to eleven people.

All Onsite programs are designed by Sharon Wegscheider-Cruse and John Cruse, M.D., well-known authors in the recovery field. Most programs are staffed by therapists trained by Sharon in techniques such as sculpting, gestalt, climbing and challenge courses, psychodrama, and equine encounters. Onsite also offers professional training institutes for therapists, counselors, and educators.

Address   16500 North Lago del Oro Parkway, Tucson, AZ 85737
Phone   (800) 341-7432. Fax (520) 792-5887.

Season   Year-round.
Programs 5- and 8-day emotional healing and personal growth work-
              shops.
Lodging   Shared accommodations usually with two adults to a room.
Rates   5 days: singles $775–795, couples $1,599. 8 days: singles
              $1,595.
Meals   3 daily buffet-style meals, each with vegetarian option.

Sedona Spirit   Sedona, AZ

In spring of 1992, Johanna Mosca drove west out of New York City, leaving behind a twenty-five-year career in education. When she reached Sedona, she began camping and living simply in an area known locally for
its healing properties. With prior NYC yoga teaching experience, Johanna began teaching mini yoga classes on the flat rocks next to a
creek. Previously certified as a Kripalu yoga instructor, she is now also
certified in Phoenix Rising yoga therapy.

Johanna currently offers at least six weeklong Sedona yoga vacations each year. Each day includes two and a half hours of morning Kripalu yoga practice plus afternoon hiking and vortex tours in the
surrounding area of red rock mountains and lush green forests. Depending on the interests of the group, some afternoons include Phoenix
Rising yoga sessions. Each vacation also includes Native American
sweat lodge and medicine wheel ceremonies, along with introductions
to local spiritual healers, psychics, and astrologers.

Address   P.O. Box 278, Sedona, AZ 86339
Phone   (520) 282-9592 or (800) 484-6677.
Season   Year-round.
Programs Weeklong vacations combining yoga and Sedona vortex
              hikes.
Lodging   Double and triple rooms at the Sky Ranch Lodge (with out-
              door pool).
Rates   Yoga vacation week $845–895.
Meals   3 daily vegetarian meals.
Services Indoor and outdoor massage.

Blue Mountain Center   Colorado Springs, CO

Located at a 7,400-foot altitude high above Colorado Springs, the Blue Mountain Center is a forty-four-acre summer workshop site dedicated to facilitating personal transformation. The center's unheated kitchen, dining, and shower house structures are surrounded by 12,000 acres of national forest. The views are spectacular from this high energy spot, where UFO sightings and powerful healings have been reported.

All workshops are led by Dr. Verna Yater, a psychic healer and trance medium whose work has been researched by the A.R.E. (Association for Research & Enlightenment). Each workshop is different, but all include such elements as discussions with spirits, meditations, chanting, and healing sounds projected through Dr. Yater or created from crystal bowls. Participants' unspoken individual concerns are often addressed with specific advice from spirits.

Dr. Yater also conducts residential workshops in Santa Barbara, California, and Sedona, Arizona—both on a stand-alone basis and as part of her yearlong transformation program that also meets at Blue Mountain.

Address   Dr. Verna Yater, 2281 Las Canoas Road, Santa Barbara, CA 93105
Phone   (805) 564-4956. Fax (805) 682-8627. Call before visiting.
Season   June through August.
Programs 7- to 9-day experiential, spiritual expansion workshops.
Lodging   Lodging provided in three-season tents. BYO sleeping bag.
Rates   Approximately $900–1,200 with discounts for early registration.
Meals   3 daily vegetarian meals.
Services Transportation to and from Colorado Springs airport or base camp—4½ miles below the center. Some workshops offer massage.

Eden Valley Lifestyle Center   Loveland, CO

Founded in 1987, Eden Valley is a homey wellness center set on 540 acres of woods and fields in the eastern foothills of the Rocky Mountains. Center facilities include a sundeck, exercise equipment, a sauna, and a Jacuzzi. On the grounds are walking trails and a garden. The Lifestyle Center shares a dedicated Seventh-Day Adventist staff with the Eden Valley senior citizens' home and with Eden Valley's small agriculture and medical missionary schools.

The center's "American Lifestyle" program includes a complete physical examination by a medical doctor, pre- and postprogram blood chemistry analyses, stretching exercises, hydrotherapy and massage sessions, health lectures, cooking demonstrations, and walks and outings in the fresh mountain air. Guests have the option of attending daily morning and evening community worship services.

"American Lifestyle" has been successful in curing or ameliorating smoking addiction, obesity, heart problems, adult-onset diabetes and hypoglycemia, high blood pressure, stress, stroke damage and stroke risk, allergies, and arthritis.

Eden Valley also welcomes personal retreatants, who may attend a health lecture and receive a combination hydrotherapy/massage treatment.

Address	6263 North County Road 29, Loveland, CO 80538
Phone	(800) 637-9355
Season	Year-round.
Programs	1-, 2-, and 3-week "American Lifestyle" programs to combat and prevent diseases brought on by unhealthy lifestyles.
Lodging	Accommodations for up to 16 guests in shared rooms with twin beds.
Rates	"Lifestyle": 1 week $370–445, 2 weeks $650–789, 3 weeks $975–1,200. Fees are prorated for partial program attendance. Personal retreat $75 per night including breakfast.
Meals	For "Lifestyle" guests, 3 daily, nondairy vegetarian buffets with fruits and vegetables from the center's organic gardens.

Filoha Meadows   Redstone, CO

This Christian fundamentalist family vacation and marital counseling center sits 7,000 feet high amid fir- and aspen-covered mountains. An indoor pool and outdoor hot tubs are fed by a natural hot mineral water spring. Also on, or adjacent to, the grounds are a par course; a beaver pond; and hiking, mountain biking, and cross-country skiing trails. Forty-five miles away are the cultural arts and skiing of Aspen.

The center offers a standard marital program featuring daily counseling with center director and clinical psychologist Robert Durham, plus meetings with a psychiatrist if necessary. There is also a special ten-day "Regeneration" program of intensive marital therapy for couples who are in the medical or dental professions. Most program guests stay for between four and seven days, with each day including two hours of counseling and time out for personal devotions and recreation.

Address	14628 Highway 133, Redstone, CO 81623
Phone	(800) 227-8906
Season	Year-round.
Programs	Health education and counseling for couples in a mountain vacation environment. Also private rentals.
Lodging	Duplex cabins. Each suite has a bedroom, family room with extra sleep space, kitchenette, and bathroom.
Rates	Nightly lodging: adults (couples or singles) $60, children under 12 $5, each additional person $15. Counseling fees negotiated in advance.
Meals	Guests make their own meals.
Services	Christian lifestyle counseling.

Rocky Mountain T'ai Chi Ch'uan   Crestone, CO

Every year since 1981, Bataan and Jane Faigao have hosted a one-week tai chi summer camp in Colorado. The most recent location has been the eighty-acre Crestone Mountain Zen Center, a high desert wilderness site looking out over the San Luis Valley from the foothills of the Sangre de Cristo peaks.

Each camp day includes periods of sitting meditation interspersed with three classes on tai chi form (or push hands and sword for more advanced practitioners). There is also time for hiking and exploring the region, which includes the Great Sand Dunes to the south and Valley View Hot Springs to the north.

Bataan and Jane studied tai chi from 1968 to 1975 under Grand Master Cheng Man-ch'ing and have been teaching tai chi since 1976. They are directors of Naropa Institute's Traditional Eastern Arts Department.

Address	2804 16th Street, Boulder, CO 80304
Phone	(303) 447-2556 or (303) 258-3023.
Season	Usually around mid-August.
Programs	6-day tai chi summer camp.
Lodging	Shared rooms and campsites at Crestone Mountain Zen Center.
Rates	$350 if camping, $375 if staying in the center facility.
Meals	3 daily vegetarian meals.

Shoshoni Yoga Retreat   Rollinsville, CO

Only a thirty-five-minute drive from Boulder, Shoshoni Yoga Retreat sits at an 8,500-foot elevation and comprises 210 acres in a valley surrounded by national forest and Rocky Mountain peaks. Dirt pathways connect hand-hewn wooden cabins to the yoga/meditation hall and the main lodge, outdoor hot tub, and sauna. Deer, elk, and red-tailed hawks floating on mountain breezes are a common sight in this wilderness area, where a forty-five-minute hike through pine and aspen forests leads to a view of the Continental Divide.

Shoshoni offers weekend retreats with a focus on yoga, healing, rejuvenation, cooking, or meditation. It also offers five-day yoga vacations plus five-day Thanksgiving and Christmas retreats. At all other times, guests are free to join in Shoshoni community healing and spiritual activities. A typical unstructured day would include group meditation before breakfast and dinner, morning and late afternoon hatha yoga and pranayama (yogic breathing) sessions, and a midafternoon hike. Evening is a time for music (on the lodge's antique piano) or a relaxing massage.

Originally built as a children's summer camp, Shoshoni is now owned and operated by a small spiritual community blending the Indian and Tibetan traditions practiced by its founder, Swami Shambhavananda. Bright prayer flags adorn buildings, and large Buddhas are painted on rock walls. A Medicine Buddha healing ritual is conducted once each week at dawn.

Address P.O. Box 410, Rollinsville, CO 80474
Phone (303) 642-0116.
Season Year-round.
Programs Weekend and 5-day yoga, meditation, and rejuvenation retreats. Also work-study options and unstructured personal retreats.
Lodging Sleeps up to 35 in cabins with carpeting, shower, bathroom, towels, and linens. Also campsites and retreat cabin with no plumbing.
Rates Weekend retreat $185–260. 5-day Thanksgiving or Christmas retreat $295. 5-day yoga vacation $475. Daily rates for classes, meals, and lodging $40–120.
Meals 3 vegetarian meals prepared each day with organically grown ingredients and in various styles: Japanese, Mexican, Indian, Italian, Chinese, and French, plus Shoshoni's own creative dishes.
Services Herbal body scrubs, aromatherapy facials, and massage.

Tara Mandala   Pagosa Springs, CO

Located 7,400–8,100 feet high near the San Juan Mountains, Tara Mandala is a 850-acre wilderness sanctuary of meadows, ponds, hills, and natural stone formations. It is also a new Tibetan Buddhist retreat center open to all for meditation retreats and other healing and spiritual programs. Buddhist practitioners are welcome for personal retreats.

The center's facilities are spare: a large yurt, a large tepee, and a large Tibetan tent to accommodate programs; a campground and meditation grove; and a spacious outdoor kitchen area with running water. The volunteer staff is planting trees to help heal the land. Guests often join center volunteers and residents for a soak in the nearby Pagosah ("land of healing waters") hot mineral pools.

Tara Mandala manifests the vision of Tsultrim Allione, ordained as a nun by H. H. Karmapa in 1970 and the author of *Women of Wisdom*. Her center attracts well-known guest teachers from primarily Buddhist and Native American spiritual traditions.

Address   P.O. Box 3040, Pagosa Springs, CO 81147
Phone   (970) 264-6177. Fax (970) 264-6169. Call before visiting.
Season   Late spring through early fall.
Programs 2- to 10-day retreats on Buddhist meditative and yogic practices, Native American wisdom, Western psychospiritual perspectives.
Lodging   Campsites. BYO tents and camping gear. Yurt (in winter) and Tibetan teacher's tent (in summer) for personal retreatants. Also motels in Pagosa Springs—15 miles away.
Rates   Program tuition (with meals): 2–3 days $95–150, 5–6 days $185–270, 9–10 days $340–500. Teacher donations customary at meditation retreats. Nightly rates for campsite: $6 during programs, $10 at other times. Yurt or Tibetan tent $22 per night.
Meals   3 daily gourmet vegetarian meals.
Services Child care for children ages 6 and up.

Lama Foundation   San Cristobal, NM

Nineteen miles north of Taos and high above the Rio Grande Gorge, one finds the Lama Foundation (founded in 1967), a colorful and growing collection of domed and adobe buildings that include a sauna and sweat lodge. Lama is also a community of people who tolerantly and conscientiously practice different spiritual traditions side by side on a daily basis. Community leadership rotates among the members, who make all major decisions by consensus.

Each year, Lama offers nearly a dozen spiritual and work retreats. The first program is usually the late-May "Community Camp," which combines physical labor with practices such as meditation, Hindu chanting, Dances of Universal Peace, Zikr, Shabbat, and Japanese tea ceremony. Other retreats focus on a single spiritual practice or on permaculture and construction projects.

Lama also welcomes personal retreatants, who, like all other Lama guests, participate in community meditations and contribute at least one hour of community work. Another option for the public is to join the summer staff, which is nearly double the size of the year-round community (which is about twenty to twenty-five residents). In nonsummer months, the community supports itself by making and selling bright-colored prayer flags, banners, and T-shirts silk-screened by hand.

Address   Box 240, San Cristobal, NM 87564

Phone   (505) 586-1269 (10 A.M. to noon). No visits without prior arrangement.

Season   Public program from mid-May to mid-September. Year-round community.

Programs   1- to 2-week scheduled camps and retreats. Also summer staff and personal retreat opportunities.

Lodging   Campsites (BYO tent) and limited dorm space (BYO sleeping bag). Clean outhouses and solar showers. Also hermitages.

Rates   8- to 10-day spiritual retreat $200–940. Weekend to 2-week work camp $100–$350. "Community Camp": 1 week $150, 2 weeks $250, or $24 per day with 3-day minimum. Lodging: tent site free, dorm $7 per night. Child care $18 per day. Hermitage $20 per night including meals.

Meals   3 daily vegetarian meals. Food mostly from Lama's organic gardens.

Services   Child care or children's camp at most work camps and some retreats.

Light Institute of Galisteo   Galisteo, NM

Though headquartered in a quiet rural village twenty-five miles south of Santa Fe, Chris Griscom and her Light Institute staff are known worldwide (from actress Shirley MacLaine's writings and Chris's own books) for their pioneering past-life regression services. In Galisteo, the Light Institute offers a variety of four-day sets of sessions (one three-hour session each day), with each set addressing a separate theme. People new to this process begin with two sets that focus, respectively, on opening to the higher self and dissolving projections of self-image onto parents. Each set consists of an emotional body balancing session followed by three multi-incarnational sessions.

On the campus of the Nizhoni School for Global Consciousness in nearby Sunrise Springs, the institute also offers residential weekend and five-day group intensives. Each intensive includes a set of four multi-incarnational sessions, a workshop with Chris Griscom, discussion groups with institute facilitators, and a cranial (a session that stimulates the body's master glands to release physical tensions and emotional holding patterns). Additional features of the six-day intensive are yoga and Tibetan exercise classes, a firewalk encounter, and a "Knowings" class.

The creation and expansion of the Light Institute was inspired by Chris Griscom's six near-death experiences, nine years in the Peace Corps, mastery of esoteric acupuncture, and her higher self. Chris is also the founder of the Nizhoni School, a boarding and day care school with curricula for all ages. Nizhoni courses include two- to four-week offerings on subjects such as "Initiating your Life Purpose."

Address   HC75, Box 50, Galisteo, NM 87540
Phone   (505) 466-1975 or (800) 983-1975. Fax (505) 466-7217.
Season   Year-round.
Programs   4-day sets of multi-incarnational sessions designed to heal, clear, and expand consciousness. Also 5-day residential intensives on themes such as "Clearing the Parents."
Lodging   Galisteo guest house accommodations (at additional cost) for Light Institute sessions. Shared Nizhoni School accommodations (covered by program fee) for intensives.
Rates   4-day sets of sessions: adults $1,200, young people (12–16) $600, children (5–11) $300. Intensives: weekend $1,000, 5 days $1,900.
Meals   For sessions, guests make their own meals at the guest house and/or dine out in nearby Santa Fe. For intensives, 3 daily gourmet vegetarian meals are provided.
Services   Cranials and spiritual guidance. Also free public meditations at the institute on Wednesday and Sunday afternoons.

Ocamora Foundation   Ocate, NM

Ocamora lies northeast of Santa Fe in the foothills of the Sangre de Cristo Mountains at an elevation of 7,500 feet. Three hundred acres of serene northern New Mexico landscape are the ideal setting for a foundation that supports solitude, deep relaxation, and inner work. The grounds include an apple orchard, garden, greenhouse, hot tub, and a pond suitable for swimming. The Cloisters guest residence complex comprises a library, meditation hall, and small kitchen.

During the summer, Ocamora hosts three- to nine-day workshops and retreats. Popular programs include dreamwork and Holotropic Breathwork workshops, Vipassana meditation retreats, and a horse clinic. Ocamora also hosts personal retreats. Silence is observed at all times in the Cloisters, and personal inner focus is encouraged by the Ocamora staff.

Address	P.O. Box 43, Ocate, NM 87734
Phone	(505) 666-2389. No visits without prior arrangement.
Season	June through mid-September for programs. Year-round for personal retreats.
Programs	3- to 9-day workshops and retreats facilitated by southwestern teachers and healers.
Lodging	Woodstove-heated private rooms and bathrooms clustered around a courtyard. BYO sleeping bag for yurt and tepees—with sleeping platforms and foam pads, nearby outhouses, and hot solar shower.
Rates	8- and 9-day meditation retreats $230–375 plus teacher donation. Fees for other summer programs set by teachers. Daily rates for personal retreats: singles $35, couples (double occupancy) $50.
Meals	3 daily gourmet (and usually lacto-ovo) vegetarian meals at workshops. BYO food for personal retreats; okay to use kitchen, which is fully stocked with kitchenware, basic supplies, and condiments.

Rose Mountain   Las Vegas, NM

Surrounded on three sides by the Santa Fe National Forest and looking out over the Pecos Wilderness, Rose Mountain is an intertraditional retreat center 8,000 feet above sea level in New Mexico's Sangre de Cristo Mountains. The center generates all its electricity through solar photovoltaics. The grounds include organic gardens, a greenhouse, a ceremonial tepee, and sweat lodge.

The center hosts men-only and women-only retreats (with sweat lodge and solo guests), tai chi retreats, retreats with a contemplative Jewish or Sufi focus, an annual "Deep Listening Retreat," plus retreats with a Buddhist meditative or psychological focus. In addition, the center offers individual private and guided retreats at a remote hermitage.

The center's director is Andy Gold, a Sufi initiate, rabbinic pastor, and former coordinator at the Lama Foundation (profiled earlier in this section). Teachers include Heloise Gold (a dancer and tai chi instructor), Shefa Gold (a composer and performer of spiritual music), as well as guest teachers like composer Pauline Oliveros.

Address   P.O. Box 355, Las Vegas, NM 87701
Phone   (505) 425-5728. No visits without prior arrangement.
Season   June through October.
Programs   Guided 6-day retreats devoted to some form of inner healing in a spiritual context. Also personal retreats.
Lodging   Private rooms and camping.
Rates   6-day group retreat $370–450. Personal retreat $35 per day.
Meals   3 daily gourmet vegetarian meals.

Takoja Institute   Questa, NM

Takoja Institute conducts summer retreats at the forty-acre Ranchos Mesclados, twenty-eight miles north of Taos. Located in the Rio Grande Valley under the peaks of the Sangre de Cristo Mountains, the ranch is at about the same altitude as Machu Pichu—the ancient Peruvian city that inspired Judith Sauceda, Ph.D., to found and direct the institute. Judith is an artist, teacher, and follower of Taoist and Lakota (Native American) spiritual traditions. From time to time, she also leads trips to Machu Pichu.

Most Takoja retreats explore the Native American "Red Road" as a spiritual path. These retreats are led or co-led by Judith and other Native American scholars and elders. Other retreat topics include "Internal Martial Arts" (a Taoist perspective on finding balance and harmony in one's life) and "Exploring the Mystic through Watercolor." At most retreats, sweat lodge and meditation are offered at no additional cost.

Takoja also welcomes personal and private group retreats. Nearby are the free hot springs at Arroyo Hondo, the 1,000-year-old Taos Pueblo, and the village of Taos—a folk arts mecca.

Address	Summer: 656 North Star Route, Questa, NM 87556
	Winter: 4495 Lakeridge Road, Denver, CO 80219
Phone	(505) 586-1086 (summer), (303) 934-3607 (winter). No visits without prior arrangement.
Season	Mid-May through October.
Programs	Weekend workshops focusing on Native American wisdom ceremonies plus other life-balancing, life-healing practices.
Lodging	Private and shared quarters in two large domed structures housing up to 16 overnight guests.
Rates	2- and 3-day scheduled workshops (with lodging and meals) $235–295. Daily rates for private retreat (includes bed and breakfast): singles $40, couples $50. Workshop with private teacher $75 per day.
Meals	Gourmet semivegetarian meals (including fish and fowl) prepared by a chef trained in London. Vegetarian options also available.

The Last Resort   Cedar City, UT

This retreat is on Midway Summit (elevation 8,700 feet) in the Dixie National Forest of southwestern Utah, a three- to four-hour drive from Las Vegas. During the resort's summer yoga retreat season, many retreatants like to travel to Pah Tempe Hot Springs on the other side of Zion National Park.

Resident retreat directors are Ed and Barbara Keays, both certified Iyengar yoga instructors. Ed is a certified rebirther, counselor, therapist, Vipassana meditation teacher, and former director of the Yoga Institute of San Diego. Barbara is a gourmet vegetarian cook and longtime student of Dr. Bernard Jensen, a leader in the fields of nutrition and natural foods cooking.

Summer yoga retreats feature twice daily yoga classes, evening and morning meditation, spectacular hikes, plus discussions of personal growth concerns (e.g., relationships and right livelihood). Other summer offerings are detoxification/rejuvenation retreats and workshops

on relationships and natural cooking. All programs include daily morning meditation and yoga. Winter silent meditation retreats employ yoga
to ease muscle tensions.

Address   P.O. Box 6226, Cedar City, UT 87421

Phone   (801) 682-2289. No visits without prior arrangement.

Season   Late December through mid-August.

Programs   Yoga, meditation, and detoxification retreats plus relationship and natural cooking workshops.

Lodging   Dorm and private room accommodations for up to 10
overnight guests.

Rates   7-day yoga retreat $695. 10-day detoxification/rejuvenation
retreat $795. 4-day relationship workshop $395. 5-day natural cooking workshop $495. Meditation retreats: 5 days
$350, 10 days $550, 30 days $1,350.

Meals   3 daily gourmet vegetarian meals. Juice fasting during
detoxification retreat.

UNITED STATES: *North Central Region*

Heartland Spa   Gilman, IL

Located eighty miles south of Chicago, the Heartland Spa is a peaceful country estate on a private lake surrounded by thirty-one acres of woods and miles of farmland. The lakefront mansion is connected by an underground passage to a high-tech, three-level fitness center housed in a renovated barn. Barn facilities include massage and steam rooms, sauna, whirlpool, and swimming pool. Among the outdoor facilities are two lighted tennis courts, a par course, a quarter-mile track, hiking/cross-country skiing trails, and paddleboats.

Guests receive casual exercise clothing and are encouraged to take only those classes that address personal goals. Most guests focus on general fitness and wellness. Some focus on relaxation and stress management through such classes as stretch and relax, tai chi, and yoga. Other classes include ballet, wushu/kung fu, and "Heartland Adventure," a series of "getting to know yourself" games and outdoor challenges designed to enhance self-confidence.

Address	225 North Wabash, Suite 310, Chicago, IL 60601
Phone	(312) 357-6465 or (800) 545-4853 (reservations).
Season	Year-round.
Programs	Personalized health and fitness programs.
Lodging	A limit of 28 guests in 14 comfortably furnished rooms with twin beds and private baths.
Rates	$280–360 per night with 30% discounts for second person (when couples attend) on weekend, 5- and 7-night packages.
Meals	3 daily gourmet vegetarian meals with dairy products and occasional fish supplements. Also daily snacks and non-alcoholic happy hour.
Services	Complimentary round-trip transportation from downtown Chicago. Package plans include free personal care services (e.g., massage, salt scrub, sea mud body mask, aromatherapy oil wrap).

U.S. North Central

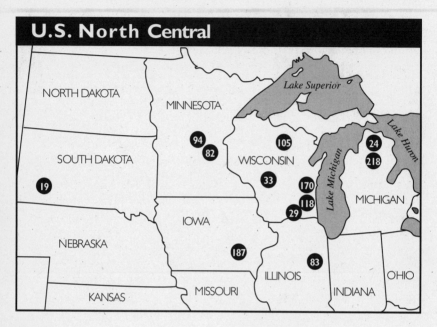

Illinois
83   Heartland Spa

Iowa
187   The Raj

Michigan
24   Camp Al-Gon-Quian
     Family/Yoga Camp
218   Song of the Morning

Minnesota
82   Hazelden Renewal Center
94   IIIHS Summer Symposium

South Dakota
19   Black Hills Health and
     Education Center

Wisconsin
29   The Center
33   Christine Center
105   Ishpiming Educational Retreat
      Center
118   Kopp Center for Continuing
      Education
170   Pathways of Light Center

The Raj   Fairfield, IA

The Raj offers rejuvenation and beauty programs based on ayurveda, the natural health-care system originally reserved for the royal families of India. Rejuvenation programs include a doctor's consultation, a health-enhancement education course (with diet, yoga, and aerobics classes), guest lectures on the science of Ayurveda, along with two hours each day of pancha karma treatments (i.e., various massages, herbalized steam bath, sound therapy, aromatherapy, shirodara—a soothing, continuous flow of herbalized oil poured slowly and gently across the forehead—and gentle oil enemas).

The Raj's "Beauty-from-Within" program assigns three specially trained technicians to each guest, focusing on internal physiological functioning to create radiant health. For all guests who have not yet received transcendental meditation training, the Raj offers an optional five-day TM course that includes two lectures, private instruction, plus three days of follow-up instruction. In addition, the Raj has special monthly "Healthy Heart" and "Weight Normalization" programs.

Address	RR 4, Box 503, Fairfield, IA 52556
Phone	(515) 472-9580 or (800) 248-9050. Fax (515) 472-2496.
Season	Year-round.
Programs	3-, 5-, and 7-day Ayurvedic rejuvenation and beauty packages.
Lodging	Capacity for approximately 50 overnight guests in single and double rooms plus various villas.
Rates	Rejuvenation program: 3 days $1,270, 5 days $2,010, 7 days $2,710. Beauty program: 3 days $1,420, 5 days $2,260, 7 days $3,600. 5-day TM course $1,000. Lodging $85–185 per night.
Meals	Gourmet vegetarian meals.
Services	Pick-up and drop-off at Cedar Rapids, Burlington, and Des Moines, Iowa, airports.

Camp Al-Gon-Quian Family/Yoga Camp   Burt Lake, MI

A summer youth and family camp facility thirty miles south of the Straits of Mackinac on the southwest shore of Burt Lake. Al-Gon-Quian's 150 acres of forests, open fields, and meadows support a full array of summer camp activities.

Two weeklong family/yoga camps are hosted each summer by the Ann Arbor YMCA. The whole family joins in the fun of swimming, sailing, campfires, archery, canoeing, horseback riding, and arts and crafts. In addition, a nationally recognized instructor leads daily advanced, intermediate, and beginner's hatha yoga classes.

Address   Ann Arbor YMCA, 350 South 5th Avenue, Ann Arbor, MI 48104
Phone   (313) 663-0536
Season   August.
Programs   Iyengar-style, hatha yoga family camp.
Lodging   Cabins with 8 bunks each and a nearby modern bathhouse. One large family per cabin, each of which overlooks the lake. Couples and smaller families may share cabins.
Rates   Adults $250–300. Youths (3–12) $100–125.
Meals   3 daily vegetarian meals.

Song of the Morning   Vanderbilt, MI

Situated beside the Pigeon River forty miles south of the Mackinac Straits is Song of the Morning, an 800-acre forest retreat operated under the spiritual guidance of Bob Raymer, a retired airline pilot and direct disciple of Paramahansa Yogananda. Ranch guests enjoy swimming, canoeing, kayaking, hiking, plus cross-country skiing in the cold, crisp Michigan winters.

The ranch's most frequent programs are three-hour Saturday meditations, weekend chanting retreats, raw juice fasting and cleansing weekends, and weekend or five-day "Clear Light Healing" retreats. "Clear Light Healing" includes breathwork sessions, chanting and mantra yoga, and satsangs (spiritual services) with Bob Raymer, as well as body purification through a fresh vegetable diet and homeovetic and vibrational healing. There are also occasional five-day meditation retreats. All programs are led by experienced teachers.

Personal retreatants are welcome at all times to visit, enjoy the facilities, and participate in daily (early morning and evening) yoga and meditation sessions. Facility rental by private groups is also an option.

Address	9607 East Sturgeon Valley Road, Vanderbilt, MI 49795
Phone	(517) 983-4107. Call before visiting.
Season	Year-round.
Programs	Weekend and 5-day retreats.
Lodging	Private single and shared apartments and rooms, men's and women's dorms, campsites, and lodge (during winter).
Rates	Retreat tuition, room, and board: weekend $295, 5 days $395–495. Weekend chanting retreat $20. Daily room and board: for adults, private $35–130, dorm $29–33, campsite $17; for children, ages 13–17 $12, under 13 free.
Meals	Daily vegetarian brunch and dinner, often with produce from the ranch's organic gardens.

Hazelden Renewal Center   Center City, MN

Nestled in the quiet lawns, pinewood forests, and quiet beauty of South Center Lake one hour northeast of Minneapolis, Hazelden Renewal Center has served since 1949 as a tranquil way station on the journey of recovery for people in all branches of the twelve-step movement. The center's grounds and facilities include miles of trails, a large print and video library, plus a fitness center with a gym, indoor track, indoor pool, whirlpool, and sauna.

Center guests can arrive anytime and stay for as long as they like. They may also participate as much (or as little) as they wish in the daily offerings, which include an early morning group meditation, a morning lecture at the Family Center, morning and afternoon and one-hour presentations or group discussions at the Renewal Center, an evening twelve-step meeting, and an evening lecture. On each visit, each guest is entitled to one consultation involving spiritual direction.

Changing from week to week, the Renewal Center's morning and afternoon programs focus on such topics as couples and singles in recovery, "Women's Spirituality," "Wellness and Self-care," and "Grief."

Address   P.O. Box 11, Center City, MN 55012
Phone   (612) 257-4010 or (800) 262-4882. Advance reservations required.
Season   Year-round.
Programs An ongoing renewal program plus focus weeks—all designed for people (and their families) in any twelve-step program.
Lodging   26 beds in 14 semiprivate and private rooms.
Rates   Program, meals, room, plus access to fitness center $125–200 per day.
Meals   3 daily meals.
Services Pick-up and drop-off at Minneapolis/St. Paul airport, train and bus terminals.

IIIHS Summer Symposium   St. Cloud, MN

Each summer since 1986, the Midwest Chapter of the International Institute of Integral Human Sciences has hosted a six-day symposium drawing well-known spiritual and personal growth authors, teachers, and healers from all over the United States. In recent years, the symposium site has been St. Johns College and its campus set on the shores of a lake in a forested region one hour northwest of Minneapolis.

The symposium offers two daily (morning and afternoon) ninety-minute work periods, with participants staying with the same workshops throughout the week. There are also intensive workshops (meeting both morning and afternoon for two days), potpourri workshops (with a different leader and topic each day), and youth workshops (for ages ten to fourteen).

Address   Michael Nelson, 6721 Amherst Lane, Eden Prairie, MN 55346
Phone   (612) 934-7355
Season   Usually late July.
Programs 6-day symposium and retreat focusing on personal and spiritual growth.
Lodging   Standard college dormitory rooms.
Rates   6-day program $375–450, with discounts for seniors, students, and youths.

Meals	3 daily cafeteria meals, including vegetarian selections.
Services	Massage, tai chi lessons, psychic and astrology readings. Also van service to and from the Minneapolis/St. Paul airport.

Black Hills Health and Education Center   Hermosa, SD

This center is located in a 450-acre valley surrounded by rimrock cliffs in southwestern South Dakota (a "banana belt" region where even winter weather is generally mild and sunny). The main lodge contains a whirlpool, a Russian steam cabinet, and a shower that alternates hot- and cold-water sprays. At least once a week, there are excursions to a large, natural indoor pool fed by a hot mineral spring.

The Black Hills Center conducts residential wellness programs designed to transform lifestyles. Each program includes an initial physical exam, daily lectures on holistic health, supervised group exercises and water therapy, massage, nutrition and stress management instruction, individual counseling, and group discussions. The center's learning-by-doing approach is also used to teach guests how to shop for and prepare nutritious meals.

The center is operated by members of the Seventh-Day Adventist Church and is affiliated with the nearby Black Hills Missionary College. The center and the college share a staff of physicians, nurses, nutritionists, therapists, and counselors. There are optional daily morning worship services and Friday vespers. A special community music program is generally offered on the last Friday night of each program.

Address	Box 19, Hermosa, SD 57744
Phone	(605) 255-4101
Season	Year-round.
Programs	13- and 20-day wellness programs for people wishing to remain healthy or to heal without drugs or surgery. Also a midsummer, 1-week "Family Health/Fun Camp."
Lodging	12 double and single rooms, with private or shared bath. Also motor home camping facilities.
Rates	13-day program: singles $1,700, couples $2,500. 20-day program: singles $2,500, couples $4,270.
Meals	3 daily buffet-style, nondairy vegetarian meals.

The Center   Elkhorn, WI

Two hours from Chicago and forty-five minutes from Milwaukee, the Center occupies forty acres of rolling wooded land next to Lauderdale Lakes in Wisconsin's Kettle Moraine region. On the grounds are canoes, hiking paths, hot tubs, and distinctive, domed buildings formerly owned by a commune.

The center hosts retreats led by the staffs of Chicago's Center for Exceptional Living (CEL) and Chicago's Human Effectiveness, Inc., counseling organizations directed, respectively, by Judith Wright and Bob Wright. Annual retreats include fall, winter, and spring spiritual weekends plus a two-week "Summer Spiritual Retreat" (with a one-week option) of meditation, chanting, singing, dancing, art, crafts, journal writing, reflection, team and life theme work, fellowship, and recreation.

Other weekend retreats may address the special concerns of women, couples, men, or "Overcoming Soft Addictions." Often in the early fall, Judith and her CEL staff also lead a pilgrimage journey to sacred places.

Address   Center for Exceptional Living, 333 East Ontario, Suite 302B, Chicago, IL 60611
Phone   (312) 664-2700 or (414) 742-2110.
Season   Year-round.
Programs Weekend and weeklong personal and spiritual growth retreats.
Lodging   Bunk room accommodations for up to 30 guests. All rooms with carpeting, electricity, woodstoves, and A/C.
Rates   Typical weekend retreat $425. "Summer Spiritual Retreat": 1 week $1,295, 2 weeks $2,320.
Meals   3 daily meals with vegetarian options.

Christine Center   Willard, WI

The full name of this facility is the Christine Center for Unitive Planetary Spirituality. It is located in central Wisconsin on 251 acres of former farmland. The barn has been converted to a library and meditation hall, and the silo is now a chapel. Hermitages, a sauna, and a Japanese deep-water bath have been built in the nearby forest.

Founded in 1980 by Franciscan Sisters, the center is an independent, ecumenical spiritual community, retreat, and education center. The resident community includes people trained in experimental and transpersonal psychology, Vipassana meditation, and Sufi practices. Spiritual guidance is available in traditional religious and transpersonal/metaphysical forms.

Each year, the center offers several two-week "Basic Life Transformation" workshops and eight-day Vipassana meditation retreats. Most other offerings are weekend workshops on subjects like sacred dance, yoga, chi gung, natural medicine, and conscious relationships. The most frequent program is the "Silent Meditation Weekend." Center facilities are also available for rent by groups or for use by personal retreatants.

Some personal retreatants participate fully in community life. A typical community day includes periods of conscious work and group and individual meditation. Sundays begin with morning communal meditation and prayer, followed by brunch, and then an afternoon of play and relaxation. Each community member also sets aside a weekly "desert day" for solitude, rest, and reflection.

Address	W8291 Mann Road, Willard, WI 54493
Phone	(715) 267-7507. No visits without prior arrangement.
Season	Year-round.
Programs	Weekend to 2-week meditation, spiritual, and personal growth workshops and retreats.
Lodging	20 hermitages, each with electricity, a wood-burning stove, and 1–3 beds. 4 of the 20 also have a toilet and bath.
Rates	"Silent Meditation Weekend" $25. Weekend workshop $55–75. 8-day meditation retreat $90. 2-week workshop $200. Personal retreat (meals included) $15–50 per day. Children up to age 6 free, ages 6–12 $5 per day, ages 13–18 $10 per day.
Meals	3 daily meals made from whole grains, nuts, seeds, organic fruits and vegetables.
Services	Spiritual guidance, reflexology, acupressure, energy balance, breathwork, massage, facial, sauna, and ofuro (Japanese deep-water bath).

Ishpiming Educational
Retreat Center   Manitowish Waters, WI

Nestled beside Turtle Lake on fifty-two acres in Wisconsin's far north woods (five hours from Milwaukee and six hours from Minneapolis) is Ishpiming, a rustic retreat that offers summer to early fall work, play, and healing seminars. A seminar room, dorm, kitchen, and dining area are housed in a large pinewood structure with a wraparound deck and floor-to-ceiling windows that afford views of water, sky, and woods. Canoes are available for use by program participants and personal retreatants. When programs are not in session, the facility can be rented by private groups.

Ishpiming ("heaven" in Ojibwa) was founded in 1991 by Sage Oh'hne, a mother, grandmother, author, and spiritual healer who gives seminars on abundance, ascension, and relationships to self, spirit, and others. Sage's seminars usually include drumming, singing, nature attunements, meditations, study of the Bible and *A Course in Miracles*, down-to-earth humor, and hands-on healing. The center's other facilitators (at least twenty each summer) include doctors, nurses, teachers, healers, artists, therapists, and businesspeople from the Midwest and other parts of the country.

Address	P.O. Box 340, Manitowish Waters, WI 54545
Phone	(715) 686-2372. Fax (715) 686-2372.
Season	June through September or October.
Programs	Weekend, 4- and 5-day work and play seminars on the healing of heart, mind, and spirit. Also work-study and apprenticeship opportunities.
Lodging	Lodging for 20–25 people in dorms, private rooms, tepees, cabins, and a loft. Also 14 primitive camping sites. BYO linens or sleeping bag.
Rates	Seminar tuition: weekend $80–250; 4 and 5 days $375–600. Nightly lodging per person: campsite $10, dorm $18, private room or tepee $35–45. Entire cabin $70–120 per night. Breakfast $7.95.
Meals	Potluck with two kitchens for preparation of personal or group meals. Optional paid breakfast.
Services	Reiki massage, self-remembering, and shamanic healing sessions.

Kopp Center for Continuing Education   Honey Creek, WI

Set on fifty-five acres in southeastern Wisconsin, eighty miles from Chicago and thirty miles from Milwaukee, Kopp Center is a country retreat of woods, meadows, and trails around a private lake. Workshop and personal retreat guests can enjoy swimming, boating, and hiking. During weekend workshops, there are daily morning Kripalu yoga sessions and Saturday aqua-aerobics in the lake.

After twenty years of offering training programs that enable healing services professionals to earn academic credits, the center has now opened its weekend workshops to the general public. Most workshops focus on applying a particular personal growth discipline, such as dance therapy, psychodrama, artistic expression, or journal writing. Facilitators include well-qualified teachers, authors, and health professionals from around the country.

Address N6360 Valley View Road, Honey Creek, WI 53138
Phone (414) 763-7591 or (800) 484-8081, code 1500. Fax (414) 763-7591.
Season June through September.
Programs Weekend workshops for personal and professional development.
Lodging Accommodations for up to 40 people in camp-style dorms and semiprivate rooms (with central toilet and washhouse) plus a few single chalet rooms with shared bathroom.
Rates Weekend workshop tuition $160. Nightly lodging $25–55.
Meals During workshops: gourmet natural foods offered at breakfast and Saturday lunch. Community kitchen facilities. Also nearby restaurants.
Services Massage.

Pathways of Light Center   Kiel, WI

Pathways of Light is a nonprofit organization founded in 1968 to facilitate spiritual awakening and growth—primarily through course offerings at a center forty miles north of Milwaukee. The center's forty acres of wooded grounds encompass a spring-fed lake, a natural amphitheater, two lodges, and three gazebos. There are also trails, canoes, and boats for guest use.

The center's major offerings are one- and two-day courses on topics like "Awakening to Your Higher Self" and "The Transforming Power of Trust." All courses include reading and group discussion, experiential processes, and guided meditations. Each is presented on weekends or as a part of occasional four-day (Thursday through Sunday) programs. Noncourse offerings include "Rest and Remembering" weekends, as well as "Migration to Freedom" meetings, based on *A Course in Miracles* (ACIM), that are held each Thursday and Sunday afternoon.

Pathways' founders and directors are Robert and Mary Stoelting, both longtime ACIM students. Others trained at the center facilitate Pathways of Light courses, offer self-awakening spiritual counseling, and lead eight-week "Self-Awakening" and "Healing Inner Child" groups in major communities throughout eastern Wisconsin and metropolitan Chicago.

Address   13111 Lax Chapel Road, Kiel, WI 53042

Phone   (414) 894-2339

Season   Year-round.

Programs   1- and 2-day experiential courses in spiritual awakening, sometimes presented within a 4-day event with meals and lodging package.

Lodging   Accommodations for up to 30 guests. Each room has 2 or 3 beds, linens, towels, and sink and is near to communal bathrooms and laundry facilities. Overflow crowds accommodated at local motel.

Rates   Course tuition: 1 day $59, 2 days $109. Lodging: $26 for 1 night, $21 per night for 2 or more nights (including sales tax). Meals and lodging for 4-day event $144 (tax included). "Rest and Remembering" weekend $142 total (tax included).

Meals   Available at nearby restaurants or on a make-it-yourself basis with shared use of center kitchen. Meals provided by center during 4-day events.

Services   Massage, acupressure, and energy work. Also spiritual counseling.

UNITED STATES: *South Central Region*

Diana's Grove   Salem, MO

Set on one hundred acres next to Mark Twain National Forest in southeastern Missouri, Diana's Grove is a rustic retreat created to support mystery school trainings and retreats in the Starhawk Wiccan tradition. Each June, during the "Week Between the Worlds" intensive, Starhawk and other nationally known teachers lead retreatants in experiential workshops and community ritual.

Other annual retreats include a weeklong "Lunacy" women's retreat in July, a weeklong "Summer's End" retreat, and a "Harvest Song" retreat during the fall equinox. These retreats include daily workshops by regional teachers on health and well-being, astrology, tarot, "Gay Men's Mysteries," dance, chanting, and trance formation. "Lunacy" and "Summer's End" may be attended on a weekend-only basis. Diana's Grove also rents its facilities for other events that are free of drugs and alcohol.

Address	P.O. Box 159, Salem, MO 65560
Phone	(314) 689-2400
Season	June through September.
Programs	Weekend and weeklong personal empowerment retreats.
Lodging	Campsites. BYO tent or use dorm marquee tents, which sleep several people.
Rates	Weekend gathering $75–100. Weeklong gathering $150–495. 3 meals $15 per day, just dinner $7.50 per day.
Meals	3 daily meals, gourmet vegetarian with chicken for meat eaters.

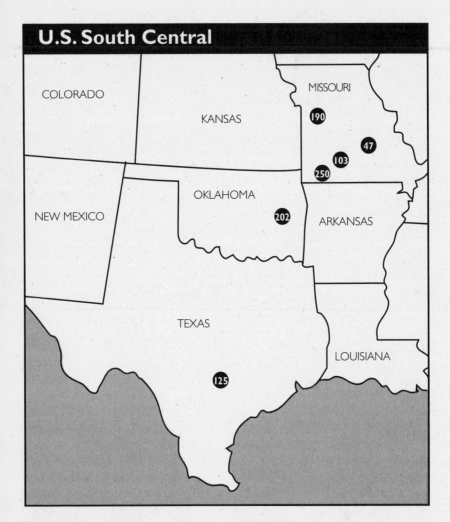

U.S. South Central

COLORADO

KANSAS

MISSOURI

NEW MEXICO

OKLAHOMA

ARKANSAS

TEXAS

LOUISIANA

Missouri
47   Diana's Grove
103   Intuition Training Workshops
190   Reforming Feelings
250   Wholistic Life Center

Oklahoma
202   Sancta Sophia Seminary

Texas
125   Lake Austin Spa Resort

Intuition Training Workshops   Springfield, MO

"Vision, Creativity, and Intuition" is a ten-day training program conducted by the Holos Institutes of Health at Brindabella Farm, eighteen miles from Springfield in southwestern Missouri. The program focuses on the use of intuitive insight to address personal power issues. It is offered in two five-day parts, with the second part optional and generally scheduled five days after the first.

Program trainers are Caroline Myss and C. Norman Shealy, coauthors of *The Creation of Health*. Caroline is an international lecturer in the field of human consciousness whose work combines an in-depth spiritual perspective with insight on the emotional, physical, and spiritual aspects of illness. Norman is a neurosurgeon, founder of the American Holistic Medical Association, a former professor at Harvard and the University of Minnesota Medical Schools, and a clinical and research professor of psychology at Forest Institute of Professional Psychology in Springfield, Missouri.

Address   HOLOS Conference Office, Route 1, Box 216, Fair Grove, MO 65648
Phone   (417) 267-2900. Fax (417) 267-3102.
Season   Year-round.
Programs   5-day trainings in intuitive insight and self-empowerment.
Lodging   Available at motels in the nearby Springfield area.
Rates   Tuition $1,050.
Meals   Lunch (vegetarian with fish and fowl) is provided.

Reforming Feelings   Independence, MO

The Franciscan Prayer Center, an eighty-two-acre campus of woods, trails, and open fields, is the suburban Kansas City site for "Reforming Feelings" weekends. Phase 1 weekends include five workshops on topics like "Understanding Self and Feeling Responsibility," "Love, Love Relationships, and Loneliness," and "Happiness and Emotions, Anger and Forgiveness." Each workshop is followed by small group sessions. Graduates of the phase 1 weekend can move on to phase 2 and then phase 3 weekends, which focus entirely on experiential work.

All "Reforming Feelings" weekends are facilitated by Gail Vaughn and her staff from the nearby Reforming Feelings Counseling and Consulting Center. Dr. Vaughn is a certified neurolinguistics therapist with a Ph.D. in psychology plus degrees in nursing and human relations. She specializes in counseling individuals and families for problems such as drug and alcohol abuse, inner-child issues, eating disorders, child abuse, and incest.

Address	1201 West College, Liberty, MO 64068
Phone	(816) 781-9494
Season	Year-round.
Programs	Weekend retreats on the origin and healthy expression of emotions.
Lodging	Accommodations for up to 45 people in single and shared rooms.
Rates	Phase 1 weekend $160. Phase 2 or 3 weekend $425. Appointments with Dr. Vaughn (at $100 per appointment, whether by phone or in-person) are required before and after each phase 2 or phase 3 weekend.
Meals	4 meals per weekend (3 on Saturday and brunch on Sunday).

Wholistic Life Center   Washburn, MO

The Wholistic Life Center occupies 900 peaceful acres of rolling Ozark countryside in southwestern Missouri. The property contains a lake, creeks, wooded trails, and abundant wildlife. Founded in 1990 to help people discover their true potential, the center hosts introductory weekend, one-week, two-week (the recommended length), and month-long programs. The resident staff includes a retired psychiatrist.

Each day there are two sessions of light movement and stretching exercises; classes on such topics as mind/body connections, nutritional intake and balance, waste elimination, and stress reduction; recreational activities like hiking, basketball, tennis, Ping-Pong, volleyball, singing, and dancing; and two herbally enriched Jacuzzi treatments. Evenings feature open-forum discussions to facilitate release of negative self-concepts and unhealthy behavior patterns.

Address   Route 1, Box 1783, Washburn, MO 65772
Phone   (417) 435-2212
Season   Year-round.
Programs Programs teaching a lifestyle of moderate exercise, healthy diet, positive mental attitude, emotional release, and spiritual growth.
Lodging   Private rooms in 10 shared cabins.
Rates   Weekend $395. 1 week $850. 2 weeks $1,600. 1 month $3,000.
Meals   3 daily nondairy vegetarian meals.

Sancta Sophia Seminary   Tahlequah, OK

This seminary is located in Sparrow Hawk Village, a spiritual community in the wooded Ozark foothills of northeastern Oklahoma. Sparrow Hawk's 432 acres are bordered on three sides by the Illinois River and centered above an energy vortex created by a star-shaped convergence of Earth ley lines. The seminary's dean is the Reverend Carol Parrish, Ph.D., a well-known author and teacher whose life was transformed by a near-death experience at age twenty-three.

Sancta Sophia teaches esoteric Christianity through a curriculum that employs home study and weeklong classes, thereby allowing anyone to enroll in a five-day week of classes. Each class meets for two and a half hours each morning or afternoon. Typical class topics are "Intuitive Development" and "Spiritual Healing." Other nondegree programs include "Special Offering" workshops (such as the perennial "Have a Complete Metaphysical"); the annual fall conference; plus an occasional intensive facilitated by Dr. Parrish, who re-visions Christianity as the path to the "Christ-within."

Address   Sparrow Hawk Village, 11 Summit Ridge Drive, Tahlequah, OK 74464
Phone   (918) 456-3421 or (800) 386-7161.
Season   Year-round.
Programs Weekend workshops and conferences, 4-day workshops, 5-day week of classes, 2-week intensive.

Lodging   Guest housing in private village homes. Also tent and ca-
bana campsites, with nearby bathhouse, at a riverside
campground.

Rates   Tuition: weekend program $60–125, 4-day workshop
$300–400, 5-day week of classes $90, 2-week "intensive"
$450. Lodging $6–15 per night. Seminary meals: lunch $4,
dinner $6.

Meals   Lunch and dinner, mostly vegetarian (some poultry and
fish), included with some workshops and all intensives.
Usually guests receive kitchen privileges, or share breakfast and dinner, at village homes. Cafeteria lunch and dinner available for purchase.

Lake Austin Spa Resort   Austin, TX

A twelve-acre facility bordering a twenty-three-mile-long lake and the
famous Steiner Cattle Ranch. LASR's physical facilities include indoor
and outdoor pools, a twenty-four-hour gym, lakeside exercise equipment, tennis and volleyball courts, paddleboats, sculls, a par course,
and horseshoe pits. Hiking trails lace the surrounding Texas hill country. Guests take their meals in the guest dining room, which offers a spacious view of the lake. Winery tours and sunset cruises can be arranged.

LASR guests are offered a large daily selection of activities, classes,
and workshops. Fitness activities include circuit classes, cross training,
Country and Western aerobics, and hill country walks. Among the
stretching and relaxation activities are water stretch, yoga, tai chi, visualization, and meditation. Classes and workshops cover art and art
therapy, cooking demonstrations, eating behaviors, body image, movement therapy, self-awareness, and inner journey.

Address   1705 Quinlan Park Road, Austin, TX 78732
Phone   (512) 266-4363 or (800) 847-5637.
Season   Year-round.
Programs   Daily holistic health workshops, relaxation and fitness ac-
tivities, plus many indoor and outdoor recreational activi-
ties.
Lodging   40 cottage rooms with B&B-style furnishings.

Rates	$200–250 per night. Packages: 4 days $925–1,075, 7 days $1,627–1,890. Add 6% room tax plus 17% service/gratuity charge.
Meals	3 daily gourmet meals. Vegetarian and other diets accommodated on advance notice. Vegetables from LASR's organic garden.
Services	Bodywork, moor therapy, Ayurveda, hydrotherapy, aromatherapy. Counseling, private medical evaluation, nutrition analysis, fitness assessment, tennis and sculling lessons. Roommate-matching service and courtesy airport transfers.

U.S. New England

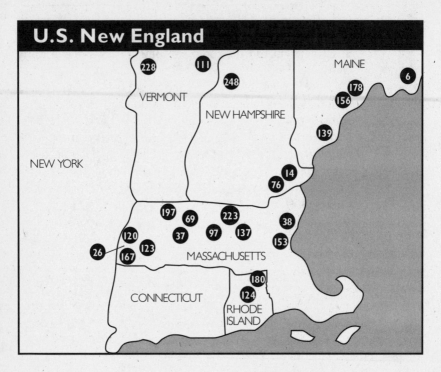

UNITED STATES: *New England Region*

Akasha Institute for Holistic Studies   Camden, ME

An hour and a half north of Portland on the picturesque coast of Maine, there is a new summer center for in-depth workshops focusing primarily on the intuitive arts and spiritual growth. The center is directed by Patti McLaine, a practicing psychic and astrologer. Although she currently hosts the workshops in her residence three blocks from the sea, plans are in the works for a full-scale residential center.

Akasha workshop presenters include gifted teachers and healers from throughout North America and overseas. The daily schedule involves sessions from 9 A.M. to noon and from 2 to 5 P.M. For the rest of the day and evening, guests are free to enjoy such midcoast Maine summer pastimes as walking on the beach, taking a hike up Mount Battie, or going for a swim in Lake Megunticook. Sailing, kayaking, or a trip to Bar Harbor and Acadia National Park are also options for an extended summer vacation in Maine.

Address	18 Limerock Street, P.O. Box 979, Camden, ME 04843
Phone	(207) 236-4036 or (800) 252-7420 (for registration).
Season	Summer.
Programs	2- to 7-day intuitive arts and spiritual growth workshops.
Lodging	Available at nearby campgrounds, cabins, motels, hotels, and inns. (Call Camden Chamber of Commerce at [207] 236-4404 for a list.)
Rates	Workshop tuition: weekend $135–210, 5 days $225–285, 7 days $340–420. Discounts for members of Friends of Akasha.
Meals	Available at nearby restaurants and cafés. Or bring lunch, store it in the fridge, and eat it in the garden or a nearby park.
Services	Intuitive counseling and bodywork services offered by local practitioners and visiting teachers.

Marie Joseph Spiritual Center   Biddeford, ME

This center is operated by the Sisters of the Presentation of Mary in the former Ocean View Hotel, overlooking a sandy Atlantic beach fifteen miles south of Portland. During the summer, the center offers weeklong guided retreats for women only, men only, and for nuns. During the rest of the year, the center hosts weekend guided prayer and scripture retreats, including retreats designed specifically for women or for men. Typical short retreats are "Becoming an Instrument of God," "Paths to Prayer," and "Grandparents as Spiritual Guides."

All retreats are led by the center's own retreat team or by guest presenters that include pastors, counselors, teachers, and writers well grounded in Catholic contemplative traditions. All retreatants are welcome to participate in community prayer and daily Eucharist.

Address	RFD 2, Biddeford, ME 04005
Phone	(207) 284-5671
Season	Year-round.
Programs	Weekend and weeklong retreats encouraging spiritual renewal in a prayerful atmosphere.
Lodging	46 rooms accommodating up to 70 guests.
Rates	Weekend retreat $60–85. Weeklong retreat $210–245.
Meals	3 daily cafeteria meals in a large dining room.
Services	Spiritual counseling on a donation basis.

Northern Pines Health Resort   Raymond, ME

Northern Pines is located near Rattlesnake Mountain and Crescent Lake, forty minutes north of Portland. The resort's seventy-acre grounds include two lodges, cedar cabins, a yurt, a sauna, and a hot tub linked by trails beneath towering pines. Along the property's one-mile lakefront, swimmers can enjoy surface waters as warm as seventy-five degrees during summer months.

The resort has been run since 1980 by owner Marlee Turner on the natural health precepts (e.g., daily exercise, healthy diet, peace of mind, and sociable fun) that helped her recover from cancer and multiple sclerosis. A typical day's menu of activities (all optional) includes early morning meditation and stretches, a prebreakfast walk, a morning class and aerobic workout, a twelve-step or *Course in Miracles* program at noon, a 2 P.M. hike (snowshoeing and cross-country skiing in the winter), yoga at 4:30 P.M., and an evening program.

Most summer weekends feature presenters on topics such as naturopathy, holistic bodywork, dance movement therapy, "Spiritual Experience in our Materialistic World," tarot, and psychic sensitivity. Weekday classes cover vegetarian cooking, biofeedback, stress management, naturopathic and ayurvedic medicine, tai chi, and folk dancing.

Address	559 Route 85, Raymond, ME 04071
Phone	(207) 655-7624
Season	Year-round except the last 3 weeks in January.
Programs	Regular daily schedule of meditation, yoga, and exercise periods plus various natural health classes.
Lodging	Overnight capacity for about 50 guests in cabins, lodge, and yurt with private or double rooms—some with fireplace or private veranda. Two are wheelchair accessible.
Rates	$130–244 per day. $780–1,462 per week. Summer bookings made by the week. Discounts on advance reservations at other times.
Meals	3 daily vegetarian meals, 50% fruits and salads. In summer, ingredients from resort's garden. 3- to 7-day fast option.
Services	Massage, seaweed wrap, reflexology, aromatherapy, rebirthing, breathwork, flotation tank. Portland pick-up and drop-off service.

Poland Spring Health Institute   Poland Spring, ME

Located thirty miles north of Portland, this institute is headquartered in a handsome three-story house surrounded by well-groomed lawns and Maine countryside. It draws its water from the same well as is used by the world-famous Poland Spring water bottling plant. A small lake is a short walk away.

The Institute operates health regeneration programs. The one-week program includes health and nutrition education, hot packs, steam baths, massage, and moderate exercise. Most guests opt for the two-week program, with an exercise regimen created on the basis of a thorough diagnostic evaluation (including an electrocardiogram). In the three-week program, treadmill stress testing is an option when it's medically appropriate and requested by guests.

Programs can be tailored to address specific guest concerns such as chronic fatigue syndrome, high blood pressure, hypertension, depression, diabetes, obesity, stress, and arthritis. There are also special smoking cessation and heart disease programs. All programs are administered by a Seventh-Day Adventist staff, which invites guests to participate in short morning worship services and Friday vespers.

Address RFD 1, Box 4300, Poland Spring, ME 04274
Phone (207) 998-2894
Season Year-round.
Programs Individualized health enhancement programs with 1-, 2-, and 3-week options. 3-week heart disease program and 2-week smoking cessation program.
Lodging 6 large, private or semiprivate rooms.
Rates 1 week $745–950 per person. 2 weeks $1,790–2,200 per person. 3 weeks $2,590–3,105 per person, $4,710 per couple when both participate, $4,125 per couple when only one member participates.
Meals 3 family-style, dairy-free vegetarian meals served each day.
Services Room service. Courtesy airport and bus terminal transfers.

Canyon Ranch in the Berkshires   Lenox, MA

A spacious 120-acre estate of broad lawns, ponds, and woods in the gentle hills of western Massachusetts. The estate's historic Bellefontaine Mansion houses medical and behavioral consultation areas, a restored library, and the dining room. The nearby spa complex features exercise rooms, indoor and outdoor tennis courts, squash and racquetball courts, indoor and outdoor pools, a suspended indoor running track, plus complete body treatment and salon facilities.

The ranch's premier offering is "Optimal Living," a personalized program created in collaboration with an interdisciplinary team of senior staff members. The program includes medical evaluation and supervision, daily indoor and outdoor exercise, daily meetings with behavioral health counselors, access to a broad array of professional health and personal/sports services, nutritional counseling, and full use of the ranch's recreational facilities. The goal of "Optimal Living" is to achieve a significant change in lifestyle.

Like its larger sister ranch in Arizona (see profile earlier in this chapter), Canyon Ranch in the Berkshires has been voted the world's best health spa by the readers of *Conde Nast Traveler* magazine. The magazine notes that Canyon Ranch offers "a rounded, holistic approach" including individual counseling, group workshops, biofeedback, and hypnotherapy. The ranch staff is composed of physicians, psychologists, registered dieticians, exercise physiologists, and certified health educators at a nearly three-to-one ratio of staff to guests.

Address	Bellefontaine, Kemble Street, Lenox, MA 01240
Phone	(413) 637-4100 or (800) 742-9000.
Season	Year-round.
Programs	3-, 4-, 5-, and 7-night packages; personalized "Optimal Living" program for 4 or more nights; also, personalized program for stays of at least 4 weeks.
Lodging	Garden units with private patios in a New England–style inn connected by glass-enclosed walkways to mansion and spa complex. Wheelchair access. Some rooms equipped for the disabled.
Rates	7-night "Optimal Living" package $2,260–3,210. Compared with the ranch's standard packages, "Optimal Living" is $195 more for 4 days, $175 more for 5 days, and no additional charge for 6 or more days. Prices do not include 18% service charge or applicable sales tax.
Meals	3 daily gourmet meals in luxurious dining room. Can accommodate supervised fasting, vegetarian, and special diets.
Services	Packages include a large selection of health and healing services plus a selection of spa and sports services.

Contemplative Dance   Amherst, MA

Located two hours west of Boston on an 800-acre campus, Hampshire College is the site of six-day summer "Contemplative Dance" workshops. Week 1 is for beginners, week 2 for "experienced movers." The daily schedule for week 1 begins with a morning warm-up session followed by a contemplative movement class. Early afternoon is free time for hiking, swimming, tennis, or just relaxing. Late afternoon offers the options of "creative forming," "dancing in the collective," and "spirit of place" classes. Evening is a time for storytelling, singing, and other forms of group play and celebration.

Workshop size is limited to twenty-four participants, who are divided into three groups facilitated by the three faculty members: Daphne Lowell, Mary Ramsey, and Alton Wasson. Daphne is an associate professor of dance/movement studies at Hampshire College. Mary leads workshops in authentic movement. Alton, a former Yale chaplain and professor of religion and humanistic psychology at Prescott College in Prescott, Arizona, is a consultant in holistic education and a counselor in active imagination. Working as a team, Daphne, Mary, and Alton endeavor to lead "Contemplative Dance" participants to "a more intimate knowledge of their embodied selves" by exploring dance as spiritual practice, as artistic resource, and as psychological narrative.

In the planning stage is a yearlong "Contemplative Dance" training, consisting of seven weekends.

Address	Professor Daphne Lowell, D.B., Hampshire College, Amherst, MA 01002
Phone	(413) 268-3294
Season	June/July
Programs	Two weeklong contemplative dance workshops.
Lodging	Student apartments with modest kitchenettes.
Rates	Workshop tuition $400. Options: on-campus housing $85, cafeteria-style meals $95.
Meals	Cafeteria-style meals with choice of vegetarian and non-vegetarian entrées. Also local restaurants.

Cowley Retreats   Cambridge and West Newbury, MA

Cowley Retreats are offered by the Society of St. John the Evangelist—the oldest Anglican religious order for men (founded in Oxford, England, by Richard Meux Benson in 1866). The retreats are held at two sites: the Monastery Guest House on the Charles River, a short walk from Harvard University and the Episcopal Divinity School; and Emery

House, on 120 acres of field and woodland adjacent to a state park, bounded by the Merrimack and Artichoke Rivers, and one hour north of Boston.

Cowley group retreats are built around themes that have included "Desire for Transformation," "Celtic Spirituality," and "How to Cultivate Hope in the Ground of Despair." Except for retreats specifically designed for men, for women, for gay men, or for lesbians, theme retreats are open to all. Directed retreats, which include a daily meeting with a spiritual director, are intended for people with retreat experience. Cowley also welcomes nondirected individual retreatants, who may participate in community worship. Silence and prayer are integral to all Cowley retreats.

Address	Monastery Guest House, 980 Memorial Drive, Cambridge, MA 02138
	Emery House, Emery Lane, West Newbury, MA 01985
Phone	Cambridge: (617) 876-3037. Fax (617) 876-3490.
	West Newbury: (508) 462-7940. Fax (508) 462-0285.
	Please call in advance of visits.
Season	Year-round.
Programs	Guided 2-, 3-, and 5-day group and directed retreats.
Lodging	Single bedrooms, each with sink. Linens and towel provided.
Rates	2- or 3-day guided retreat $100–155. Directed retreat: 3 days, $180, 5 days $275–300. Individual retreat $45–50 per night.
Meals	3 daily silent meals, accompanied by readings at midday and in the evening.

Gateways to Creativity   Deerfield, MA

In this six-day residential workshop, art making is used as a catalyst for personal transformation. It is held every year on the New England country campus of Eaglebrook School, where every day begins with an optional early morning yoga session. Each workshop is limited to sixteen to eighteen participants, who work with a variety of art materials in an environment that encourages creative self-expression. No prior art experience is required.

The program is facilitated by Dale Schwarz and Guillermo Cuellar, directors of the New England Art Therapy Institute (NEATI), along with a guest yoga instructor. Dale is a multimedia artist and registered art therapist. Guillermo's expertise includes the fields of art expression and creative behavior, gestalt and family therapies. Along with art therapist Peter London, Dale and Guillermo also conduct a six-day "Sacred Art—Sacred Places" exploration of artistic creativity in Oaxaca, Mexico.

Address	The New England Art Therapy Institute, 216 Silver Lane #25, Sunderland, MA 01375
Phone	(413) 665-4880
Season	Usually in late July and/or early August.
Programs	6-day art workshop exploring creativity as a catalyst for personal transformation.
Lodging	Simply furnished, private campus rooms.
Rates	$785 with early registration.
Meals	3 wholesome meals each day (Sunday dinner through Friday lunch), all with vegetarian options. Home-baked bread.

Insight Meditation Society   Barre, MA

Insight Meditation Society (IMS) is a Vipassana meditation retreat center set on eighty wooded acres in the quiet countryside of central Massachusetts. Retreats up to nine days long are designed to be comfortable for beginners. Meditation periods alternate sitting with walking meditation. The sittings may be done on floor cushions, benches, or chairs.

An IMS retreat day begins at 6 A.M. with forty-five minutes of sitting meditation followed by breakfast and free time—an opportunity to perform one's daily forty-five minutes of required maintenance work. From 8:15 A.M. to noon there are periods of meditation combined with instruction. Following lunch and a short rest break, meditation/instruction resumes from 2 to 5 P.M. After a light evening supper, there is usually a one-hour evening discourse.

All retreats are led by highly qualified visiting teachers, including several current and former Buddhist monks. Three teachers, Joseph Goldstein, Jack Kornfield, and Sharon Salzberg, were IMS cofounders.

Address	1230 Pleasant Street, Barre, MA 01005
Phone	(508) 355-4378. Fax (508) 355-6398. No visits without prior arrangement.
Season	Year-round except for January.
Programs	Teacher-led Vipassana meditation retreats, most 2–9 days long. 3-month retreats can be taken on a partial, 6-week basis.
Lodging	Capacity for 100 overnight guests in double rooms (some singles) with men and women housed in separate quarters. Renovations have been made to accommodate the disabled.
Rates	Center retreat fees: 2 or 3 days $95–125, 5 days $165, 7 days $215, 9 days $265. Students make teacher donations at end of retreat.
Meals	3 daily vegetarian meals.

Kripalu Center   Lenox, MA

Housed in a former Jesuit monastery, Kripalu Center overlooks Lake Mahkeenak in the Berkshires region of western Massachusetts. Its 320 forested acres contain walking trails and a private beach for summer swimming. Facilities include a twenty-four-hour meditation room plus separate men's and women's whirlpools and saunas. The center's teachers and staff are all members of a yogic spiritual community of roughly 200 people.

For a guest in the popular "Retreat and Renewal," or "R&R," program, a full day (all activities optional) would include early morning and midafternoon sessions of Kripalu yoga, yogic breathing, and meditation; a gathering after breakfast to discuss issues relating to spiritual living; a session exploring Kripalu yoga's eight pathways to high-level health and transformation; DansKinetics (yoga stretches combined with aerobic dance); an early afternoon guided walk or community service opportunity; and an evening community satsang (devotional worship) service or other event.

Most of Kripalu's many other programs focus on various branches and disciplines of yoga, bodywork, holistic health and well-being, self-discovery, and spiritual attunement. Multiple-day conferences address subjects like "Psychotherapy and Spirituality." Monthlong teacher trainings are conducted in the arts of Kripalu yoga, bodywork, and holistic living. There is also a "Spiritual Lifestyle Training" that serves as a residency introduction program.

Address   Box 793, Lenox, MA 01240
Phone   (413) 448-3400 or (800) 967-3577 (reservations).
Season   Year-round.
Programs   3- and 4-day, weeklong, and 2-week "Retreat and Renewal," spiritual and holistic health programs and conferences. Monthlong professional trainings.
Lodging   Capacity for more than 310 overnight guests in dorms (with bunk beds), rooms for two (with double or twin beds, lake or forest views), and a few rooms with private baths.
Rates   R&R $64–195 per night. Other programs: 2 nights $160–390, 3 nights $270–675, 6 nights $495–1,395, 7 nights $560–1,295, 13 nights $1,001–2,431, 27-day training $2,052–4,941.
Meals   3 daily vegetarian buffets, high in fiber and protein, low in fats and sweeteners. Fresh-baked bread. Most meals are silent.
Services   Massage and shiatsu therapy, footcare reflexology, energy balancing, and yoga therapy. Daily children's and teen programs from late June to early September. Weekend child care at other times. Also occasional reduced fare limo service to and from the airport in Albany, New York.

Kushi Institute   Becket, MA

Housed in a former Franciscan abbey on 600 acres of Berkshire meadows and woodlands, the Kushi Institute is the major center in the eastern United States for macrobiotic research and education. Institute directors Michio and Aveline Kushi personally lead several of the residential seminars. In all seminars, mornings begin with Japanese do-in, or self-massage and stretching exercises, and classes open with a meditation.

The institute's seven-day "Way to Health" seminar is recommended for those new to macrobiotics. It explores the relationship between diet and health, the basics of oriental diagnosis, and the fundamentals of a natural lifestyle. It also includes daily cooking classes. Weeklong cooking seminars offer a more detailed treatment of "Homestyle Cooking," "International Cuisine," or "Healing Foods."

Those wishing full immersion in the Kushis' teachings can attend the "Dynamics of Macrobiotics" seminars. There are three levels of these seminars, and each requires a one-month stay. Guests at every level take classes on natural home gardening, food processing, cooking, health diagnosis principles, family health issues, holistic health-care methods, shiatsu and chi energy practices, and macrobiotic lifestyle principles. Other "Dynamics" elements include a guided journal-writing exercise, a "Relating and Resolving" workshop, a private guidance session, and weekly nondenominational spiritual practices.

Address	P.O. Box 7, Becket, MA 01223
Phone	(413) 623-5741. Fax (413) 623-8827.
Season	Year-round.
Programs	7-day "Way to Health" and cooking seminars. 4-week "Dynamics of Macrobiotics" seminar. Occasional short "Spiritual" and year-end "Predictions" seminars.
Lodging	Main building has 10 simply furnished 1- and 2-bed guest rooms, a few with private bath or shower. A separate dormitory facility can accommodate another 20–30 guests.
Rates	7-day "Way to Health" $830–985. 7-day cooking seminar $910–985. 4-week "Dynamics of Macrobiotics" $2,950–3,250.
Meals	3 daily macrobiotic meals.
Services	Shiatsu massage and personal education sessions.

Maharishi Ayur-Veda Health Center   Lancaster, MA

This center is housed in a luxurious redbrick mansion set on 200 acres of well-kept lawns and woodlands thirty miles west of Boston. It is staffed by doctors and nurses trained in both Western and traditional Indian (Ayurvedic) health practices.

The center's basic offering is its ongoing, one-week "Perfect Health" program. This program includes an initial Ayurvedic evaluation of body type and body/mind imbalances; daily two-hour pancha karma rejuvenation treatments (massages, steam bath, pouring of warm oil across the forehead, and a mild enema); gentle hatha yoga sessions; sound and aroma therapies; classes on such topics as diet, exercise, daily and seasonal routines; plus practice of transcendental meditation. Departing guests receive specific recommendations for designing a health maintenance program at home.

Address   679 George Hill Road, P.O. Box 344, Lancaster, MA 01523
Phone   (508) 365-4549. Fax (508) 368-0674.
Season   Year-round.
Programs 1-week Ayurvedic "Perfect Health" program. Also transcendental meditation training for those not yet initiated.
Lodging   Luxurious single and double bedrooms and suites, all with A/C.
Rates   "Perfect Health" program $2,850–3,950. TM training $1,000.
Meals   3 daily vegetarian meals, prepared to stimulate all 6 tastes and served in the dining room or guests' private rooms.
Services Outpatient evaluation and consultations by phone or mail.

New Life Health Center   Boston, MA

Occupying a spacious three-story building in the Jamaica Plain section of Boston, the New Life Center contains an organic vegetable garden, a natural food kitchen and dining area, guest rooms, a yoga and meditation hall, an infrared sauna, lecture and physical therapy rooms, and treatment rooms. Treatments include acupuncture, acupressure, cupping (for energy, blood circulation, and toxin removal), moxa heat (for strengthening the immune system), herbal teas, and homeopathic remedies.

The center's resident program offers guests an initial health evaluation, daily morning meditation, prescribed morning treatments, afternoon treatments (if necessary), yoga classes five days each week, and lectures and workshops on holistic self-healing. Maladies that have been reportedly healed through this program include chronic pain, weight problems, ulcers, substance dependencies, immune disorders, cancer, and diabetes.

Center director Dr. Bo-In Lee is a respected acupuncturist trained in the Eastern and Western healing arts, psychology, and spiritual disciplines. His staff includes several health-care assistants, his wife and codirector Namye Lee, and Asha Saxena, M.D. Namye is the creator of Mahayana yoga, which combines yogic breathing and postures with partner work, acupressure massage, and meditation. Asha is a general practitioner and acupuncturist educated in her native India and New England.

Address	12 Harris Avenue, Boston, MA 02130
Phone	(617) 524-9551. Fax (617) 524-0345.
Season	Year-round.
Programs	1-, 2-, and 3-week resident programs using both Eastern and Western medicine to promote self-healing of various physical conditions.
Lodging	Capacity for 16 overnight guests in double occupancy rooms and a few private rooms.
Rates	1 week $995, 2 weeks $1,990, 3 weeks $2,985. Additional fees for additional treatments (if necessary). Special arrangements for companions of program residents.
Meals	3 daily meals, mostly vegetarian with occasional fish and chicken. A fasting program may be prescribed.
Services	Outside lab tests and X rays, acupressure massage, herbal teas and nutritional supplements, corrective exercises to balance posture and reduce muscular tensions—all as prescribed by Dr. Lee.

Option Institute   Sheffield, MA

An eighty-five-acre hillside estate in southwest Massachusetts, less than a three-hour drive from both Boston and New York City airports. Housed in handsome, comfortable structures amid sweeping lawns, meadows, and forests, institute guests can enjoy swimming, cross-country skiing, and hiking. Summer program participants can also enjoy the many theaters and festivals of the surrounding Berkshire region.

The institute was founded in 1983 by Barry and Samahria Kaufman to help singles, couples, and families learn how to increase their happiness through enhancing self-confidence and interpersonal skills. Programs include "The Happiness Option" (three-day weekend), "Loving You/Loving Me" (a three-day program for couples), "Empowering Yourself" (a five-day program), and "Living the Dream, Instead of Just Dreaming It" (a two-part training, with each part four weeks long).

The institute's full-time staff of more than forty include certified "Option Process" mentors, apprentices, and resident volunteers. The heart of the Option Process is a nondirective dialogue technique encouraging self-acceptance and suspended judgment. The ramifications and applications of this approach are described in Barry Kaufman's many books.

Address	2080 South Undermountain Road, Sheffield, MA 01257
Phone	(413) 229-2100. Fax (413) 229-8931.
Season	Year-round.
Programs	3-day, 5-day, 4-week, and 8-week life enhancement workshops. Customized programs for families with children suffering from various dysfunctions. Also 4-month resident volunteer program.
Lodging	Accommodations for up to 60 in guest houses, including double rooms, triple rooms (generally used only on weekends), and a few private rooms available on special request. Limited wheelchair access.
Rates	Program rates: 3 days $465, regular 5-day rate $995, 5-day rate with personalized program for small groups $1,275, 4 weeks $3,800, 8 weeks $7,200.
Meals	3 daily vegetarian meals.

Rowe Camp & Conference Center   Rowe, MA

This center is located in northwest Massachusetts next to 1,400 acres of Berkshire forests. On the grounds are a white clapboard farmhouse, a recreation hall, camp cabins, and a sauna. The program schedule is managed by a small resident community that includes codirectors Prue Berry and Doug Wilson. Prue is a singer, guitar player, and mother. Doug is a Unitarian minister, comedian, and political activist.

A Unitarian summer camp since 1924, Rowe Camp now offers both children's and adult camps from late June through August. There are four weeklong adult camps: "Men's Wisdom Council" for men only, "Womencircles" for women only, "Recovery Camp" as a complement to various twelve-step programs, and "Liberation Camp" for singles and couples seeking better communication between men and women. "Liberation Camp" includes a program for parent-accompanied children ages eight to eighteen.

Rowe Center hosts weekend workshops nearly every week except during camp season. Workshop facilitators include well-known authors, teachers, healers, and musicians. Perennial offerings include Wavy Gravy's "Clowning and Compassion," relationship workshops with Joyce and Barry Vissell, pre- and postsummer workweeks (free for full-time workers), and the Labor Day weekend retreat for gay and bisexual men.

Address	Kings Highway Road, Box 273, Rowe, MA 01367
Phone	(413) 339-4954 or (413) 339-4216 (registration). Fax (413) 339-5728.
Season	Year-round.
Programs	Weeklong women's, men's, "Liberation," and "Recovery" gatherings and camps. Weekend workshops on spirituality, healing, relationships, self-expression, and self-acceptance. Also workshops for specific gender and sexual preference groups.
Lodging	Capacity for 120 in farmhouse and cabin dorms plus a few private bedrooms with shared baths. Several dorms are coed. There are also campsites. BYO bedding.
Rates	Weeklong adults' gathering or camp $355–405. Weekend program tuition $125–185. Weekend room and board $65–155.
Meals	3 daily vegetarian meals.

Spring Hill   Ashby, MA

Set on high ground with sweeping vistas of New Hampshire and the Boston skyline (one and a half hours to the southeast), Spring Hill is an eighty-acre retreat of high meadows, rolling hills, and wooded trails. The center offers "Opening the Heart," or "OTH," workshops, as originally developed in 1976 by Robert and Judith Gass. Each workshop generally has about thirty participants and ten staff, drawn from a pool of nearly one hundred therapists and counselors. And each participant's background information is reviewed in advance to ensure that his or her needs are addressed.

The most frequently presented workshops are "OTH—Individuals" and "OTH for Couples." Other offerings include "Silencing the Inner Critic," "Finding the Self," plus many workshops for specific groups such as women, men, gay men, lesbians, abused women, and adult children of alcoholics. All workshops draw on Western psychological methods such as gestalt, psychodrama, bioenergetics, music and creative art therapies, and small group and individual exercises. Meditation, witnessing, and inner work are also employed.

Additional programs include trainings for prospective staff members and other therapists, plus introductory one-day OTH workshops in major cities throughout the Northeast. Spring Hill center is also available for rental by other groups.

Address	Spring Hill Road, P.O. Box 130, Ashby, MA 01431
Phone	(508) 386-0244 or (800) 550-0244. Fax (508) 386-7567. No visits without prior arrangement.
Season	Year-round.
Programs	Weekend workshops focusing on opening the heart.
Lodging	Side-by-side, futon-style mats in separate men's and women's sleeping quarters in conference center barn. Also tent sites.
Rates	Weekend workshop $295.
Meals	5 vegetarian meals each weekend.

Aryaloka Buddhist Retreat Center   Newmarket, NH

Located sixty miles north of Boston on thirteen acres of wooded property laced by paths and streams, Aryaloka is housed in a spacious building formed by two connecting geodesic domes with wood interiors. The structure includes guest quarters, a movement/workshop room, a top-floor meditation hall, a small library, and a well-stocked Buddhist bookstore.

Anyone may participate in the frequent introductory "Meditation Day" and "Buddhism Day" seminars. Other programs open to the public include weeklong women's, men's, and open summer retreats. Those familiar with Aryaloka meditation practices may also participate in additional weekend and weeklong meditation retreats. All programs are conducted by resident and local teachers from the Aryaloka spiritual community.

For men and women willing to commit to a Buddhist spiritual life by joining Friends of the Western Buddhist Order (FWBO), there are also weekend and weeklong retreats that combine meditation, study, and devotional practice. FWBO emphasizes Vipassana meditation and development of compassion. The center also offers free working weekends plus a comfortable cabin for solitary retreats in wooded seclusion.

Address	14 Heartwood Circle, Newmarket, NH 03857
Phone	(603) 659-5456. No visits without prior arrangement.
Season	Year-round.
Programs	Weekend and weeklong meditation retreats, working retreats, and Buddhist studies workshops.
Lodging	Capacity for at least 20 overnight guests in private rooms.
Rates	1-day seminar $45. Weekend retreat $80–90. Weeklong retreat $210. Nonprogram, daily guest rate (1 night and meals) $35.
Meals	3 daily vegetarian meals. Meals may be taken in one's room or in the communal dining area.

Green Pastures Estate   Epping, NH

Like other Emissary communities around the world, the fifty or so people at Green Pastures Estate share a commitment to living in harmony with life's creative process. The estate's 160 acres of buildings, pastures, woodland, orchards, and gardens are owned by the community as a whole. Major decisions are made by consensus, and most members are employed in community endeavors such as organic gardening, turkey raising, and running workshop/retreat facilities at this center one hour north of Boston.

As a center for spiritual growth and renewal, Green Pastures hosts mostly two- or three-day workshops on subjects like deep ecology, relationships, and various modes of spiritual and holistic healing. There are also occasional five- to seven-day programs on subjects (such as firewalking) that require intense concentration and total immersion.

Lodging is an option at most workshops, though it sometimes is included in the program fee (especially with longer workshops). All visitors are accommodated in community households, each with several individuals and families sharing living space. The entire community eats together in a large dining hall and worships together on Sunday mornings and Wednesday evenings in ever-changing, cooperatively created services.

Address	38 Ladds Lane, Epping, NH 03042
Phone	(603) 679-8149. Fax (603) 679-5138.
Season	Mid-February through early December.
Programs	Mostly weekend workshops on spiritual growth, healing, and human potential. Occasional 5- to 7-day programs.
Lodging	Single and double guest rooms in communal living facilities.
Rates	2- or 3-day workshop tuition $150–195. Nightly lodging (with 3 meals) $35–80. Commuters charged $5 per day plus $10 per meal.
Meals	Communal lunch and dinner with vegetarian options. Breakfast supplies available on a "help yourself" basis.

Wellspring Foundation of New England   Lyme, NH

This nonprofit community health services organization hosts six-day retreats to encourage spiritual, emotional, and physical healing among people with cancer. Until the construction of Wellspring's own center, the retreats are being held at Gove Hill—a 200-acre mountaintop country estate in Thetford, Vermont.

At each retreat—known as "WCHP," for "Wellspring Cancer Help Program"—sessions include meditation and progressive deep relaxation exercises, gentle yoga, massage, and other therapeutic touch. There are opportunities for group sharing and support, as well as self-exploration through music, poetry, art, sand-tray therapy, and dreamwork. There are also informative sessions on nutrition and cancer therapy options. If necessary, emergency care is available at the Dartmouth-Hitchcock Medical Center in nearby Lebanon, New Hampshire.

Wellspring's program is modeled after California's Commonweal program (see profile earlier in this chapter), where Wellspring directors

Bob Rufsvold, M.D., and Deb Steele, M.A., both received training. So just as at Commonweal, each WCHP is limited to eight participants who all must be under the care of a primary-care physician or oncologist and be well enough to benefit from the program.

Address	P.O. Box 70, Lyme, NH 03768
Phone	(603) 795-2144
Season	Year-round.
Programs	6-day self-healing program for people with cancer.
Lodging	Shared accommodations (3 or 4 per room) at Gove Hill.
Rates	$1,500 per person.
Meals	3 daily vegetarian meals.

Kushi Summer Conference   Smithfield, RI

After many years in Vermont, the one-week summer conference of the Kushi Institute (profiled earlier in this chapter) is now held on the campus of Bryant College, a 300-acre facility an hour's drive southwest of Boston. The guest faculty of fifty teachers, counselors, and authors present workshops, classes, and lectures on all aspects of macrobiotic lifestyle (e.g., organic gardening, cooking, physical and mental health); and on exercise and centering disciplines like tai chi, chi gung, aikido, Alexander Technique, and bio-breath energetics. There are also evening programs such as contra dancing and a talent show.

Address	P.O. Box 390, Becket, MA 01223
Phone	(413) 623-5741. Fax (413) 623-8827.
Season	One week in August.
Programs	Macrobiotic conference/camp.
Lodging	Clean, quiet dormitories with separate dorms for families with children. Also double rooms, single rooms, and limited campsite space (near showers and bathrooms).
Rates	Meals and tuition: adults $525, children ages 2–17 $275, children under 2 free. Rooms: adults $200–275, children ages 2–17 $100. Tent sites $75–125.
Meals	3 daily macrobiotic meals.

Services   Dietary guidance, shiatsu massage, private yoga sessions. Also children's activities.

Providence Zen Center   Cumberland, RI

Set on fifty wooded acres fifteen miles north of Providence, Rhode Island, this center is headquarters of the international Kwan Um School of Zen—founded in 1983 by the seventy-eighth patriarch in the Korean Chogye order. It is also home of Diamond Hill Zen Monastery and a small community of lay Zen practitioners, who operate public walk-in and residential programs.

People new to meditation may attend monthly Sunday morning meditation instruction or occasional one-day retreats. Beginner meditators may also participate in meditation retreats of two or three days that require a stay of at least one full night and day. The daily retreat schedule includes sitting, chanting, walking and bowing meditation, talks, and work practice.

Diamond Hill is a long-term retreat facility and residence for monks and nuns. This facility hosts "Kyol Che" retreats over three-week summer and three-month winter periods. A "Kyol Che" day consists of chanting and sitting and walking meditation punctuated by short work and break periods from 4:45 A.M. to 9:40 P.M. The general public may participate for a minimum of one week in the winter and a minimum of three days in the summer.

Address   99 Pound Road, Cumberland, RI 02864
Phone   (401) 658-1464. Fax (401) 658-1188. Call before visiting.
Season   Year-round.
Programs   Meditation retreats ranging from a day or a weekend up to 3 months. Also Buddhist monastic residential training.
Lodging   Dorms with mattresses or futons on carpeted floors. Semiprivate rooms or beds for people with special needs. Men and women in separate rooms. Tent sites. BYO sleeping bag, pillow, and towel.
Rates   3-week retreat $800 or $40 per day. 3-month retreat $2,500 or $280 per week. Other meditation retreats $40 per day. Guest visit or solo retreat $175 per week or $25 per day. Residential training $460 per month.

Meals   3 daily buffet-style vegetarian meals, eaten out of bowls, served on retreats. Short-term overnight guests prepare own meals.

Karme-Choling   Barnet, VT

Set on 540 acres of meadows and woodlands in northern Vermont, Karme-Choling is a large meditation and Tibetan Buddhist studies center that each year offers more than sixty programs—most given over a weekend and most open to first-time visitors. There are programs in traditional Japanese arts, "Dharma Art" trainings in the art of everyday life, "Gateway" programs for beginner and intermediate meditation students, and "Shambala" trainings in "The Heart of Warriorship" and "The Sacred Path of the Warrior." One-month meditation retreats are also offered. Center days begin at 7 A.M. with group meditation, and guests are asked to contribute an hour and a half of daily work.

Karme-Choling is run by a nonmonastic spiritual community of fifty to sixty people. It was established by the late Chogyam Trungpa, former abbot of Tibet's Surmang monasteries, founder of Colorado's Naropa Institute, and author of *Shambala: The Sacred Path of the Warrior*. The center's programs are conducted by both resident and visiting teachers, many from Naropa.

One can also stay at Karma-Choling through weeklong summer camps for families and young people (ages 10 and older), residency and work-study programs, plus personal retreats for authorized students.

Address   Star Route, Barnet, VT 05821
Phone   (802) 633-2384. Fax (802) 633-3012. Call before visiting.
Season   Year-round.
Programs   Weekend programs on meditation and conscious and creative living from a Tibetan Buddhist perspective; weeklong summer family and youth camps; 1-month meditation retreats; residency and work-study.
Lodging   Overnight guest capacity of up to 200 at Karme-Choling and a guest house in nearby Barnet. Accommodations consist of dorms and shared rooms with floor mattresses (BYO sleeping bag), a few 1- and 2-bed private rooms, solo retreat cabins, and tent sites.

Rates	Weekend program $90–185. 6- to 8-day workshop $175–375. Weeklong camp: adults $200, young people ages 10–17 $250, children up to age 10 $100. Kids at other times: under 3 free, others $14 per day. 1-month retreat $600 or $190 per day. Residency: short-term $24 per day, 1+ month $15 per day.
Meals	3 meals, vegetarian or meat, plus a teatime snack each day.
Services	Child care for ages 3 to 11 included in child lodging/meal rates. Low-fee rides to and from airports, train and bus stations.

Sunray Peace Village   Lincoln, VT

Sunray Village is an annual ten-week summer encampment set on twenty-seven acres of meadows, woods, ponds, and streams bordering the Green Mountain National Forest in central Vermont. The village fosters a sense of cooperation, harmony, and practical spirituality through Native American ceremonies, morning and evening community meditations, and the practice of working with others for an hour each day before the various workshops and training programs.

Annual village events include a weekend gathering of Native American elders and the one-week "Peacekeeper Mission" (a training in personal and planetary transformation based on Cherokee meditations, chanting, and community dream practice). Other programs include two-day workshops such as "Crystal Study and Healing," the family "Star**Child Gathering," "Men and Women Walking in Balance," and "Tibetan Fire Puja Teachings." At other time of the year, Sunray hosts weekend Peacekeeper Mission residentials at various sites around North America and abroad.

The village is sponsored by Sunray Meditation Society under the guidance of the venerable Dhyani Ywahoo—a full-blooded Cherokee trained by her grandparents in the Ywahoo lineage, a Tibetan Buddhist teacher of both the Nyingma and Kagyu schools, an author, and a Peace Village workshop leader.

Address	Sunray Meditation Society, P.O. Box 269, Bristol, VT 05443
Phone	Numbers change from year to year and differ among various camp programs.

Season   Late June through early September.

Programs   1- to 7-day trainings, workshops, and ceremonies focusing on how to live in peace with oneself, others, and the Earth. Programs led by Sunray summer faculty and visiting teachers.

Lodging   BYO tent and sleeping bag. Nearby toilets, sinks, and hot showers.

Rates   Tuition (including camping) ranges from $50 for 1-day workshop to $420 for 7-day retreat. Additional camping $10 per night per person.

Meals   Large tent for communal cooking and dining. BYO food, cooking equipment, and utensils.

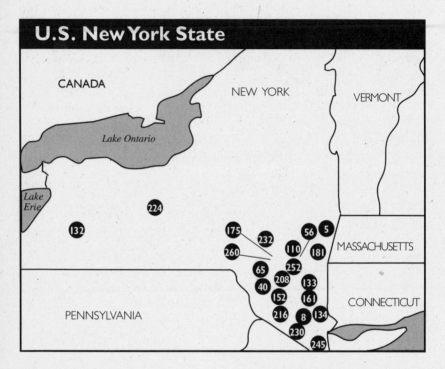

U.S. New York State

CANADA

NEW YORK

VERMONT

Lake Ontario

Lake Erie

MASSACHUSETTS

CONNECTICUT

PENNSYLVANIA

UNITED STATES: *New York State*

Aegis at the Abode   New Lebanon, NY

Aegis is headquartered in a mountaintop retreat center and former Shaker village on 430 forested acres in the Berkshire Hills. During the summer, weekend and weeklong programs are conducted at the mountaintop site in classroom pavilions. The grounds also include a sweat lodge, a camp kitchen, and a dining pavilion. In cooler months, Aegis shares space with its parent Sufi community in the 150-year-old village.

Summer weekend retreats and camps focus on subjects like spiritual healing, sacred dance, and Christian mysticism. In July there is usually a ten-day "Summer Celebration Camp" with yoga, meditations, singing, Dances of Universal Peace, women's councils, sweat lodge, and many workshops. Late in August there is a one-week "Spiritual Music Camp" cofacilitated by Pir Vilayat Inayat Kahn—head of the Sufi order. All programs are led by resident and visiting members of the international Sufi community.

Aegis's parent community, the Abode of the Message, consists of about twenty-five children and fifty adults. Every adult is free to follow his or her own spiritual path. Each day of the week includes scripture readings, prayers, and chants from a different religion. There are three daily worship periods, and grace is sung before each meal.

Personal retreat visits to this community are welcomed throughout the year.

Address	RD 1, Box 1030D, New Lebanon, NY 12125
Phone	(518) 794-8095.
Season	Year-round with scheduled programs offered from late March through early September.
Programs	2- to 10-day programs exploring and celebrating spiritual freedom and diversity, musical expression, and healing. 1- to 3-month work exchange. Also personal retreats and private group rentals.

Lodging	Overnight guest capacity of 175 in summer and 125 in winter. June–September: tent sites, huts, and log cabins with separate washhouses, hot showers, and outhouses. October–May: single or shared rooms in main Shaker buildings complex. BYO towels and bedding.
Rates	Tuition: 2- and 3-day programs $135–185, 6-day "Spiritual Music Camp" $200 or $35 per day, 10-day "Summer Celebration Camp" $150 or $20 per day. Meals and lodging $20–40 per day. Personal retreat $40–65 per day (with meals).
Meals	3 daily vegetarian meals with dairy and nondairy options.
Services	Child care. Children's camp during "Summer Celebration Camp."

Ananda Ashram   Monroe, NY

Ananda Ashram lies one hour northwest of New York City on eighty-five acres of meadows and woodlands surrounding a lake with an island. There are nature trails, orchards, a vegetable garden, a swimming pool, sweat lodges, a meditation room, and a yoga health center with a eucalyptus sauna (for use by members of the Yoga Society of New York). The ashram was founded by the late Ramamurti Mishra, M.D., as the country retreat of the YSNY. Today it is operated by a small residential community of families and single adults.

Overnight guest fees cover meals and all ongoing activities: daily early morning chi gung and hatha yoga sessions; weekly classes in yoga, tai chi, chi gung, Kathak dance, Sanskrit and Hindu scripture studies; evening lectures and cultural programs; plus daily morning and evening satsang (fire ceremony, meditation, chanting, and readings). All overnight guests are asked to donate one hour each day to service. And all guests staying at least one month must belong to the Yoga Society of New York or San Francisco.

Especially during the summer, there are also special tuition programs facilitated by guest teachers. Such programs have included weekend art retreats, artist/writer workshops, and "Nada Yoga" (science of sound frequencies) silent retreats, as well as a weeklong "Taoist Meditation" intensive and a two-week "Classical Indian Music" course. The ashram does not offer children's programs except during special (and tuition-free) family events, such as "Family Weeks."

Address   RD 3, Box 141 (Sapphire Road), Monroe, NY 10950
Phone   (914) 782-5575
Season   Year-round.
Programs Daily selection of free (with stay) holistic health, spiritual, and cultural activities, classes, and events. Also occasional daylong or multiple-day workshops (requiring tuition).
Lodging   Capacity for 35 overnight guests in dorms and a few semi-private rooms with shared bath. Also campsites.
Rates   Guest stay: 1 day $32–46, 1 weekend $80–115, 1 week $185–265. Tuition programs: 2 days $70–100, 7 days $200, 2 weeks $300.
Meals   3 daily lacto-vegetarian, buffet-style meals prepared in various styles with fresh fruits, vegetables, and accompanying salad.

Dai Bosatsu Zendo   Livingston Manor, NY

Dai Bosatsu Zendo is the first traditional Rinzai Zen Buddhist monastery established in the West. It is set on 1,400 acres at the quiet edge of Beecher Lake, the highest lake in the Catskill Mountains. The architectural style is traditional Japanese. The abbot is Eido Shimano Roshi, who also presides over midtown Manhattan's New York Zendo.

Twice each year, Dai Bosatsu hosts three-month training periods (kessei) that can be attended on a monthly basis. During each month of kessei, there is a silent weeklong intensive meditation retreat (sesshin) with options for shorter five-day and weekend stays. Every year there are also four "Introduction to Zen" weekends, two "Healing and Wellness" weekends for HIV-positive people, four twelve-step weekends, and the August "O-Bon Festival."

Guest students are expected to participate fully in the daily monastic schedule. Beginning with wake-up at 5 A.M., an average day includes morning and evening chanting services; morning and afternoon work periods; plus sitting meditation (zazen) before breakfast, lunch, and bedtime. Other guests, and people in private groups renting the zendo's conference center, may participate in Zen practices if they wish to do so.

Address   HCR 1, Box 171, Livingston Manor, NY 12758
Phone   (914) 439-4566. Fax (914) 439-3119. Call before visiting.

Season   Year-round.

Programs 100-day Zen practice periods, 5- and 7-day intensive meditation retreats, weekend introductory workshops, plus special programs for 12-step and HIV-positive people.

Lodging   Accommodations for about 100 in single and double
monastery rooms, a lakeside guest house with kitchen, and
a cottage.

Rates   Practice period: 3 months $1,500, 1 month $750. Intensive
meditation retreat: 7 days $350, 5 days $250, weekend $150.
"Introduction to Zen" weekend $150. Monastery room and
board: guests $60 per day, work-study students $40 per day.

Meals   3 daily vegetarian meals taken in silence.

Elat Chayyim   Accord, NY

Elat Chayyim offers courses that explore spirituality, healing, and creative expression. Most courses are presented in the context of (or at
least with reference to) Jewish tradition, with a few exceptions (e.g.,
yoga and meditation retreats, and a "Writing Our Own Stories" workshop). Retreatants may take one or two courses, each of which meets
for three hours every morning or afternoon for two to six days. They are
also free to abstain from taking any course at all.

The center is located thirty-five minutes southwest of Woodstock,
New York, on a thirty-five-acre Catskills property with meadows, tennis
courts, a volleyball court, Ping-Pong table, an indoor Jacuzzi, and a
large outdoor pool. Daily activities include a hike before breakfast,
yoga, classes in basic Jewish spirituality, and a prayer/meditation session before dinner. Each guest is also a member of a mispocha (family)
group that meets daily for discussion and reflection on the retreat experience. There are optional mispocha groups for gay/lesbian and twelve-
step guests.

Most retreats end with a spirited Shabbat (Sabbath) celebration.
Shabbat preparation and celebration are a major focus of the daily children's program. In the spirit of "the more the merrier," Elat Chayyim offers singles' Shabbat retreats. The center also rents space for special
gatherings and retreats (e.g., weddings, family reunions, and synagogue
retreats).

Address   P.O. Box 127, Woodstock, NY 12498
Phone   (914) 679-2638 or (800) 398-2630 (phone and fax).
Season   May through November.
Programs   Primarily courses ranging from 2 to 6 days. Also work-exchange weeks, internships, and food services apprenticeships.
Lodging   Accommodations for more than 100 people. Mostly double occupancy rooms with A/C. A few single, quadruple, and 5-bed family rooms. Wheelchair accessible housing. Also campsites.
Rates   Courses: 2 days $90–170, 3 days $175–275, 4 days $340–465, 5 days $420–575, 6 days $470–645. Second course in 1 week, add $120. Children and teens for 2–6 nights $85–205.
Meals   3 daily gourmet Kosher vegetarian meals, prepared as much as possible from locally grown organic produce.
Services   Daytime children's program and evening child care.

Foundation for "A Course in Miracles"   Roscoe, NY

A place for study and reflection on a book first published in 1975 by the Foundation for Inner Peace. *A Course in Miracles* (*ACIM*) was written over a seven-year period of dictation (from an inner voice identifying itself as Jesus) to the late Helen Schucman, an atheist and a professor of medical psychology at Columbia University's College of Physicians and Surgeons. In close consultation with Helen, Dr. Kenneth Wapnick edited the manuscript for publication. Since then, Dr. Wapnick has written many ACIM commentaries.

Ken and his wife, Gloria, are the hosts of the Foundation for "A Course in Miracles," which is situated on the edge of Catskill Forest Park, roughly two and a half hours from metropolitan New York. The center's ninety-five acres of lawns and forest rim the shore of Tennanah Lake, and guests are free to hike, swim, or canoe between their morning and late afternoon classes. To ensure a quiet atmosphere, children and pets are not allowed at the center.

The foundation has a dual focus: teaching of ACIM's principles of forgiveness, which is accomplished primarily through workshops; and application of these principles to one's personal life, which is the focus of the foundation's Academy classes. All programs are conducted by the Wapnicks and the foundation staff.

Address   1275 Tennanah Lake Road, Roscoe, NY 12776
Phone   (607) 498-4116. Fax (607) 498-5325. Call before visiting.
Season   April through early December.
Programs   ½-, 1½-, and 2½-day "A Course in Miracles" workshops. 7-, 8-, 10-, 12-, and 14-day ACIM Academy classes. 20-day ACIM intensive. Individualized study retreats and 3-month long-term study program.
Lodging   Accommodations for over 130 guests. Academy students and personal retreatants housed in kitchenette apartments. Workshop students housed in double occupancy rooms. All rooms have private bathrooms, most with both a shower and a tub, but a few with shower only. Linens and towels provided.
Rates   Personal retreat $30–40 per day. Workshops: ½ day $20, 1½ days $146–166, 2½ days $216–246. Sample Academy rates: 7 nights $220–280, 10 nights $348–438, 14 nights $405–509.
Meals   3 daily meals, with vegetarian options, served only during 1½- and 2½-day workshops. Lunches served during Academy courses. Otherwise, Academy students and retreatants prepare meals in their kitchenettes or the common kitchen.

Karma Triyana Dharmachakra   Woodstock, NY

Located ninety miles north of New York City on a twenty-acre site amid the meadows and forests of the Catskill Mountains, Karma Triyana Dharmachakra is a Tibetan Buddhist monastery and retreat center in the Karma Kagyu tradition. The center's resident abbot is Khenpo Karthar Rinpoche, who emigrated to the United States in 1976 to become spiritual director of all Karma Thegsum Choling centers. Also resident at the center is lama Bardor Tulku Rinpoche.

The center offers weekend and two- to ten-day Tibetan Buddhist teachings and empowerment seminars plus occasional "Introduction to Meditation" weekends. During these programs, the daily schedule is as follows: breakfast at 7:30 A.M., meditation from 10 to 10:30, teachings from 10:30 to noon, meditation between 3 and 3:30 P.M., teachings from 3:30 to 5, supper at 6, and Chenrezig practice between 7 and 8. Some seminars are designed specifically for people new to meditation and/or Buddhist teachings. Most are taught by a resident lama. All guests are asked to donate one and a half hours of daily work to help maintain the center.

Address	352 Meads Mountain Road, Woodstock, NY 12498
Phone	(914) 679-5906. Fax (914) 679-4625. Call before visiting.
Season	Year-round.
Programs	Weekend and 7- to 10-day seminars on meditation practice, Buddhist philosophy and psychology.
Lodging	Generally shared rooms. Sometimes private rooms are available. Floor and tent space also available. BYO sleeping bag.
Rates	Program tuition: weekend $45–75, 7 to 10 days $150–250. Room and board: $25–45 per day, $145–270 per week.
Meals	3 daily vegetarian meals.

Lily Dale Assembly   Lily Dale, NY

This tranquil spiritualist community in western New York (one hour south of Buffalo and three hours east of Cleveland) has hosted public programs every summer since 1879. These offerings now include a full schedule of workshops, classes, and lectures by well-known authors and teachers of the intuitive arts, channeled wisdom, spiritual and holistic healing, and spiritual and personal growth.

The community's cozy and quaint nineteenth-century atmosphere is enhanced by charming old hotels and a lakeside park with a swan shelter, picnic pavilion, bandstand, and gazebo. There is also a beach and beach house, nature trails, meditation garden, and sweat lodge. Daily community activities include healing and meditation services plus "message services" conducted by guest and resident mediums. There are also weekly concerts, thought-exchange circles, and Sunday worship.

Address	5 Melrose Park, P.O. Box 248, Lily Dale, NY 14752
Phone	(716) 595-8721. Fax (716) 595-2442.

Season   May through September.

Programs Workshops (2 days on average) ranging from an evening to
            5 days.

Lodging   Two hotels, private guest houses, and trailer park.

Rates   Tuition for ½-day to 5-day program $18–275. Lodging: hotel
            $21–43 per night or $140–290 per week; trailer park $6 per
            day or $40 per week; guest houses, call (716) 595-8722 for
            referrals.

Meals   At community cafeteria or Pagoda Snack Bar. Or make
            your own at guest houses with kitchens or kitchen privi-
            leges.

Services Private consultations with mediums tested, approved, and
            registered by the Lily Dale Assembly.

Linwood Spiritual Center   Rhinebeck, NY

Located two hours north of New York City in the Hudson River Valley,
this sixty-five-acre hilltop property is operated by the Sisters of St. Ur-
sula as a nunnery and retreat center for men and women. On the
grounds are a large main building, a guest house, a cottage, a large outdoor pavilion, a swimming pool, and tennis courts.

Linwood offers retreats with a holistic orientation that include a one-
week summer "Human Wellness" retreat and a number of two-day
(mostly weekend) programs of ongoing twelve-step retreats, Enneagram study retreats, plus theme retreats such as "Dance as Prayer,"
"Spiritual Journals," and "Life Regeneration." Other programs, of a
Catholic religious orientation, consist of weeklong directed prayer retreats, guided weekend women's retreats, and the weeklong "Ignatian"
guided retreat.

Address   139 South Mill Road, Rhinebeck, NY 12572

Phone   (914) 876-4178. No visits without prior arrangement.

Season   Year-round.

Programs 2-day and weeklong retreats on spirituality and human
            development.

Lodging   Single room accommodations for over 25 people. Also one
            double room plus a cottage for private retreats.

Rates   Weekend retreat $115–130. Weeklong retreat $260.

Meals	3 daily meals. Option to dine alone in silence.
Services	Spiritual counseling. Massage available on weekends.

Living Springs Lifestyle Center Putnam Valley, NY

A health reconditioning center nestled among the trees on the edge of a quiet lake one hour north of Manhattan. Guest recreation opportunities include hiking on the nearby Appalachian Trail, canoeing, boating, plus ice-skating and cross-country skiing during winter months.

The center's "Wellness" program includes a blood chemistry analysis, consultation with a physician, daily exercise, spa treatments (e.g., steam bath, sauna, and massage), as well as classes on such subjects as natural remedies, vegetarian cooking, and nutrition. Individual programs can be designed to focus on weight or stress management problems. There is also a "Smoking Cessation" program.

All guests are invited (but by no means required) by the Seventh-Day Adventist staff to participate after breakfast in short inspiration periods of song, prayer, and scripture readings illustrating spiritual growth principles. Most guests stay for the recommended two-week period.

Address	22 Living Springs Lane, Putnam Valley, NY 10579
Phone	(914) 526-2800 or (800) 729-9355 (reservations).
Season	Year-round.
Programs	"Wellness" and "Smoking Cessation" programs, both 1 or 2 weeks.
Lodging	8 single or double occupancy "standard" and "superior" rooms in a two-level lodge.
Rates	1 week $995–1,445. 2 weeks $1,795–2,595. 50% discount for a supportive spouse who participates in the program.
Meals	3 daily, buffet-style vegan (nondairy vegetarian) meals.
Services	Train station and airport pick-up/drop-off service.

New Age Health Spa Neversink, NY

This 155-acre converted farm lies two and a half hours northwest of New York City in the foothills of the Catskill Mountains. On or near the spa grounds are indoor and outdoor swimming pools, five miles of wooded trails, and an "alpine tower"—a freestanding, fifty-foot-high, hourglass-shaped climbing structure made of two interlocking log tripods. A barnlike building houses a full array of spa beauty treatments. There are also sauna and steam rooms.

A New Age day can begin with Zen meditations at 6:30 A.M., a three- to six-mile power walk at 7, and yoga at 8. Following breakfast at 9, guests can depart for an all-day guided easy or moderate hike in some of the Northeast's most beautiful wilderness areas. Those who stay behind can select activities that typically include fitness and nutrition seminars, body and low-impact-aerobic conditioning, water aerobics, stretch class, afternoon yoga or tai chi, and predinner guided meditation. Evenings often feature a talk or a movie.

Address	Route 55, Neversink, NY 12765
Phone	(914) 985-2467 or (800) 682-4348 (reservations).
Season	Year-round.
Programs	Guests design their own holistic health program by selecting from daily lectures; hikes and other fitness activities; meditation, yoga, or tai chi sessions.
Lodging	Approximately 40 simply furnished single, double, and triple cottage rooms—all with private bath, no phone or TV.
Rates	$114–226 per day. $697–1,423 per week. Plus 15% service charge and 8% sales tax.
Meals	3 daily meals. Choice of vegetarian or nonvegetarian entrées. Greens and vegetables from spa's own gardens.
Services	A large variety of spa body treatments and salon services. Also body therapies (shiatsu, reflexology, aromatherapy, and therapeutic massage), fitness or nutrition consultations, yoga therapy and hypnotherapy, astrology and tarot readings.

Omega Institute for Holistic Studies   Rhinebeck, NY

Situated in the Hudson River Valley two hours north of Manhattan, the Omega Institute is a large summer learning community that combines education and vacation. The institute's faculty includes many well-known teachers and authors from the international human potential movement. Its eighty-acre property is graced with flower and vegetable gardens, tree-lined paths, and a lakeside beach for swimming and boating. There are also volleyball, tennis, and basketball courts.

All Omega guests are required to enroll in a weekend or 5-day workshop. The workshops are varied and are grouped under six general subject categories: personal health and development; gender, relationships, and family; nature and society; spiritual understanding; sports; and the arts. The many subject subcategories include holistic health, relationships, dance/movement, caring for the Earth and our communities, and spiritual retreat. Typical workshop topics are "Immune Power," "Conscious Loving," "Dancing Our Stories," "Healing Environments," and "Meditation for Beginners."

The institute's most popular offering (held several times each season) is the 5-day "Wellness Week" covering diet, nutrition, fitness, exercise, lifestyle, attitude, and time perception. The week includes low-impact aerobics, muscle strengthening, stretching, and creative movement. Following mornings of core program workshops, participants can opt in the afternoons for more of the same or for sessions of massage, movement, or fitness activities.

An average day at Omega can begin at 6:30 or 7 A.M. with a yoga, tai chi, or meditation session followed by breakfast. Workshops meet from 9 to noon and from 2 to 4:30 P.M. There are optional movement, yoga, and meditation classes at 12:15, 5:15, and 5:30. Following dinner, the day ends with a sample workshop, concert, community gatherings, dance, or film.

Address	260 Lake Drive, Rhinebeck, NY 12572
Phone	(914) 266-4444 or (800) 944-1001 (reservations). Fax (914) 266-4828.
Season	June through October.
Programs	4–12 workshops and retreats each week and weekend for a total of more than 250 per season on all aspects of holistic health.
Lodgings	Accommodations for over 350 guests in tent sites, dorms, and double occupancy cabin rooms with private or shared bath. Also a few cabins specifically for single parents and their children. BYO towels and linens for dorms. Some cabins and other facilities equipped for the disabled.

Rates   Program tuition: weekend $155–270, 5 days $250–375, "Wellness Week" $290. 10% discounts for students, senior citizens, and early registrants. Lodging: 2 days $81–175, 5 days $162–350.

Meals   3 daily, mostly vegetarian meals with produce from the garden.

Services   Massage, bodywork, nutrition counseling, wellness evaluations, flotation tanks, and other therapies at Omega's Wellness Center. Summer child-care program for preregistered children under 15.

Phoenicia Pathwork Center   Phoenicia, NY

This 300-acre Catskill Mountain Forest retreat is two and a half hours northwest of New York City. The primary purpose of the center is to facilitate "Pathwork," a spiritual path based on 258 lectures channeled through the late Eva Pierrakos. Pathwork includes individual sessions, group lectures and discussions, prayer, and meditative exercises.

Pathwork introduction weekends are held five times each year. The center hosts other Pathwork weekends and one-week intensives, and a one-month "Pathwork Experience" (personal retreat with two Pathwork sessions each week) on a regular basis from September through May. There is also a "Pathwork Studies" program consisting of one weekend each month from September through June. All programs are facilitated by trained Pathwork teachers.

The center's grounds include trails, a sweat lodge, spa facilities, tennis courts, and a swimming pool. When not in use for Pathwork programs, the facility is available for personal retreats and for rental by outside groups.

Address   P.O. Box 66, Phoenicia, NY 12462
Phone   (914) 688-2211. Fax (914) 688-2007.
Season   Year-round.
Programs   Pathwork: 2- and 3-day workshops, 1-week individual intensives. Also opportunities for work exchange plus short- and long-term residency.

Lodging	Capacity for up to 170 overnight guests in 16 motel-type rooms and 42 shared bedrooms (2–4 people per room). Private rooms and cottages available for couples and retreat leaders.
Rates	Pathwork programs (including room and board): weekend $210–415, 1-week intensive $2,100, 1-month "Pathwork Experience" $1,275.
Meals	3 daily buffet meals with vegetarian options.

Pumpkin Hollow Farm   Craryville, NY

Ever since its founding in 1937, Pumpkin Hollow Farm has been a peaceful haven honoring the theosophical lifestyle of study, service, and meditation. Close to the Massachusetts border two and a half hours north of New York City, "the Hollow" covers 130 acres of fields and forest. On the grounds are a stream and waterfall, a central farmhouse, a meditation center, and rustic cabins all connected by a network of nature trails.

During warm months, the Hollow offers as many as three workshops each weekend on subjects like meditation, tai chi, "Levels of Consciousness," "Healing Dream and Ritual," "Celebration of Family," and therapeutic touch, a mode of healing conceived at Pumpkin Hollow by Dora Kunz and Dolores Krieger. Facilitators come from throughout the Northeast and beyond.

There are also spring and fall work weekends, summer residency programs, and work scholarships. Personal retreatants are welcome for midweek stays or longer—weekend space permitting.

The rhythm of life at the Hollow includes sunrise ceremonies, morning yoga and group meditations, swimming, games, singing and storytelling, sunset walks, evening talks and campfires.

Address	1184 Route 11, Craryville, NY 12521
Phone	(518) 325-3583 or (518) 325-7105. Please call before visiting.
Season	Late March through early December.
Programs	2- and 3-day weekend workshops on spiritual philosophy, growth, and healing.

Lodging	Cabins and houses with dorms, shared rooms, and a few single rooms. Also campsites.
Rates	Program tuition: 2 days $20–35, 3 days $45–55. Room and board: weekend $55–85, extra days and weekdays $25–40, kids under 12 at half price.
Meals	3 daily vegetarian meals.

Shalom Mountain   Livingston Manor, NY

This fifty-four-acre retreat center in the Catskill Mountain foothills is lo-cated two and a half hours northwest of New York City. Offered nearly every month, the center's three-day "Shalom" retreat is designed to cre-ate a loving community where personal work can be initiated. Special programs focus on such themes as "Sexuality and Spirituality," "Inte-grating Life Choices," and "Path of the Mystic." Other programs are lim-ited to men, women, couples, families, or therapists.

Most retreats are led by center hosts Joy Davey and Lawrence (Lau-rie) Stibbards. Joy is a psychologist. Laurie is a marriage and family counselor with a background in pastoral counseling. Also on staff is Carol Jud, a teacher and therapist trained in Core Energetics and Bioen-ergetics. Guest retreat leaders include people trained in past-life regres-sion, vision quest, yoga, voice/song, and clowning. In conjunction with Timshel (see profile later in this chapter), Shalom Mountain also leads occasional winter trips to Mexico and Nicaragua.

Address	664 Cattail Road, Livingston Manor, NY 12758
Phone	(914) 482-5421. No visits without prior arrangement.
Season	Year-round.
Programs	3- to 8-day retreats designed to release blocked feeling and foster body/spirit integration. Also work weekends and personal retreats.
Lodging	12 bedrooms sleeping up to 18 people.
Rates	Weekend women's festivals and men's gatherings: $95–125 (BYO tent and sleeping bag). 3-day "Shalom Retreat": men's retreats and women's retreats $460. 3- to 8-day special pro-grams: $325–775. 3- to 8-day couples' retreats: $810–1,390 per couple. Personal retreat $55 per day.

Meals   3 daily meals. Vegetarians accommodated with advance notice.

Sivananda Ashram Yoga Ranch   Woodbourne, NY

A peaceful country retreat in the Catskill Mountains a hundred miles northwest of Manhattan. The main building is a turn-of-the-century farmhouse heated in the winter by a brick Bavarian-type stove. Two larger, unheated buildings contain summer guest rooms and a large yoga hall. In warm weather, yoga classes are held outdoors on a large wooden platform with the scenic Catskill Mountains as a backdrop.

A day at the ranch begins at 6 A.M. with meditation, chanting, and a talk. The first hatha yoga session is at 8. After brunch at 10, guests are invited to donate one hour of service to the ashram community. From noon till the second yoga class at 4 P.M., guests can rest, take a swim in the pond, walk or cross-country ski through the surrounding eighty acres of fields and forest, or thaw out in a Russian-style wood-burning sauna. Dinner is followed by meditation, chanting, and a talk, with lights out at 11.

Virtually every weekend a theme is explored in afternoon classes and workshops, often led by visiting teachers and healers. Typical themes are "Yoga and Chiropractic," "Healing Plants," and "The Art of Relaxation." Some weekends include sweat lodge ceremonies. Special ranch programs include five-day "Family Yoga" and "Mini Yoga" vacations, a summer "Sadhana Week" of intense group yoga practice, and an occasional nine-day "Detoxifying Fast."

Address   P.O. Box 195, Budd Road, Woodbourne, NY 12788
Phone   (914) 434-9242. Fax (914) 434-1032.
Season   Year-round.
Programs   Regular daily schedule, with mandatory attendance at satsangs and yoga classes. Special weekend, 5-day, and weeklong programs. Also residency program and monthlong training course for yoga teachers.
Lodging   40 double and 3- to 6-person rooms, some with private bath. Campsites in back field (BYO tent).

Rates	Adults $25–40 per day, $175–220 per week. Special programs: 4 nights $150, 7 nights $275, 9 nights $400. Children up to age 5 free, ages 5–12 half-price.
Meals	2 daily, buffet-style vegetarian meals with vegetables and greens from the ranch's organic garden and greenhouse (in season).
Services	"Kid's Yoga Days" on second Sunday of each month.

Springwater Center   Springwater, NY

This nonsectarian meditation retreat center is located on 230 acres of open fields and woods forty-five miles south of Rochester in New York's Finger Lakes region. Set on a quiet hillside, the house contains a meditation room, glass-walled solarium, and a hot tub. Several miles of trails are easily accessible for walking, hiking, and cross-country skiing.

Always open for private meditation retreats, the center also conducts guided group retreats that are usually about seven days long. Center director Toni Packer is present at most weeklong retreats to give talks and meet privately and/or in small groups with participants. Prior to founding Springwater Center in 1981 with a group of friends, Toni was director of Rochester Zen Center. She has since dropped all Zen forms.

Author of the book *The Work of the Moment*, Toni encourages meditative inquiry into the nature of self. There is no talking among retreat participants. Meals and work, exercise and rest, teacher talks and meetings are all interspersed with short sittings (chairs allowed) throughout the day. Except for work periods, all activities are optional.

Address	7179 Mill Street, Springwater, NY 14560
Phone	(716) 669-2141. No visits without prior arrangement.
Season	Year-round.
Programs	4-, 7-, and 10-day meditation retreats. Also personal retreats.
Lodging	16 bedrooms, each with 2 mattresses. BYO bedding and towel.
Rates	4 days $180. 7 days $300. 10 days $430. Personal retreat $14 per night or $84 per week plus $7.50 per day for meals.

Meals 3 daily vegetarian meals. Meal preparation and house-cleaning done by retreatants during daily 1-hour work period.

Tai Chi Farm   Warwick, NY

Tai Chi Farm occupies more than one hundred acres just north of the New Jersey/New York border in southeastern New York. The property contains forest trails, a stream, a small waterfall, and a pond. A Chinese-style mountain gate, garden, pavilion, gazebo, and outdoor tai chi practice area serve as gathering sites. A renovated barn containing a shrine to Zhang San-Feng (tai chi's creator and "patron saint") is used as a large indoor practice area.

Following "Early Bird" weekends in late May, the three-month summer season gets under way with the annual "Zhang San-Feng Festival" on the first weekend in June. At the festival, workshops are offered by at least a dozen well-known teachers of tai chi and related disciplines. Most of the twenty-five or so workshops offered over the balance of the summer are best suited for intermediate and advanced students, but all are also open to beginners.

Tai Chi Farm was founded in 1984 by Master Jou, Tsung Hwa to serve as a place for those interested in tai chi to study and practice together. Master Jou, Tsung Hwa leads five workshops. A few workshop leaders come from as far away as California, but most are from the northeastern United States.

Address Tai Chi Foundation, P.O. Box 828, Warwick, NY 10990
Phone (914) 986-3908. Best to write.
Season Workshops late May through early October. Open for personal retreats on weekends throughout the year.
Programs Weekend, 3-day, and 5-day workshops—mostly on tai chi but also on related subjects such as Taoist meditation and acupressure.
Lodging 8 primitive wooden cabins with no heat, electricity, or running water. Hot showers on the grounds. Campsites. BYO bedding. Also nearby motels, hotels, B&B inns.
Rates Workshop tuition: weekend $85–100, 3 days $120–140, 5 days $180–200. Cabin $10 per night. Campsite $5 per night.

Meals   BYO food, camp stoves, and coolers. Barbecue pit. Small
deli/grocery store within walking distance.

Services   During "Zhang San-Feng Festival" weekend, all who wish
to display their goods along "Tai Chi Avenue" may do so for
a small fee.

Tai Chi on the Lake   Andes, NY

This three-week summer camp hosted by New York City's School of Tai
Chi Chuan is located two and a half hours northwest of New York City.
The site is a 160-acre former children's camp set on a hillside hugging
the south side of a lake and facing the majestic Catskill Mountains to
the southeast.

The camp is primarily for beginners, who are taught the basics of tai
chi form. Beginner sessions include courses in "Breathing and Chi" and
the "Eight Ways." (The latter is easier to learn than tai chi form, requires
less time and space for practice, and is ideal for people recovering from
injury or illness.) Classes meet in the morning and for an hour after
lunch. Afternoons are free for practice and recreation. Evenings feature
a teacher-led practice period followed by tai chi–related demonstrations
and films.

The camp also offers "Time in the Art" days, weekends, and 5-day
weeks to encourage students to practice the art of tai chi at their own
rate. Mornings include classes by senior teachers plus meditation and
practice periods. An additional master class meets after lunch, and the
evening program (shared with the beginners) rounds out the day.

Address   School of Tai Chi Chuan, 46 West 13th Street, New York, NY
10011

Phone   (212) 929-1981. Fax (212) 727-1852.

Season   3 weeks in August.

Programs   Weekend and 5-day tai chi learning and practice sessions
for beginner and experienced students. Also mid-July to
early August work-study programs.

Lodging   Simple rustic cabins (most with more than 1 bedroom) with
shared or private bath. Also platform campsites with use of
bathrooms.

Rates   Camp tuition, room, and board: beginner's weekend $150, 5 days $350; "Time in the Art" day $75, weekend $150, 5 days $350; work-study day $50, weekend $100, 5 days $250. Children's program (ages 3–14): 5-day tuition $180, board $15 per day, room free with parents.

Meals   3 daily meals with extensive salad bar and vegetarian options.

Services   Children's program allows parents to participate fully in all camp programs while having meals and some free time with their children.

Wainwright House   Rye, NY

A handsome stone mansion overlooking Long Island Sound, Wainwright House is a short drive or train ride north of New York City. Each year Wainwright offers more than one hundred evening, half day, daylong, and weekend workshops on subjects pertaining to the arts, health and healing, and psychological and spiritual development. About twenty of these offerings are two- and three-day workshops. In most workshops, meals and lodging are optional rather than part of the program. Program teachers and facilitators include many leaders in the human potential field.

The center was founded by the Laymen's Movement "for the purpose of bringing ethical and spiritual values into public life." Today, Wainwright offers a two-year "Guild for Spiritual Guidance" program. Guild participants attend one weekend retreat each year plus nine twenty-four-hour (overnight) sessions. Wainwright also has an annual "Receptive Listening" program, which meets one day each week for eight weeks and concludes with a weekend retreat.

Address   260 Stuyvesant Avenue, Rye, NY 10580
Phone   (914) 967-6080. Fax (914) 967-6114.
Season   Year-round.
Programs   Evening, half day, full day, and weekend workshops—mostly on topics relating to personal and spiritual growth.
Lodging   Dorm and double rooms. Meals and lodging available to program participants by advance reservation.

Rates   Weekend workshops (excluding room and board) $85–190.
Room $35–45 per night. Meals: breakfast $7.50, lunch $9.50,
dinner $15.

Meals   3 daily buffet-style meals.

Wise Woman Center   Woodstock, NY

Wise Woman Center is a densely wooded, Catskill Mountains goat farm
and learning center. It is also the home of Susan Weed—an initiated
high priestess of Dianic Wicca, editor of Ash Tree Publishing, and best-
selling author of books on the ancient "green witch" paths to healing.
The center's fifty acres include herb gardens, meeting and moon lodge
tepees, and a sundeck by a large swimming pond. Swimmers can find
privacy in a river near a waterfall.

The way of the wise woman seeks to nourish the wholeness of the
unique individual through the use of compassionate intuition, personal
and community ritual, and common local plants (weeds). "Problems"
are viewed as solutions pointing the way to the original question,
thereby allowing new answers to emerge. Each season the center offers
workshops, intensives, apprenticeships, and correspondence courses.
Guest teachers include Z. Budapest and Vicki Noble. Workshop groups
are usually small and intimate. Some are open to men as well as women.

Address   Susan S. Weed, P.O. Box 64, Woodstock, NY 12498.

Phone   (914) 246-8081 (also accepts fax). Call before visiting.

Season   Spring through fall.

Programs   Daylong herbal medicine and spirit healing workshops for
men and women, 2- and 3-day weekend intensives usually
for women only, and apprenticeships of more than 6 weeks
for women only. Also work-exchange programs and correspondence courses.

Lodging   Dorm and campsites (BYO tent and sleeping bag). Room in
house for the physically challenged. (Signing can also be
arranged.)

Rates   Daylong workshop $40–55. Weekend workshops or inten-
sive $195–450. Apprenticeship $450 per week for 6 weeks
and $350 per week thereafter.

Meals   3 daily "country vegetarian" meals.

Zen Mountain Monastery   Mount Tremper, NY

Zen Mountain Monastery (ZMM) is a building of blue stone and white oak set on 230 acres of Catskill Mountain Forest Preserve. ZMM is also a monastic training center, weekend retreat center, and home for twenty to thirty male and female monks and lay residents. The monastery's founder and abbot, John Daido Loori, is an American Zen master, naturalist, artist, and workshop leader.

Frequent weekend retreats and occasional five- and six-day retreats are conducted by visiting teachers and artists on themes of artistic expression; on practical/artistic skills like Zen gardening, mindful photography, and aikido; on wilderness and meditative awareness; and on Taoist practices such as chi gung and tai chi.

The weekend retreats begin with Friday supper and an evening orientation talk. Retreatants then conform to the Zen schedule: up at 5 A.M. on Saturday for meditation followed by a service, a silent work assignment after breakfast, workshops from 10 A.M. to noon and from 1:30 to 5 P.M., evening meditation and then worship. A 6:45 Sunday breakfast is followed by work practice, morning service, and a formal talk. Retreatants depart after lunch.

There are also "Introduction to Zen Training" weekends, weekend and six-day meditation intensives, one-month retreats, and extended residential programs. The introductory weekend, included in the one-month retreat, is a prerequisite for the meditation intensives. One-month retreatants receive one or two days off each week and may participate in theme workshops.

Address	P.O. Box 197PC, South Plank Road, Mount Tremper, NY 12457
Phone	(914) 688-2228. No visits without prior arrangement.
Season	Year-round.
Programs	Weekend retreats leaning to practical and artistic spirituality. Also Zen training weekends, weekend and weeklong meditation intensives, 1-month retreats, 1- to 12-month residency programs.
Lodging	A 100-bed dormitory, with linens and blanket provided. Private or semiprivate rooms reserved for residents of 1 month or more.
Rates	2- and 3-day weekend retreats $195–245. 5- and 6-day retreats $265–325. 6-day meditation intensive $250 or $50 per

day. Residency program and one-month retreat, each $575–675 per month or $175 per week.

Meals   3 daily, primarily vegetarian meals with a vegetarian alternative when meat or fish is served. Vegetables and greens from garden.

UNITED STATES: *Mideast Region*

Kordes Enrichment Center   Ferdinand, IN

Set in the rolling rural countryside of southern Indiana, Kordes Enrichment Center is a retreat facility and corporate ministry of the Sisters of St. Benedict. The spacious grounds include a lake, outdoor swimming pool and tennis courts, and miles of trails. Rooted in the Benedictine traditions of care and hospitality, Kordes provides rental facilities and public workshops for people of all faiths.

Residential workshops include seven-day guided and directed retreats that employ body prayer, music, art, and guided meditations. The more frequent, two-day workshops cover topics such as centering prayer, Enneagram spirituality, healing the inner child, personal empowerment, and relationships. Facilitators include visiting therapists and teachers plus members of the Kordes staff, who also provide guidance for individual, directed retreats.

Address   841 East 14th Street, Ferdinand, IN 47532
Phone   (812) 367-2777. Fax (812) 367-2313. Please call in advance.
Season   Year-round.
Programs   2- and 7-day workshops and retreats promoting growth in wholeness, holiness, and service as people of God.
Lodging   Up to 60 beds in rooms that each have 2 beds and a shared bath.
Rates   2-day program $70–120. 7-day program $300–350. Private directed retreat $45 per day.
Meals   3 daily meals with no red meat.

Oakwood Farm   Selma, IN

Once a 326-acre working farm, Oakwood is now a natural sanctuary staffed by members of a resident community that is more than thirty

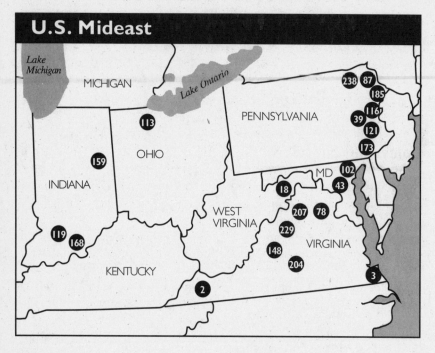

U.S. Mideast

Lake Michigan

MICHIGAN

Lake Ontario

PENNSYLVANIA

238 87 185 116 39 121 173

113

OHIO

159

INDIANA

MD 102

18 43

WEST VIRGINIA

207 78

229

VIRGINIA

148

204

119 168

KENTUCKY

2

3

years old and affiliated with the Emissaries. Bordered on one side by the White River, the property harbors orchards, organic gardens, and a teeming wildlife population. The site is located fifteen minutes from Muncie in east-central Indiana.

Programs sponsored by the community itself include weeklong "Flower of Life" workshops; weekend "Quickening" workshops; and the annual four-day "Midwest Drum and Dance Festival," a harvest celebration that draws talent from around the country. Oakwood-sponsored programs include bonfires, hayrides, sweat lodges, picnics, and wildflower and wildlife sanctuary excursions. Oakwood also hosts private and public programs organized by outside groups.

Address	3801 SCR 575 East, Selma, IN 47383
Phone	(317) 282-7027. Fax (317) 282-0484. Please call before visiting.
Season	Year-round.
Programs	Weekend to weeklong seminars and workshops on Earth stewardship, community building, personal and spiritual growth.
Lodging	50 guest beds in private and shared rooms. Separate family spaces with equipped kitchen. Also campsites.
Rates	Weekend workshop $80-150. Most weeklong programs $400–650. Personal retreat $30–65 per day including meals.
Meals	3 daily meals with vegetarian options. Homegrown organic food available in season.
Services	Massage, reiki, and attunements.

Orbis Farm   Mauckport, IN

A retreat center and workshop facility on seventy-five acres of woodland forty miles southwest of Louisville, Kentucky. The farm has a large organic garden, and neighboring Mount Tom offers miles of walking trails.

The center hosts weekend workshops throughout most of the year. A majority of the offerings focus on aspects of hatha yoga, spiritual healing, or holistic healing. From late January through mid-March (as well as scattered throughout the rest of the year), the farm also offers kundalini intensives. These weekends explore kundalini philosophy and meditation under the guidance of Orbis Farm's founder Helen Mc-Mahan.

Orbis Farm is directed by Helen McMahan and Betty Cole. Betty is a longtime meditator, gardener, herbalist, and cook who sometimes leads a one-day "Come Play in the Garden" workshop. Helen teaches yoga and meditation at both the farm and Orbis Personal Growth Center in Louisville, Kentucky. Farm workshops are also led by highly qualified guest teachers.

Address	8700 Ripperdan Valley Road, SW, Mauckport, IN 47142
Phone	(812) 732-4657. No visits without prior arrangement.
Season	Late January to mid-November.
Programs	Weekend yoga, spiritual healing, and holistic healing workshops.
Lodging	Dormitory accommodations for up to 20 people.
Rates	Programs: 1 day $55, 2 nights $175 and $205, 3 nights $250.
Meals	3 vegetarian meals, with fish and chicken options. Vegetables from own gardens. Lunch included only in 1-day programs.

Dayspring Retreat Center   Germantown, MD

On the edge of Washington, D.C.'s northern suburbs, Dayspring Retreat Center's Inn and Lodge of the Carpenter rest amid 200 acres of woods, fields, and still waters. The center hosts more than forty two-day/two-night silent retreats each year. Most are weekend retreats exploring themes like "The Stranger in Us" and "Awakening to the Presence." The rest are primarily Sunday-through-Tuesday "Spiritual Life" retreats focusing on "The Beloved," "The Burning Heart," or "The Carefree Living."

Weekend retreats begin with supper on Friday evening. The leader then sets the theme and guides the retreatants into silence. Saturday is a time of rest, contemplation, wandering, study, or guided journal writing. There are two sessions of leader-guided prayer, meditation, or scripture reading. Retreatants leave the silence with a Sunday worship service followed by a noon meal and departure at 2 P.M. "Spiritual Life" retreats have the same schedule but on different days.

Dayspring retreat leaders come from many Christian denominations.

This reflects the ecumenical spirit of the retreat's parent Church of the Savior, a nondenominational, inner-city Christian church praised by author M. Scott Peck for its commitment to service and building community. Dayspring also welcomes personal retreatants (particularly during August) and rental of its facility by private groups.

Address	11301 Neelsville Church Road, Germantown, MD 20876
Phone	(301) 428-9348. No visits without prior arrangement.
Season	February through December.
Programs	Guided 2-day silent theme retreats. Guided 1-day weekday silent mini-retreats. Also a few totally silent leaderless retreats.
Lodging	Capacity for 18 overnight guests (16 retreatants and 2 leaders) in men's and women's dorms.
Rates	Weekend guided retreat $90. 2-day weekday "Spiritual Life" retreat $75. Weekday miniretreat, no charge but donations accepted. Personal retreat $25 per night (BYO food).
Meals	6 natural, fresh, nutritionally balanced meals at each retreat. A minimum of meat. The choice to fast is respected.

International Meditation Center   Westminster, MD

This center is set in the rural Maryland countryside one hour northwest of Baltimore and ninety minutes north of Washington, D.C. It hosts ten-day Vipassana meditation retreats that include eight to ten hours of meditation each day (a rigorous schedule but not, according to the center, beyond the capabilities of even a beginner with a sincere interest in meditation).

The first five days of each retreat focus on calming the mind, the last five days on developing awareness. During any meditation period, students may get up to stretch or walk around. All students, however, are expected to refrain from talking with other students and to adhere to the daily schedule: wake-up at 4 A.M., meditation and a teacher talk from 4:30 to 6:30, group and individual meditation periods during most of the morning and afternoon, a teacher talk at 6 P.M., group meditation from 7:30 to 8:30, and lights out at 9.

All meditation teachers have been trained by Sayamagyi Daw Mya Thwin and Sayagyi U Chit Tin, who have practiced and taught Vipassana meditation for over thirty years in the Burmese Theravada Buddhist tradition.

Address   438 Bankard Road, Westminster, MD 21158
Phone   (410) 346-7889. Fax (410) 346-7282. No visits without prior arrangement.
Season   Usually 4 or 5 retreats spaced throughout the year.
Programs 10-day silent Vipassana meditation retreats.
Lodging   Separate men's and women's dorms.
Rates   10-day retreat $225–300.
Meals   Ample food at daily vegetarian breakfast and lunch. Also a late-afternoon tea break.

Kerr House   Grand Rapids, OH

An antiques-filled Victorian mansion and holistic rejuvenation retreat that is a half-hour drive from Toledo in northwestern Ohio. The standard five-day programs are directed by owner/hostess Laurie Hostetler, a yoga teacher and student of the well-known American yoga teacher Indra Devi.

During a Kerr House program, the morning features hatha yoga and low-impact aerobics followed by a session of body treatments. Lunch is served in the café. An afternoon might include counseling on reducing stress or building self-esteem, followed by a walk on the nearby towpath. There is another yoga session at 5 P.M. The evening's candlelight dinner is served in the formal dining room, often to the accompaniment of a harpist. Guests may then enjoy a whirlpool and sauna before retiring for the night.

While most Kerr House programs are for women, there are occasional weeks and weekends for couples or men only. The house is otherwise available for rental by private groups. With three staff members per guest, the house has the relaxed and elegant atmosphere of a private club.

Address   P.O. Box 363, 17777 Beaver Street, Grand Rapids, OH 43522
Phone   (419) 832-1733.
Season   Year-round.
Programs 5-day and weekend rejuvenation programs with gentle hatha yoga, body treatments, and lifestyle enhancement classes.
Lodging   An 8-guest capacity in 5 guest rooms, 3 suitable for couples.

Rates   5 days $2,150. Weekend $575–675.

Meals   3 daily meals, mostly vegetarian, sometimes with fish or chicken.

Services Programs include a generous selection of spa body treatments. Additional treatments may be purchased at additional cost.

Creative Energy Options   White Haven, PA

Creative Energy Options (CEO) hosts a variety of professional and personal growth training programs. Typical of the four-weekend programs open to the general public are "Creativity and Health" (with a different teacher each weekend) and "Cross-Cultural Practices and Health" (with Angeles Arrien). Other CEO offerings include two-weekend programs such as "Power Couples" and the one-weekend "Bridges to Remembering" with Emmanuel as channeled by Pat Rodegast.

"Power Couples" is facilitated by CEO directors Herb Kaufman and Sylvia Lafair, who also lead an annual nine-day New Mexico adventure into Native American culture (with storytelling, drumming, sweat lodge, and vision quest). All CEO weekend programs are held at the Country Place, a Poconos farmhouse retreat set on fifty acres of woodlands with a pond and hiking trails. The Country Place is about an hour and a half from both Philadelphia and New York City.

Address   909 Sumneytown Pike, Suite 105, Spring House, PA 19477

Phone   (215) 643-4420. Fax (215) 643-7031.

Season   Year-round.

Programs 1-, 2-, and 4-weekend personal growth and professional training retreats. (The 2-weekend program is spaced over 5 months, the 4-weekend program over 9 or 10 months.) Also an annual "Power of the Southwest" New Mexico vacation.

Lodging   Dorm accommodations for up to 50 guests in large, modernized 19th-century farmhouse.

Rates   Tuition: single weekend $300, 2-weekend program $1,500 per couple including room and board, 4-weekend program $1,650. Room and board $130 per weekend. 9-day New Mexico vacation $1,850.

Meals   3 daily gourmet vegetarian meals and snacks.

Himalayan Institute   Honesdale, PA

This institute rests on a plateau in the softly rolling hills of the Pocono Mountains. Its 422 acres include tennis and basketball courts plus a pond where guests can swim or, in winter, ice-skate. Year-round, the favorite outdoor recreation is a long walk or jog in the miles of surrounding woods and meadows, often opening onto majestic vistas.

Each month the Himalayan Institute offers a variety of multiple-day retreats and seminars, all taught by institute faculty. Residential programs allow guests to attend classes and seminars while living and working (four or five hours each day) in this spiritual community. Personal meditation retreats (a two-night minimum) are open to anyone who has attended an introductory meditation course in the institute tradition.

A day at the institute begins with silently guided yoga at 6:45 A.M. or breakfast at 8. There are workshops and/or lectures in the late morning, midafternoon, and again in the evening. Silence is observed from 5 to 6 P.M. and again from 10 P.M. to 8 A.M. the next morning. Every day there is ample unstructured time for rest, reading, fellowship, and outdoors recreation.

The institute was founded by Indian yogi Swami Rama to create a bridge between Western science and the ancient teachings of the East. Its staff includes Western doctors and psychologists. Originally built as a Catholic seminary, the institute's three-story main building houses offices, classrooms, an auditorium, medical facilities, and guest and resident bedrooms.

Address   RR 1, Box 400, Honesdale, PA 18431
Phone   (717) 253-5551 or (800) 822-4547. Fax (717) 253-9078.
Season   Year-round.
Programs Mostly weekend, 3-, and 5-day seminars and retreats on yoga, meditation and holistic health, self-development, and spiritual unfoldment. Also residential programs and personal meditation retreats.
Lodging   Main building has 100 beds in simple 1- and 2-bed rooms, each with a sink. Communal toilets and showers. Families with children accommodated in nearby family house.
Rates   Seminars and meditation retreats: 2 nights $90–130, 3 nights $135–195, 4 nights $180–260, 5 nights $225–325, 6 nights $270–390, 7 nights $315–455. Residential programs:

10 days $350, one month $736 ($300 per month after the first month), one-year internship $1,750. Personal meditation retreats are at high end of seminar/meditation retreat rates, meals not included.

Meals   3 vegetarian meals per day, nutritionally balanced and with vegetables from the organic garden. A few tables reserved for silent meals.

Services   Stress assessment profiles and biofeedback sessions. Also holistic health outpatient services.

Kirkridge Retreat and Study Center   Bangor, PA

More than fifty years old, this nondenominational retreat center is committed to fostering personal growth and social change. It lies eighty-five miles north of Philadelphia on 270 acres containing seven buildings connected by trails and roads. The center's lodge building is at the top of a ridge, near the Appalachian Trail. In a valley, gentle pastureland surrounds the center's 180-year-old farmhouse.

Kirkridge is especially known for workshops that give voice to society's "outsider" groups (such as gay men and lesbians). Founded by a Presbyterian minister, the center also offers programs addressing various issues (e.g., sexuality, disability, simple living, and contemplative prayer) from a biblical perspective. Additional workshops are on subjects like healing through dance or song, storytelling, deep ecology, and social justice.

Most Kirkridge workshops include sharing in small groups, silence and reflection, hiking, hearthside conversations, and morning and evening prayers. Personal retreats and rentals by private groups are also welcomed.

Address   2495 Fox Gap Road, Bangor, PA 18013
Phone   (610) 588-1793
Season   Year-round.
Programs   Weekend, 4-, and 5-day workshops on personal and social transformation.
Lodging   For group retreats, 4 facilities accommodating 100+ guests. For personal retreats, five 1- and 2-bed accommodations, each with kitchen and bath. BYO linens.

Rates   Workshops: weekend $195–275, 4 and 5 days $295–445.
              Daily rate for personal retreat (meals not included): singles
              $50, couples $70.
Meals   3 nutritious daily meals. No red meat.
Services   Pastoral counseling. Also Book Nest bookstore.

Kripalu Community at Sumneytown   Sumneytown, PA

Located on sixty-eight acres of wooded hills one hour northwest of
Philadelphia, Kripalu Community at Sumneytown hosts weekend workshops and retreats on Kripalu hatha yoga, meditation, selfless service,
and conscious relationship as vehicles for personal growth. There are
also yoga teachers' retreats and trainings. Most programs are facilitated
by people who have lived or trained at Kripalu at Sumneytown or the
Kripalu Center in Massachusetts.

Kripalu Community's residents (some twenty adults and several children) enjoy a yogic lifestyle while pursuing schooling and careers in
the surrounding area. Community holiday celebrations and Saturday
evening satsangs—chanting, meditation, lectures, and sharing—are
open and free to the public. Overnight visitors on personal retreat may
participate in community projects and early morning yoga sessions.

Address   P.O. Box 250, 2109 Walters Road, Sumneytown, PA 18084
Phone   (215) 234-4568. No visits without prior arrangement.
Season   Year-round.
Programs   2- to 4-day workshops on yoga, meditation, and yogic
              lifestyle.
Lodging   Capacity for roughly 40 people in dorms, double and single
              rooms with shared or private bath. BYO linens, blankets,
              and towels.
Rates   Workshop tuition (including meals and dorm-style hous-
              ing): full weekend $180–195, 4 days $250–530. Single-day
              workshop (with lunch) $70. Personal retreat (meals not in-
              cluded) $20–50 per night.
Meals   3 vegetarian meals with mostly organically grown ingredi-
              ents, dairy and nondairy options. Personal retreatants may
              use kitchen.
Services   Private yoga classes and massage.

Pendle Hill   Wallingford, PA

Pendle Hill has occupied a wooded twenty-three-acre campus in the
Philadelphia suburbs for more than sixty years. Here education is envisioned as a means of transforming people and society. Each quarter and
particularly during the summer, Pendle Hill hosts workshops on subjects such as comtemplative dance, emotional healing, the concerns of
men and families in transition, "Friendly Clowning," and Quaker values.
In addition, personal retreat "sojourns" (of up to three weeks) allow full
participation in community life and also in some classes.

Pendle Hill's "Resident Study" program is conducted over ten- and
eleven-week fall, winter, and spring terms. Each term offers five or six
noncredit classes on Quaker and biblical studies, spiritual practice and
social concerns, plus crafts like pottery and weaving. Term students are
encouraged to take two or three classes, each of which meets as a group
once each week. Term projects may take the form of written work, music or dance presentations, or craft displays.

Pendle Hill students are of many ages, creeds, nationalities, and professions. During the nine-month school year, students and faculty live
and work together as a community. Everyone has a daily kitchen job, a
weekly housekeeping job, and a half-day stint on a campus work pro-
ject. Each morning there is an optional Quaker worship service—a period of communal silence while waiting for the "inner light" of God.

Address	338 Plush Mill Road, Wallingford, PA 19086
Phone	(610) 566-4507 or (800) 742-3150.
Season	Year-round, with a summer break for those in the "Resident Study" program.
Programs	Weekend and 4-day workshops. Term "Resident Study" courses.
Lodges	Private, simply furnished study-bedrooms; linens and bedding provided. Also 2 small hermitages for personal retreats.
Rates	Weekend and 4-day workshops $145–235. Daily rate for sojourns: singles $49–54, couples $79–84. "Resident Study": 1 term $3,780, full year $11,030.
Meals	3 communal meals each day, all with vegetarian options.
Services	Free 1-hour consultation on learning objectives is required each week for resident students and optional for sojourners.

Rainbow Experience   Bushkill, PA

An annual event for many years, the Rainbow Experience is a week of nonsectarian spiritual rejuvenation and celebration—held in recent years at Tamiment resort in Pennsylvania's Pocono Mountains. Set on a ninety-acre lake, the resort offers swimming, paddleboats and canoes, nature walks and fitness trails, horseback riding, tennis, and golf. Some twenty-five teachers, healers, and entertainers come from all over the United States to contribute to the experience.

Sandwiched between Sunday opening and Saturday closing, the Rainbow Experience is a full five days of morning lectures and workshops, afternoon seminars, evening speaker programs, and late evening entertainment. Other program activities include network lunches, bonding through music and drumming, breathwork, movement, labyrinth, sweat lodge, medicine wheel, group visioning, and Rainbow Arts Emporium.

Address   Life Spectrums, P.O. Box 373, Harrisburg, PA 17108
Phone   (800) 360-5683
Season   Generally in mid-July.
Programs   Workshops, seminars, and talks on centering, creativity, natural healing, self-empowerment, and the spiritual journey.
Lodging   Double and triple occupancy rooms, all with A/C and bath.
Rates   Tuition: ages 9 and older $270, ages 6–8 $200, under 6 free. Meals and room: ages 18 and older $325, children and teens (sharing room with 2 adults) $30–200, depending on age.
Meals   3 daily meals.
Services   Bodywork and massage. Free sessions with spiritual counselors and healing arts practitioners. Youth and children's programs.

Timshel   Lawton, PA

Timshel is a retreat center set in a forested valley with ponds, a stream, and scenic vistas of the Endless Mountains in northeastern Pennsylvania. All retreats here are centered in loving community, spiritual disciplines, and communion with nature. Each day includes community meetings and discussions, practice of yoga and meditation, invention and practice of worship, plus free time.

Retreats are led by Jerry and Georgeanne Judd along with Liza Braude. Jerry is a former pastor, the founder of Shalom Mountain Center (profiled earlier in this chapter), and a published author with a Ph.D. from Yale in the psychology of religion. Georgeanne is an artist who teaches art as a creative expression of the spiritual journey. Liza is a process-oriented teacher and leader of yoga and song.

Address   RD 5, Box 81, Montrose, PA 18801
Phone   (717) 934-2275. No visits without prior arrangement.
Season   June through mid-October.
Programs   5- and 8-day retreats to explore and experience the divine presence.
Lodging   Private and shared room accommodations for at least 15 guests in the large main house and a cottage.
Rates   5 days $480. 8 days $750. Work scholarships available.
Meals   3 daily meals. Vegetarians accommodated on advance notice.

A.R.E. Camp   Rural Retreat, VA

Each summer A.R.E. (Association for Research & Enlightenment) conducts camps for children, adults, and families at a secluded fifty-acre site adjoining a national forest in southwest Virginia. The rustic environment includes cabins, a recreation hall, an arts and crafts building, a meditation grove, a pond, an organic garden, a volleyball court, and a soccer field.

There are three one-week "Family Camps" for families and single adults. Each camp has a different theme (e.g., holistic health, spiritual centering, and family concerns within a spiritual context). Each camp combines traditional camp activities for all ages (nature exploration, arts and crafts, swimming, hiking, drama, and music) with nontraditional camp activities (mostly for adults) such as daily dream exploration, meditation/quiet time, and study and discussion of the Edgar Cayce material.

The A.R.E. Camp season concludes with a two-week session on "Creative Transformation" staffed by faculty from the A.R.E.-affiliated Atlantic University. Offered concurrently with the final week of the university session is an adult meditation retreat that combines mantras, chanting, and meditation instruction with yoga and energy-balancing techniques.

Address   A.R.E., P.O. Box 595, Virginia Beach, VA 23451
Phone   (804) 428-3588
Season   Mid-June through August.
Programs   1-week "Family Camp" (also for single adults), 1-week meditation retreat, 2-week Atlantic University session.
Lodging   Capacity for 110 people in screened-in, 6- to 8-bunk cabins. During family weeks, some families sleep in cabins, but most sleep in their own tents or campers.
Rates   "Family Camp" adults $200, children ages 10–17 $170, children under 10 $100. Meditation retreat $200.
Meals   3 daily, mostly vegetarian meals with fresh herbs and vegetables from the organic garden.

A.R.E. Conferences   Virginia Beach, VA

At its headquarters a short walk from the Atlantic Ocean, the Association for Research & Enlightenment each year hosts at least twenty conferences on topics relating to personal growth and spiritual evolution. Most feature noted authorities in a particular field—such as Harvard's John Mack on UFOs or English archaeologist Robert Bauval on ancient Egypt. Other presenters include experts on the Edgar Cayce materials.

A typical day at the popular "Finding Your Life Mission" conference begins with breakfast and dream discussion groups at the nearby Ramada Inn. Workshops are held from 9:15 A.M. to noon. Before lunch, attendees may meditate with center staff members in the center's Meditation Garden. Lunch is an opportunity for discussions and fellowship in small groups, each serving as a minifamily for interested conference attendees. Between afternoon and evening presentations there is a break for free time and dinner.

Another facet of A.R.E.'s Virginia Beach operation is the Reilly School of Massage, which has begun offering residential "Temple Beautiful" programs similar to those at Arizona's A.R.E. Medical Clinic (see profile earlier in this chapter).

Address   P.O. Box 595, Virginia Beach, VA 23451
Phone   (800) 333-4499
Season   Year-round.
Programs 3- to 5-day conferences on spiritual and personal growth topics.
Lodging   Nearby motels, campgrounds, and room rentals.
Rates   Conference tuition $255–315.
Meals   Lunches may be purchased on site. Many restaurants in the area for breakfast and dinner.
Services Massage, steam baths, facials, hydro- and colon therapy at A.R.E.'s Reilly School of Massage.

Hartland Wellness Center   Rapidan, VA

Situated on 760 wooded acres in the quiet foothills of the Blue Ridge Mountains is Hartland, a combination wellness center and missionary college operated by a team of Seventh-Day Adventist professionals: nurses, hydro- and massage therapists, nutritionists, and health educators. The facility includes a fully equipped cooking lab, exercise room, indoor swimming pool, sauna, and sundeck. The grounds include a garden and walking trails.

Hartland's "Lifestyle to Health" programs cover massage and hydrotherapy, nutrition and cooking instruction, stress management and health education, individual counseling, and supervised exercise. They also include "God's answer to stress management," namely, daily morning and evening gatherings devoted to stretching, prayer, and scripture readings. There is also an optional Saturday morning worship service.

Many folks come to Hartland simply for a healthy vacation. Others come to address and ameliorate serious health concerns—such as weight problems, smoking, stress, heart disease, hypertension, and diabetes—in a drug-free natural health environment.

Address   P.O. Box 1, Rapidan, VA 22733
Phone   (703) 672-3100 or (800) 763-9355
Season   Year-round.
Programs 10- and 18-day lifestyle modification programs tailored to each guest's specific health risks and problems.

Lodging   5 single rooms and 10 rooms with 2 beds in each. All rooms have a private bath.

Rates   "Lifestyle to Health": 10 days $1,500, 18 days $2,500, 10% off for second family member. "Stop Smoking": 10 days $1,700, 18 days $2,700.

Meals   3 daily, nondairy vegetarian meals.

Services   Airport, train, and bus station pick-up/drop-off services.

Monroe Institute   Faber, VA

The Monroe Institute rests on 800 acres in the misty, rolling Blue Ridge foothills twenty-five miles south of Charlottesville. The property includes forest, walking trails, meditation spots along a creek and atop the ridges, and a lake where guests can swim. But the focus of the institute is the development of sound wave technology that alters brain waves to induce different states of consciousness. Through this technology, institute program participants experience these different states while remaining "awake"—somewhat akin to lucid dreaming. One program alumnus, a Zen Buddhist monk, attests that states of consciousness usually attainable only after years of meditation can be realized within one week at the institute.

The first and most popular of the institute's six-day programs is "Gateway Voyage," which guides participants through states of expanded awareness to explore in depth both human consciousness and other energy systems. "Guidelines II" facilitates communication with distinct intelligences (e.g., one's inner self–helper, nonphysical friends, or universal consciousness). "Lifeline" allows participants to become familiar with other levels of existence and to offer assistance to entities they meet in those states. "Guidelines II" and "Lifeline" also offer training in the use of dolphin energy for healing oneself and others.

All explorations take place in private chambers totally isolated from light and extraneous sound. Skilled facilitators guide participants through the five or six daily forty-five-minute tape exercises, experiential and discussion sessions, and individual meetings. Also in residence is institute founder Robert A. Monroe, a former broadcast industry executive (and engineer by training) whose life was altered in 1958 by the onset of involuntary out-of-body states.

Address   Route 1, Box 175, Faber, VA 22938
Phone   (804) 361-1252
Season   Year-round, with recess from mid-December to early January.
Programs 6-day programs designed to expand human consciousness by inducing states of nonphysical awareness through a carefully controlled brain wave–altering sound wave technology.
Lodging   Sleeping space for 24 guests in individual Controlled Holistic Environmental Chambers (CHECs), each with adjustable fresh air input, adjustable (in both color and intensity) lighting, plus soothing sounds emanating at night from the CHEC speaker system.
Rates   6-day program $1,495.
Meals   3 meals per day, vegetarian option available on advance notice.
Services   Courtesy pick-up/drop-off at Charlottesville, Virginia, airport and bus and train station.

Satchidananda Ashram   Buckingham, VA

Also known as Yogaville, Satchidananda Ashram is a rustic spiritual community of some 50 children and 250 adults living and working on 750 acres of wooded hills in rural Virginia. Hilltop clearings offer sweeping vistas of the Blue Ridge Mountains, the James River, and the riverside Light of Truth Universal Shrine (LOTUS)—a lotus-shaped temple honoring the world's major religions. Yogaville's founder and spiritual director is Swami Satchidananda, a prolific author and recipient of the Martin Buber Award for Outstanding Service to Humanity.

Yogaville residential workshops and retreats focus primarily on hatha yoga and meditation. There are one- to three-week yoga teacher training programs. Two special summer programs are a two-week children's camp and a monthlong classical Indian dance camp. The Lotus Retreat and Conference Center is available for rental by outside groups. Yogaville also welcomes overnight guests, most of whom come for special holiday celebrations or "Welcome Weekend" (every weekend) activities.

A day at Yogaville can begin at 5 A.M. with silent meditation, at 6:30

with yoga, or with breakfast from 8 to 9. All are welcome at the noon LO-
TUS meditation followed by the day's main meal. Guests are invited to
practice selfless service by working alongside community members during the day. "Welcome Weekend" activities include a nature walk, an
ashram tour, a talk on integral yoga, and guided meditation and hatha
yoga classes for beginners.

Address	Route 1, Box 1720, Buckingham, VA 23921
Phone	(804) 969-3121 or (800) 858-9642
Season	Year-round.
Programs	2- to 10-day hatha yoga and meditation workshops, retreats, and trainings led by resident teachers.
Lodging	Accommodations for 100+ people in private efficiency apartments, dorms, and campsites. Unmarried men and women in separate quarters.
Rates	Programs: weekend $150–500, week $320–1,070. Guest stay: weekday $25–60, weekend day $25–65, full week $135–370, low kids' rates.
Meals	3 daily vegetarian meals eaten in silence. Fruits and vegetables from Yogaville's 1-acre orchard and organic garden.
Services	A combination café/mini–health food store.

Sevenoaks Pathwork Center   Madison, VA

This 130-acre retreat center in the Shenandoah foothills is about one
hundred miles southwest of Washington, D.C. The property encompasses forest, meadows, and a cleared quadrangle surrounded by the
center's buildings. There are hiking trails, a volleyball court, and a pond
where guests can swim in the summer. The grounds also contain a
sweat lodge and Native American medicine wheel.

Sevenoaks focuses primarily on "Pathwork"—the study and practice
of concepts and exercises presented in 258 lectures channeled through
the late Eva Pierrakos. Center directors Donovan and Susan Thesenga,
both authors of Pathwork-related books, lead or co-lead most programs, including the ten-weekend "Transformation" program. Guest
teachers lead workshops on other psychospiritual subjects such as
shamanism, past-life therapy, and men's and women's empowerment.

Address   Route 1, Box 86, Madison, VA 22727
Phone   (703) 948-6544
Season   Year-round, with most workshops from spring through fall.
Programs 2- to 5-day workshops on Pathwork and other psychospiritual subjects. Plus a 10-weekend, 9-month "Transformation" program.
Lodging   Accommodations for 40+ people. Most rooms have 2 twin beds. Couples may receive a private room. Also campsites.
Rates   Workshops: weekend $235–275, 4 and 5 days $335–595.
Meals   3 daily buffet meals with vegetarian options.

Swannanoa   Waynesboro, VA

Located twenty miles west of Charlottesville, Swannanoa is a marble palace surrounded by terraced gardens overlooking the Shenandoah Valley. This is the site of the home-study University of Science and Philosophy, which also holds the paintings and sculptures of the university's founders, Walter and Lao Russell. A friend of Ralph Waldo Emerson, Walter was a highly versatile genius and mystic. Lao, his British-born wife, shared Walter's vision for humankind to "find happiness and peace through knowledge and practice of the Love Principle of Giving and Regiving which Nature alone practices and man defies."

Swannanoa programs include daylong, weekend, and weeklong seminars on applying the Russells' prescriptions for health and happiness. Most programs are led by Timothy Binder, a naturopathic physician and doctor of chiropractic, and Shirley Smith, an evolutionary tutor and transformational breathwork facilitator. From time to time, Swannanoa also hosts symposiums that include nationally known spiritual and holistic healers. All programs offer yoga, meditation, healing circles, and other activities.

Address   P.O. Box 520, Waynesboro, VA 22980
Phone   (703) 942-5161. Fax (703) 942-8705.
Season   Year-round.
Programs Daylong, weekend, and weeklong seminars based on the principles of natural science and philosophy.
Lodging   Available at nearby motels and inns.

Rates   Program tuition: 1 weekend $100–125, 1 week $500–575.
Meals   Lunches provided.

Bhavana Society   High View, WV

A monastic retreat and meditation center two hours west of Washington, D.C. In keeping with the ancient Buddhist "forest tradition," this rustic center is tucked away in a secluded and heavily wooded area. The grounds include a house, a combination dining room and meditation hall, plus several small huts used primarily for personal retreats. The center is staffed by American monks and Bhante Gunaratana, a senior Sri Lankan monk who is the author of the book *Mindfulness in Plain English*. The society hosts weekend and ten-day guided group retreats, but only the weekend retreats are suitable for beginners.

Weekend retreatants arrive by 7 P.M. on Friday for orientation. Saturday begins with a 5 A.M. wake-up bell and 5:30 group meditation. Breakfast is at 7, with meditation resuming at 8. A three-hour lunch and recess period begins at 11, followed by another hour of meditation, an hour of teacher interviews, and a hatha yoga session at 4:30 P.M. Following a tea break at 6, the day ends with a sitting and then a talk at 8. Meditation periods alternate between one-hour sittings (chairs permitted) and half-hour walking meditations. Retreatants may talk only with teachers. Retreatants depart on Sunday after lunch.

Address   Route 1, Box 218-3, High View, WV 26808
Phone   (304) 856-3241. Fax (304) 856-2111. Call before visiting.
Season   Year-round.
Programs Weekend and 10-day group meditation retreats, 5 of each per year.
Lodging   Accommodations for 25+ retreatants in double rooms and small huts, each sleeping 1–3 people. Every hut has a small heater. BYO bedding and (in winter) heater fuel.
Rates   In accordance with the Vipassana tradition, all retreats (including meals and lodging) are free of charge. But donations are accepted and necessary to support the center.
Meals   Vegetarian breakfast and lunch, as well as a tea break.

UNITED STATES: *Southeast Region*

Hawkwind Earth Renewal Cooperative   Valley Head, AL

This seventy-seven-acre campground and retreat center is set in the mountains of northeast Alabama. The property includes indoor and outdoor sheltered teaching areas, gardens, Native American ceremonial grounds, and a place for meditation. The facilities are available for rent.

Hawkwind is also a membership organization that sustains a food co-op, an artists' co-op, Will's Creek Trading Post, a barter co-op, and support groups (with several annual weekend retreats) for men, women, and parents. Other regular Hawkwind community programs include solstice gatherings, spirit healing dances, plus "Family Lodge" (sweat lodge) gatherings with a moon lodge for women in their sacred time, talking-circle support for parents, and a potluck dinner.

Hawkwind's directors are John Tarwater and Charla Hermann. John is a craftsman, drum maker, and ceremonial leader of Lakota/Scottish heritage. Charla directs Hawkwind's outreach/crisis services and support group programs. Non co-op members are welcome at most Hawkwind retreats, gatherings, and workshops, some of which are led by well-known teachers of Native American medicine ways, spiritual ecology, and personal healing.

Address	P.O. Box 11, Valley Head, AL 35989
Phone	(205) 635-6304. Reservations required for all visits.
Season	Year-round.
Programs	Weekend workshops and member community events, most involving Native American medicine ceremony.
Lodging	Campsites and tepees with nearby outhouses and solar shower. Also a 12-bed bunkhouse.
Rates	Weekend program tuition $20–170. Camping: $20 per person or $30 per family for a onetime pass, $50 per person or $80 per family in membership fees for use of the campground 4 times within 1 year. Kids' programs $7–11 per day.

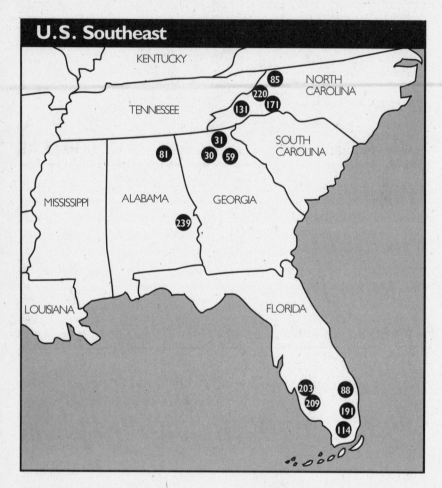

U.S. Southeast

KENTUCKY

TENNESSEE

NORTH CAROLINA

SOUTH CAROLINA

MISSISSIPPI

ALABAMA

GEORGIA

LOUISIANA

FLORIDA

Alabama
81 Hawkwind Earth Renewal
    Cooperative
239 Uchee Pines Lifestyle Center

Florida
88 Hippocrates Health Institute
114 Keys Institute
191 Regency Health Resort
203 Sanibel Island Yoga Vacation
    Retreat
209 Shangri-La Natural Health Resort
    & Spa

Georgia
30 Center for New Beginnings
31 Center for Spiritual Awareness
59 Eupsychia Institute

North Carolina
85 Heavenly Mountain—The
    Spiritual Center of America
131 Lighten Up! Yoga Vacation &
    Retreats
171 Pavillon International
220 Southern Dharma Retreat Center

Meals   All meals are community potluck during weekend programs.

Services No charge for participation in Native American ceremonies.

Uchee Pines Lifestyle Center   Seale, AL

Located fifteen miles southwest of Columbus, Georgia, Uchee Pines Lifestyle Center is a warm and friendly healing facility situated on 200 acres of quiet woodland. Also known as Anvwodi (Cherokee for "get well place"), the center invites guests to rediscover the natural rhythms of their bodies through rest, temperance, proper diet (including plenty of water), sunlight, country hiking, and outdoor work such as gardening, tending the orchard, or chopping wood.

Anvwodi regularly offers eighteen-day lifestyle programs that include physical exams, blood chemistry profiles, physiotherapy, health lectures, regular physician consultations, and natural remedy and cooking classes. All lifestyle programs are customized to address each guest's goals (e.g., weight loss, smoking cessation, blood pressure, or diabetes control). There are also five-day natural health seminars plus nine- or twelve-month student training programs.

Uchee Pines Institute was founded by Calvin and Agatha Thrash, devout Christians, medical doctors and coauthors of several books on natural remedies and preventive medicine. Respecting the healing power of faith in God, the center offers daily morning and evening worship services, Friday and Saturday vespers, a Bible-based "Keys to Happiness" class, plus Saturday morning church services. In addition, each lifestyle program guest is assigned a counselor who can also serve as a prayer companion.

Address   30 Uchee Pines Road, #75, Seale, AL 36875
Phone   (205) 855-4764
Season   Year-round.
Programs 18-day, physician-directed lifestyle programs using natural healing methods, including optional Christian services. Also spring and fall 5-day seminars on "Simple Remedies and Preventive Medicine."

Lodging   7 rooms with twin beds, modern furnishings, and private baths. Campsites and trailer hookups available for seminar attendees.

Rates   Lifestyle program: guest $2,595, second participating family member $2,395, nonparticipating family member $1,495. Seminar: tuition $100, meals $50, housing $75, trailer hookup $25, campsite $10.

Meals   3 daily family-style vegetarian meals free of dairy products.

Services   Seminar services at additional cost: physical exam, consultation, blood chemistry analysis, pap smear.

Hippocrates Health Institute   West Palm Beach, FL

More than thirty years old, this subtropical, wooded estate includes cottages, winding walkways, and an expansive hacienda with swimming pool, sauna, and Jacuzzi. Reflecting the commitment of its director, Brian R. Clement, a longtime living foods advocate, the institute encourages guests to reach personal goals through self-healing techniques that can be maintained at home. Benefits of institute visits have included tension release, improved digestion, greater emotional stability, reduced back pain, and reversal of degenerative disease.

The institute's "Health Encounter" program begins with a complete health appraisal. Other individualized services include nutritional counseling. Each day there is early morning yoga or stretching and exercise; two or three classes on subjects like internal awareness, stress management, visualization, and positive thinking; plus afternoon aquacise in the outdoor pool. Each week there is a massage session and group discussions with the institute's psychologist, physician, and chiropractor.

Address   1443 Palmdale Court, West Palm Beach, FL 33411

Phone   (407) 471-8876 or (800) 842-2125 (reservations)

Season   Year-round.

Programs   3-week health maintenance/restoration program that can be taken in 1-week pieces and tailored to specific goals (e.g., weight reduction, cleansing, rebuilding).

Lodging   Shared and private bedrooms (with shared baths), some in a house with a private pool. Also shared and private suites.

Rates	1 week $1,300–2,500. 2 weeks $2,400–3,750. 3 weeks $2,900–4,500.
Meals	3 daily high-enzyme, organic vegetarian meals. Wheat grass and fruit juices between meals.

Keys Institute   Key Largo, FL

Sixty miles south of Miami, the Keys Institute hosts growth potential workshops during the colder months of the year. The institute's rented bayside facility offers salt- and freshwater swimming, Jacuzzi, canoeing, and paddleboating. And long afternoon breaks allow time for fishing, snorkeling, diving, wind surfing, and sailing.

Formerly a popular Esalen Institute employee, institute director Dorothy Thomas attracts a small but top-notch faculty from around the country. Regular facilitators include regression therapist/author Roger Woolger, Tao psychologist/author John Heider, and gestalt practitioner Christine Price. Workshop participants help out with workshop set-up and take-down chores. Work-scholar opportunities require a four- to six-month time commitment.

Address	P.O. Box 3150, Key Largo, FL 33037
Phone	(305) 451-3519
Season	Early November through late March.
Programs	3- to 5-day workshops involving bodywork, breathwork, gestalt, group process work, and meditation.
Lodging	Private rooms, double (2-bed) rooms, and sleeping bag space.
Rates	Most workshops $350–475.
Meals	Daily self-serve continental breakfasts. First lunch provided. Other lunches and dinners purchased and prepared as a "structured potluck" by the participants, who also clean up after meals.

Regency Health Resort   Hallandale, FL

A fifteen-minute drive from Ft. Lauderdale airport, Regency Health Resort is an oceanside body/mind health spa. Facilities include a heated outdoor pool, Jacuzzi, sauna, shuffleboard, and Nautilus gym with treadmill and Stairmaster. There is also a spacious poolside/seaview wooden deck. The resort's staff includes licensed nutrition counselors as well as chiropractic and medical doctors.

A typical Regency morning might begin with a walk on the beach, followed by breakfast, a health talk, low-impact "funercise" session, and then a light workout in the pool. The afternoon could include a question-and-answer session on the gym's equipment, a food preparation class or private nutritional consultation, tone and stretch or dancercise class, plus yoga and meditation sessions. Evenings feature a movie, a musical event, or a talk on subjects like behavior modification and stress reduction techniques.

Address   2000 South Ocean Drive, Hallandale, FL 33009

Phone   (305) 454-2220 or (800) 454-0003. Fax (305) 454-4637.

Season   Year-round.

Programs   1-week program focusing on weight loss, detoxification, fitness, nutrition, and relaxation. Shorter stays at daily rates.

Lodging   Rooms with view of ocean or court, some with living room, and all with at least 2 double beds, private bathroom, cable TV, phone, and A/C.

Rates $140–219 per day. $895–1,395 per week. Lower rates in summer.

Meals   3 daily gourmet vegetarian meals, with option of juice or water fast.

Services   Massage, reflexology, sea-salt body scrub, therapeutic facial.

Sanibel Island Yoga Vacation Retreat   Sanibel Island, FL

"Sparkling days and starry nights on magical Sanibel Island" is usually an accurate description of the annual spring Sanibel Island Yoga Vacation Retreat. Vacationers stay in villas on one of the best shelling beaches in North America. Yoga classes are taught twice daily in a bright hall, a two-mile walk or bike ride (bicycles can be rented) from the villas.

An annual event since 1982, the retreat is led by Bobbi Goldin, a certified Iyengar yoga teacher and director of the Yoga Institute of Miami.

Bobbi is assisted on Sanibel by Kandy Love of the Health and Harmony Center in Fort Myers.

Address	The Yoga Institute of Miami, 9350 South Dadeland Boulevard, Suite 207, Miami, FL 33156
Phone	(305) 661-9558
Season	Generally the first week in May.
Programs	Iyengar-style, weeklong hatha yoga vacation.
Lodging	2-bedroom, 2-bath beachside villas with full kitchen, washer and dryer, A/C, TV, and phone. Full linens provided.
Rates	Shared room $488. $225 extra for private room or housing for a companion not doing yoga.
Meals	Make own meals or eat out at nearby restaurants.

Shangri-La Natural Health Resort & Spa Bonita Springs, FL

Set in a tropical locale of white sandy beaches, lush gardens, and freshwater mineral springs, Shangri-La is a newly renovated spa retreat near Naples, Florida. The historic main hotel sparkles with original art and Italian Saturnia marble. There is a new state-of-the-art fitness center offering personalized weight training and toning programs. Also new is a beauty and massage center, and a sauna and steam room will be opened soon. Some guests sign up for the cosmetic surgery vacation plan: one week of presurgery relaxation and detoxification followed by one week of postsurgery recovery.

The resort's new European owners have expanded Shangri-La's original commitment to lifestyle education and improvement. Each day includes trips to nearby Gulf Coast beaches for morning "flexorcise" and invigorating walks, aqua-aerobic classes in the outdoor pool followed by health talks by guest speakers, afternoon workshops and classes, late afternoon yoga and meditation, plus evening lectures, entertainment, or informal discussions. All activities are optional. The new owners have also enhanced the resort's traditional focus on natural diet and detoxification by the introduction of "phasing," a gradual process toward a healthier diet.

Address	P.O. Box 2328, Bonita Springs, FL 33959
Phone	(941) 992-3811 or (800) 279-3811. Fax (941) 947-9079.

Season   Year-round.

Programs   Daily beach trips, exercise classes, health talks and workshops, and tai chi, yoga, and meditation sessions.

Lodging   Main hotel luxury rooms (with cable TV, digital phones, art, and tasteful furnishings) plus garden accommodations (including 2-room suites) elsewhere on the estate—all with A/C.

Rates   Weekly double occupancy rates: garden rooms $499–999, luxury rooms and suites $799–1,299.

Meals   3 daily vegetarian meals prepared by an award-winning chef. Special diets offered for such disorders as PMS, candida, and chronic fatigue syndrome.

Services   Massages, body scrubs and wraps, facials, manicure, and pedicure.

Center for New Beginnings   Dahlonega, GA

This center was established in 1985 on forty-five acres of North Georgia woodlands sixty-five miles northeast of Atlanta. The property contains hiking trails, flower and vegetable gardens, hot tubs, and a fire circle. Center owners Joseph and Katherine Whitner create a warm "down home" atmosphere. They also lead couples workshops and holiday singles retreats. Joseph is a pastoral counselor and ordained Presbyterian minister who has developed the "Integrative Model of Spiritual Reality." Katherine is also the center's business manager.

The center hosts frequent public workshops led by guest facilitators from around the country. These programs include yoga and meditation retreats, cancer healing retreats, artistic self-expression workshops, plus other offerings that encourage harmony of body, mind, emotions, and spirit. The center also welcomes individual and private group retreats.

Address   Route 1, Box 1692, Porter Springs Road, Dahlonega, GA 30533

Phone   (706) 864-5861. No visits without prior arrangement.

Season   Year-round.

Programs   2- to 7-day workshops and retreats on personal and spiritual growth.

Lodging	Cabins, main house, and lodge with single and shared bedrooms.
Rates	3-day singles retreat $225. Couples weekend $350 per couple. Guest teacher workshop: 4 days $295, 7 days $495. Nightly rate for personal retreat: singles $60, couples $100.
Meals	3 daily meals with vegetarian options.
Services	Counseling for couples and individuals. Massage can be arranged.

Center for Spiritual Awareness   Lakemont, GA

Located two hours northeast of Atlanta in a secluded mountain setting, the Center for Spiritual Awareness hosts retreats structured by Roy Eugene Davis, a direct disciple of the late Paramahansa Yogananda. Each retreat day begins with early morning meditation followed by hatha yoga (optional) and breakfast. There are classes at 10 A.M. and 1 P.M. Afternoon is free time—for reading, reflection, a walk, or a swim at nearby Lake Rabun beach. A 7 P.M. session is followed by fellowship and educational videos.

Davis himself teaches most of the classes, though guest presenters sometimes facilitate workshops. The theme is always the same: living a natural, God-centered life, with emphasis on practices and routines to facilitate awakened spiritual consciousness. People new to CSA retreats are advised to familiarize themselves with the philosophy and practices of Kriya yoga as explained in Davis's books. During weeklong retreats, Kriya yoga initiation is offered every Thursday evening.

Address	P.O. Box 7, Lakemont, GA 30552
Phone	(706) 782-4723. Fax (706) 782-4560. No visits without prior arrangement.
Season	May through early September.
Programs	Weekend and weeklong meditation and spiritual awakening retreats.
Lodgings	Double occupancy rooms in guest house. Also motels 10 miles away.
Rates	Accommodations, programs, and meals on a donation basis.

Meals   Vegetarian breakfast and lunch. For dinner, guests may use kitchen facilities or go to local restaurants.

Eupsychia Institute   Dahlonega, GA

This institute offers six- and fourteen-day retreats designed to encourage psychological and spiritual integration that includes self-healing and personal growth. The site for these retreats is Forrest Hills Mountain Hideaway, a Blue Ridge Mountains retreat center eighty miles northeast of Atlanta near Dahlonega, Georgia. All programs are directed by Eupsychia's founder Jacquelyn Small, a prolific writer, former faculty member of the Institute of Transpersonal Psychology in Palo Alto, California, and past training director of the Texas Commission on Alcoholism and Drug Abuse.

Eupsychia's fourteen-day "Healing into Wholeness" intensive is generally offered three times a year by six staff members guiding twenty to twenty-five participants and trainees. This retreat includes daily yoga classes, bodywork, exercise, meditation, silent time, nature outings, nutritional counseling, and twelve-step meetings. The somewhat larger, spring and summer six-day intensives vary in focus according to the expertise of the guest teachers and healers (often well-known authors) appearing as copresenters with the Eupsychia staff. And virtually all programs contain the elements of breathwork, guided imagery, artwork, sacred ceremony, and group process.

Eupsychia's programs have proven to be particularly helpful in addressing birth or childhood trauma, repressed incest and abuse issues, burnout, and food and process addictions (e.g., gambling and sex). A high percentage of program participants return as trainees, viewing training as just another dimension of self-healing. The institute also hosts a six-day training workshop on transpersonal counselor skills once each summer.

Address   P.O. Box 3090, Austin, TX 78764
Phone   (512) 327-2795 or (800) 546-2795. Fax (512) 327-6043.
Season   Intensives usually offered in spring, summer, and fall.
Programs   6-day and 14-day intensives for people interested in healing and awakening more fully to their potential.

Lodging Shared accommodations.
Rates   6-day intensive $995. 14-day intensive $3,295.
Meals   3 daily meals.

Heavenly Mountain—
The Spiritual Center of America   Blowing Rock, NC

Spread across 1,500 acres in the ancient and rolling Blue Ridge Mountains of North Carolina, this beautifully landscaped health resort and spiritual center is envisioned by its founders as a source of spiritual inspiration for U.S. leaders.

The Heavenly Mountain portion of this new development is a luxurious family resort community with health spas offering treatments (such as pancha karma) based on the time-tested Ayurvedic system of natural health. Other amenities include tennis courts, swimming pools, horseback riding, and walking trails. Golf, skiing, river sports, and cultural events are abundant in the surrounding area.

An additional benefit of a stay at Heavenly Mountain is the soothing atmosphere generated by the several hundred practitioners of transcendental meditation housed in separate men's and women's communities at opposite ends of the resort. Known as the Spiritual Center of America, the two meditation communities also welcome guests at residential programs—such as a six-day TM training and "Breath of Serenity" women's weekends. Center guests may also use the health spa and other facilities at Heavenly Mountain.

Address Heavenly Mountain, P.O. Box 708, Blowing Rock, NC 28605
Spiritual Center of America, P.O. Box 2287, Blowing Rock, NC 28605
Phone   Heavenly Mountain: (704) 264-6040. Fax (704) 265-3213. Spiritual Center of America: (800) 241-5420. Fax (704) 265-0046. Advance reservations required.
Season   Year-round.
Programs Ayurvedic health spa facilities.
Lodging Luxury rooms and suites, all with private baths. Private house rentals also available.
Rates   As of late 1995 rates not yet set; the resort and spiritual center will open sometime in 1996. Rates at a predecessor

facility: 6-day TM training $1,600, "Breath of Serenity" weekend $430.

Meals   3 daily vegetarian meals served in elegant dining facilities.
Services Ayurvedic health treatments.

Lighten Up! Yoga Vacation and Retreats   Western NC

Asheville's Lighten Up! Yoga Center sponsors a six-day summer yoga vacation at a rustic camp and conference center looking out over the Blue Ridge Mountains of southwestern North Carolina. The vacation includes four hours of daily yoga, three evening yoga programs, a celebration on the final night, and free time to enjoy a lake for swimming and boating, guided hikes, a botanical garden, and summer theater. The teachers are certified Iyengar yoga instructors.

Lighten Up! also hosts weekend yoga retreats in the early summer and fall at a Lake Junaluska retreat center twenty-six miles west of Asheville. Each retreat includes five yoga classes plus enough free time for a walk along (or around) the 200-acre lake. The retreat yoga teacher is Lillah Schwartz, an Iyengar yoga instructor for more than twenty-five years and the founder/director of Lighten Up!

Address 60 Biltmore Avenue, Asheville, NC 28801
Phone   (704) 254-7756
Season   Summer and fall.
Programs Iyengar-style, hatha yoga getaways, including 6-day vacation and 2-weekend retreat.
Lodging Double occupancy rooms in deluxe lodge, rustic 6-person cabins, and small apartments.
Rates   6-day vacation: adults $760–870, children and teens $55–295. Weekend retreat $195 per adult.
Meals   3 daily vegetarian meals in a casual, private setting.
Services Children's program during the 6-day vacation.

Pavillon International   Britten Falls, NC

On 160 forested acres roughly thirty miles southeast of Asheville, Pavillon International is welcoming guests as of July 1, 1996, after twenty years of successful operation in Val David, Quebec. The new grounds and facility include a ten-acre lake, forest trails, and exercise room.

Pavillon programs are for people who are (or might be) in twelve-step recovery programs. The twenty-eight-day "Inner Journey" program includes step work, meditation, breathwork, introspective self-exploration, grief work and healing sessions, and accountability/empowerment support groups. Similar disciplines are used in one-week programs focusing on "Awakening the Spirit Within," "Heart Connections," and "Expanded Spirituality." There are also weekend programs.

All programs are facilitated by Gilles and Liliane Desjardins with the assistance of a well-trained team of counselors. Known for their innovative recovery work, Gilles and Liliane are themselves graduates of recovery programs, as is Pavillon's spiritual director, Father Leo Booth. Pavillon's on-site medical director is Yale-educated Dr. Martin Waugh. Program aftercare includes support group meetings plus visits and workshops by Pavillon staff with Pavillon graduates throughout North America.

Address   New address not available at press time.
Phone   (800) 392-4808. Advance reservations required.
Season   Year-round.
Programs Weekend, weeklong, and 4-week recovery programs for people with addiction, codependency, or dysfunctional family problems.
Lodging   Accommodations for up to 30 program participants in double occupancy rooms, each with private bath.
Rates   1 weekend $250. 1 week $1,000–1,500. 4 weeks $8,400.
Meals   3 daily meals accommodating all diets.
Services Massage.

Southern Dharma Retreat Center   Hot Springs, NC

One hour north of Asheville in a remote region of the Great Smokey Mountains, Southern Dharma Retreat Center (SDRC) hosts meditation retreats ranging from a weekend to seven days. All are suitable for beginner meditators, and all are held in an atmosphere of silence except for group discussions and meetings with teachers. From time to time, SDRC also hosts public workshops (e.g., "Women and Spirituality") sponsored by other organizations.

While meditation is the common thread of SDRC retreats, most retreats explore a specific theme. Mindfulness in daily life, stillness and movement, meditation as a path of the heart, and our relationship to fear are just a few of the topics covered. In addition to monks and teachers from all Buddhist traditions, SDRC teachers have included people on the Christian, Hindu, and other spiritual paths.

Address	Route 1, Box 34-H, Hot Springs, NC 28743
Phone	(704) 622-7112. No visits without prior arrangement.
Season	April through December.
Programs	2- to 7-day guided meditation retreats.
Lodging	Dormitory, small cabin, and primitive creekside campsites with a nearby shower.
Rates	2- and 3-day retreats $105–135. 7-day retreat $225–275. Teacher donations accepted at the end of each retreat.
Meals	3 daily nondairy vegetarian meals.

MEXICO AND THE CARIBBEAN

Casa Radha   Cordemex, Yucatan, Mexico

This two-story pink stucco residence is twenty minutes from Gulf of Mexico beaches and a half hour from the Spanish colonial "white city" of Merida (where people customarily wear white). On the quiet grounds are a swimming pool bordered by coconut palms and an orchard of mango, banana, and avocado trees. Casa Radha is an intimate and informal retreat center operated by teachers trained at British Columbia's Yasodhara Ashram (see profile in next section).

Each morning there are sessions in dream interpretation and "hidden language hatha yoga" (a reflective type of yoga practiced at Yasodhara Ashram). Afternoons are free for beach trips and visits to Merida, a vibrant cultural center where streets are blocked off on Sundays for traditional dancing and singing. In the evenings, guests may participate in an Indian-style satsang worship service.

Each week features a trip to the ancient Mayan temples at Dzibilchaltun. There is also a weekly workshop on a topic (e.g., kundalini yoga or spiritual aspects of hatha yoga) agreed on by the guests (usually numbering no more than four) from the many workshop subjects covered at Yasodhara.

Address	Apartado Postal 44, Cordemex, Yucatan 97310, Mexico
Phone	011 52 (994) 95-551 (also accepts fax).
Season	Year-round.
Programs	A selection of optional activities including daily yoga and dreamwork sessions and a weekly workshop.
Lodging	Accommodations for up to 6 guests.
Rates	1 day $110. 1 week $700. 2 weeks $1,200 (in Canadian $). 15% discount for groups of 3 to 5 people.
Meals	3 daily meals, 100% vegetarian if so requested.
Services	Airport pick-up/drop-off. Excursions to Mayan sites.

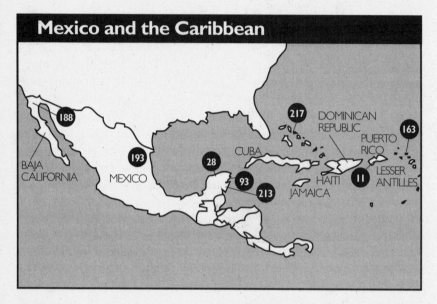

Mexico and the Caribbean

Hotel NaBalam   Isla Mujeres, Quintana Roo, Mexico

On a tiny Caribbean island only a fifteen-minute ferryboat ride from Cancun, Hotel NaBalam offers a tranquil location for weeklong yoga retreats. The instructor is Alvaro Escalante, founder of yoga centers in Italy and Mexico, and a leading teacher of musicosophy (listening to music in a manner that facilitates spiritual growth). Alvaro's morning and late afternoon yoga sessions, including meditation through music, are geared to beginners and intermediates. These sessions are conducted in a spacious, thatched-roof yoga/meditation studio overlooking the sea.

Hotel NaBalam is on North Beach, a "clothing optional" expanse of whispering palm trees, white sands, and turquoise waters. Vacationers can rent kayaks and wind surf boats, or snorkel and dive around one of the world's great coral reefs. In addition, visits to the mainland Mayan ruins of Tulum, Coba, and Chichen Itza are adventures that can be enjoyed in a single day.

Address   Calle Zazil-Ha No. 118 Playa Norte, Isla Mujeres, Quintana Roo 77400, Mexico
Phone   011 52 (987) 70-279. Fax 011 52 (987) 70-446.
Season   Year-round.
Programs   Weeklong guided yoga retreats.
Lodging   Standard rooms, oceanfront and poolside suites, each with A/C, ceiling fans and a private patio or balcony.
Rates   1-week retreat $490 shared occupancy. Single supplement $140.
Meals   3 daily lacto-vegetarian meals. Fresh seafood option each day.

Rancho La Puerta   Tecate, Baja, Mexico

This 300-acre landscaped oasis is set among rock-strewn hills and mountains near the California/Mexico border. The site was cleared in 1940 by Ed and Deborah Szekely for the Essene School of Life whose grounds consisted of a spartan adobe hut and campground. Renamed (in Spanish) Ranch of the Open Door, the property later became the site of the hemisphere's first par course, first circuit training, and first exercise program set to music. Not only was the ranch the first modern fitness resort, it was also the birthplace of spa cuisine.

Today the ranch is a villagelike complex of residence and administrative buildings, outdoor swimming pools, lighted tennis courts, separate men's and women's health centers (each with sauna, steam room, whirlpool, and private rooftop sunbathing area), fitness gyms, beauty treatment center, and a new "quiet" gym for stretching, yoga, and meditation sessions. There are also acres of gardens and miles of hiking trails, some leading up the nearby sacred Mount Kuchumaa.

During the resort's weeklong program, guests are advised to choose at least one daily class from each of five categories: aerobic workouts, toning and strengthening, stretching and flexibility, coordination and balance, and relaxation. A typical day begins with yoga or a hike, includes up to six hours of organized group and class activities, winds down with a meditation session before dinner, and ends with an evening film or guest speaker. Summers feature the popular family week. There are also visits by well-known holistic health and fitness teachers.

Address	P.O. Box 463057, Escondido, CA 92046
Phone	(619) 744-4222 or (800) 443-7565. Fax (619) 744-5007.
Season	Year-round.
Programs	Weeklong holistic health spa programs.
Lodging	Accommodations for up to 150 guests in studio bedroom rancheras, 1-bedroom haciendas and villa studios, and 2-bedroom villa suites. All have private bath (suites have 2). All except rancheras have a kitchenette, living room, and fireplace. No phones or TVs.
Rates	Winter weekly rates $1,440–2,265. Rates 12–16% less from late June through mid-September.
Meals	3 daily vegetarian meals with fish served 3 times each week. Breakfast and lunch buffets, sit-down dinner with silent tables. Vegetables picked daily at dawn from own organic gardens.
Services	Roommate-matching service and courtesy San Diego airport pick-up and drop-off. Tennis lessons, Pilates sessions, craft classes, massage, herbal wrap, facials.

Rio Caliente   Primavera Forest, Guadalajara, Mexico

In the subtropical national forest of a Sierra Madre mountain valley 5,000 feet up is Rio Caliente, a twenty-four-acre retreat that was once a spiritual center for the Huichol Indians (the "healing people"). On the grounds are hot volcanic streams and waterfalls of soft, odorless waters feeding four soaking pools and an Aztec steam room. The grounds also include guest rooms with handcrafted beds and chairs, spa facilities, and a physician-directed miniclinic.

The atmosphere at Rio Caliente is informal and relaxed. Dress is casual, and nude sunbathing is permitted within two enclosed pool areas, one for men and one for women. All holistic health and fitness programs are optional. Other activities include van excursions to the local market, picturesque Lake Chapala, and Tlaquepaque, Mexico's arts and crafts center. Meals are convivial, and evenings are free for conversation, a movie, or a soak.

Though only one hour by microbus taxi from Guadalajara's international airport, Rio Caliente is far away from the modern world. There are no phones, and mail is extremely slow. Everyone is asked to bring a flashlight and insect repellent. Clothesline and pins are provided, though guests may pay the room attendant a small fee to wash their laundry.

Address	c/o Marian Lewis, P.O. Box 897, Millbrae, CA 94030
Phone	(415) 615-9543. Fax (415) 615-0601.
Season	Year-round.
Programs	Holistic health and fitness spa with optional daily yoga, tai chi (in some months), meditation, guided hikes, and aquatic aerobics.
Lodging	48 small, single and double rooms: "patio rooms" near dining room and "pool rooms" near the pools. Private baths. Limited wheelchair access. No phones. Satellite TV.
Rates	$70–96 per night. May through October: 7-night "Classic" $499–599, 10-night "Stress Buster" $715–855. Tips included, but add 10% sales tax.
Meals	3 daily vegetarian buffets with eggs, dairy, or raw foods options. Garden greens. Tropical fruits in season.
Services	Horseback riding, sightseeing trips, and spa services (mud wrap, massage, beauty treatments, and antistress and antiaging therapies).

Sian Ka'an Oasis   near Tulum, Quintana Roo, Mexico

Located an hour and a half south of Cancun International Airport, Sian Ka'an (Mayan for "where the sky is born") is a Caribbean beachside vacation retreat neighboring a national park of lagoons, mangroves, tropical rain forests, and beaches. Only a few miles away are such ancient Mayan ruins as the royal city of Tulum and the jungle pyramids of Coba. Other diversions include swimming, snorkeling, and sailing in a luxurious catamaran yacht. But for many, just being in the natural beauty and wildlife of an untouched seaside wilderness is sufficient reason for a Sian Ka'an vacation.

Several times throughout the year, Sian Ka'an Oasis hosts a weeklong "Healing Holiday" that includes three daily meditations, three yoga classes, a one-hour massage or energy session, plus side trips. At other times, guests may participate in a daily community meditation. Massages and yoga classes (taught three times a week by a local instructor) are available at an additional fee. And from time to time, well-known personal growth organizations and yoga instructors (such as the Feathered Pipe Foundation and Angela Farmer) rent the facility for public programs.

Address   Osho Travel, P.O. Box 352, Mill Valley, CA 94942
Phone   (415) 381-9861. Fax (415) 381-6746.
Season   Year-round.
Programs Weeklong yoga and meditation vacations.
Lodging   Single and double occupancy, standard and deluxe cabanas.
Rates   Weeklong holiday package $600–880. Daily room rate $38–90. Breakfast $7, lunch $9, dinner $13–15. Add a 10% hotel tax.
Meals   Buffet-style vegetarian meals with fresh seafood on request.
Services Massage and yoga classes at extra cost during personal retreats.

Sivananda Ashram Yoga Retreat   Paradise Island, Bahamas

A Caribbean camp set on a beach of pure white sands and clear blue waters, Sivananda Ashram Yoga Retreat is a four-acre paradise for yoga students who do not mind discipline. Everyone is up with the sun for meditation at 6 A.M., followed by hatha yoga on a wooden deck shaded by palms and looking out over the sea. After brunch at 10, vacationers may attend a noon yoga coaching class. There is a lecture/workshop at 2 P.M. and yoga again at 4. Evenings feature meditations (and sometimes bonfire meditations on the beach) plus a talk on yogic practice or philosophy.

In their ample free time, guests can explore Paradise Island or nearby Nassau, take a boat excursion, play tennis or volleyball at the compound, swim and snorkel at the beach, or just relax on an airy veranda facing the sea. After meals, guests wash their own plates and utensils and put them out to dry on open-air racks. Though just a short walk from glamorous hotels and casinos, Sivananda Ashram Yoga Retreat is a world away in spirit. "Health is wealth, peace of mind is happiness, and yoga shows the way" is its guiding philosophy.

Address	P.O. Box N-7550, Nassau, Bahamas
Phone	(809) 363-2902 or (800) 783-9642. Fax (809) 363-3783.
Season	Year-round.
Programs	Hatha yoga retreat with regular daily schedule. Attendance required at classes and meditations. Special holiday programs. 4-week teachers' training in February is open to all.
Lodging	103 beds in beachside wooden cabins and main building dorms. Linens and towels provided. Also 50 tent sites in a coconut grove. Communal bathrooms and showers.
Rates	$40–75 per day, with rates $10 higher during Christmas and Easter periods. Teachers' training: tent $1,350, dorm $1,950.
Meals	Midmorning and evening vegetarian buffets. Snack canteen.
Services	Shiatsu and reflexology bodywork.

Ann Wigmore Institute   Rincon, Puerto Rico

This institute is housed in two white stucco buildings surrounded by coconut, papaya, and banana trees in a quiet neighborhood of cottages
and fishermen's homes on tropical Puerto Rico's west coast. Fifty yards
away, the ocean is visible from the second-story veranda of the institute's guest residence quarters.

The institute offers a twelve-day "Living Foods Lifestyle" program designed to rejuvenate body and spirit in accordance with the Hippocratic
wisdom "Let nature be the doctor of disease." The program encourages
gentle self-healing in a learn-by-doing environment. It was established
by the late Dr. Ann Wigmore, who could perform somersaults to demon-
strate her flexibility right up to the time of her death, in a 1993 fire at age
eighty-four.

A "Living Foods Lifestyle" day begins with wheat grass juice, light exercise, yoga, or beach walks. Participation in certain personal growth
classes (e.g., journal writing, inner-child and reflexology work) is required for a diploma. Other morning and evening classes focus on nutritional theory, colon care, and techniques for growing and preparing
living foods meals. Afternoons are for free time or optional classes, including sessions on massage and relaxation techniques. Each course
ends with a graduation ceremony banquet.

Address	P.O. Box 429, Rincon, Puerto Rico 00677
Phone	(809) 868-6307. Fax (809) 868-2430.
Season	Year-round.
Programs	12-day "Living Foods Lifestyle" program that can be re-peated for a 26-day stay. Also 1-week personal retreats and 1-week intensive certification programs for LFL graduates.
Lodging	Capacity for about 25 overnight guests in dormitory, semi-private (shared with one other), and private rooms. Shared and private rooms may have full, half or no bathroom.
Rates	12-day program $945–1,750. 26-day program $1,650–3,250. Rates 10–15% lower from late May through early September.
Meals	3 daily living foods meals. The staple is energy soup—a blended mix of fruit, greens, enzyme-rich Rejuvelac, avo-cado, dulse, and pea/lentil sprouts. The regimen is comple-mented by fruit smoothies, nut pâtés, seed yogurts, coconut milk, and fresh salads.

Services   Reflexology, rebirthing, massage, colonic irrigation, colonic wheat grass implants. Free transportation to and from airports.

Omega in the Caribbean   St. John, U.S. Virgin Islands

Tucked amid mahogany and bay trees above a secluded bay, Omega in the Caribbean is a midwinter tropical village of canvas cottages at Maho Bay Camp Resort. It is run by the Omega Institute for Holistic Studies (profiled earlier in this chapter). Part of Virgin Islands National Park, the campground has hillside boardwalks that connect to miles of well-marked hiking trails along and above pristine sandy beaches.

The day begins with sunrise meditation, yoga, or tai chi. Meals and workshops are in open-air pavilions overlooking the sea. There are two daily two-hour workshop periods plus informal talks or concerts in the evenings. Each week, at least six ongoing workshops are presented, and vacationers may sample all workshops or focus on one or two.

The one workshop usually offered during all six weeklong sessions is "Creating Time for Wellness," facilitated by Omega Institute's president, Stephan Rechtschaffen, M.D. Through visualization, mindfulness, and awareness exercises, Stephan encourages vacationers to discover "island time—the natural rhythm that comes from living in the present moment."

When they are not in workshops, most vacationers disperse to enjoy the beaches, snorkel among Trunk Bay's coral reefs, or explore the island. Island attractions include Bordeaux Mountain's rain forest and spectacular views, the ruins of eighteenth-century sugar mills, and old-style farms owned and worked by descendants of Danish settlers.

Address   Omega Institute for Holistic Studies, 260 Lake Drive, Rhinebeck, NY 12572

Phone   (914) 266-4444 or (800) 944-1001 (reservations). Fax (914) 266-4828.

Season   6 weeks from January to mid-February.

Programs   6 weeklong holistic health vacations, each with weeklong workshops led by well-known visiting teachers, healers, and artists.

Lodging   96 wooden-floored canvas cottages, each with 2 beds, bedding and linens, a living/dining area, lounge chairs, and sofa. Boardwalks connect to toilets, showers, and dining pavilion.

Rates   1-week vacation (including food, lodging, and round-trip airfare from New York City) $1,374–1,490.

Meals   3 lavish vegetarian buffets each day, including some fish and dairy products. Tropical fruits available throughout the day.

Services   Massage and nutrition counseling. Land transport between island airport and Maho Bay.

BRITISH COLUMBIA, CANADA

In this section, all prices are in Canadian dollars. Translated into U.S. dollars, these prices would be substantially (20–35 percent) lower.

Hollyhock   Cortes Island, British Columbia

Hollyhock is a family vacation and learning center on Cortes Island, one hundred miles north of Vancouver in the Georgia Strait. Handcrafted buildings blend into an environment of old-growth trees and herb, flower, and vegetable gardens. An orchard sanctuary is being created for contemplation and meditation. Across the waters to the east, the skyline is shaped by the rugged contours of the Coastal Mountains.

From spring through fall, Hollyhock hosts more than fifty seminars and workshops. Most programs are facilitated by well-known artists, authors, educators, and healing arts practitioners from throughout North America and other parts of the world. Typical titles for these three- to nine-day programs are "Shamanism—Spirits of Nature," "The Couples' Journey," "Meditation, the Drum, and Ecstasy."

The center also offers one-week holiday packages that include yoga, tai chi, or a bird-watching walk each morning; a guided walk through Hollyhock gardens; naturalist tours, including sailboat trips to neighboring islands; swimming in the strait's ocean waters, warmed in summer up to seventy-two degrees Fahrenheit; a bodywork or massage session; unlimited hot tubbing; evening talks, music, or stories at the fire circle on the beach.

During the six-week spring "Open Community," Hollyhock becomes an extended family of guests, staff, and island residents. Each week includes arts, crafts, writing, and storytelling classes; afternoon teas and a special entertainment evening; music, singing, and drumming events; plus ritual celebrations. From mid-May through August there are weeklong kayaking camps and expeditions; in July and August, weeklong "Kids Camps" on Read Island.

Canada—British Columbia

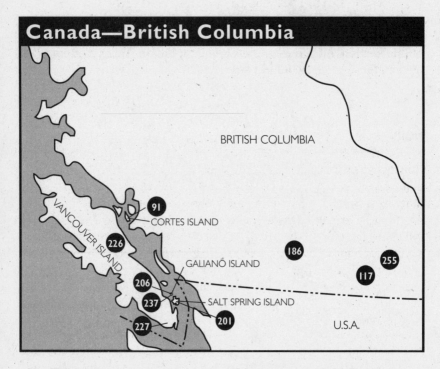

Address   Box 127, Manson's Landing, Cortes Island, B.C. V0P 1K0, Canada
Phone   (604) 935-6533 or (800) 933-6339. Fax (604) 935-6424.
Season   March through October.
Programs   3- to 9-day seminars and workshops in the practical, creative, and healing arts. Weekend and weeklong holiday packages. Also 90-day work exchange for Canadian citizens and landed immigrants.
Lodging   Accommodations for about 70 people in single rooms with or without bath, double occupancy rooms, and dorms that sleep 3 to 6 people. There are also campsites (BYO tent and bedding).
Rates   3- to 9-day program tuition $195–745. Daily rate for room and board: adults $44–124, children ages 4–12 $29–64, children under 4 free.
Meals   3 daily gourmet vegetarian meals. Seafood served twice each week and at Friday night beach barbecues.
Services   Massage, Hellerwork, emotional release, integrated bodywork, natural skin care.

Kootenay Lake Summer Retreats   Nelson, British Columbia

These retreats are held at Camp Koolaree in the mountains of southeast British Columbia. Camp facilities include a lodge for indoor classes and fireside socializing, a kitchen and dining area, a large meadow for tai chi practice, and a private beach for swimming and canoeing. Nearby are hiking trails and a natural hot spring.

In recent years, the camp has consisted of two weeklong retreats: one on tai chi and the other on pa kua, a tai chi "sister art." Both retreats offer daily sessions in forms (mostly for beginners), push hands (for all levels), weapons, and applications (for intermediate and advanced). Other daily sessions are early morning chi gung, late afternoon meditation and philosophy, after-dinner group discussions, and evening healing and bodywork presented by guest instructors.

The head instructor is Rex Eastman, who has taught tai chi since 1975. "Mad Dog" Eastman also hosts winter weekend "Tai Chi/Snowboard Playshops" at Big White ski area near Kelowna, British Columbia;

two-week spring "Ski and Tai Chi Vacations" in the French Alps; and weeklong midsummer "Tai Chi/Surfing Funshops" on Maui.

Address	Kootenay Tai Chi Centre, Box 566, Nelson, B.C. V1L 5R3, Canada
Phone	(604) 352-3714 (also accepts fax).
Season	August.
Programs	Weeklong tai chi and pa kua retreats. Beginners welcome.
Lodging	Tents and shared cabins. BYO warm sleeping bag and mattress.
Rates	Tuition, meals, lodging, and boat transportation: 1 week $395, 2 weeks $750.
Meals	3 daily, well-balanced vegetarian meals.

Rainbow Medicine Wheel Camp   Kelowna, British Columbia

Located sixty miles northwest of Kamloops, Rainbow Medicine Wheel Camp is set on sixty acres of traditional Native healing grounds beside the Salmon River at the north end of the Vernon Okanogan Reservation. A camp weekend extends from Thursday evening through Sunday noon with medicine wheel explorations and meditations, talking and healing circles, sweat lodges, breathwork sessions, a Saturday evening feast and celebration, plus time out for crafts, herb walks, swimming, and free massages.

The primary camp facilitators are Neil Farstad, a sweat lodge and medicine wheel keeper of Meti descent, and Estella Mueller, a breathwork teacher and spiritual counselor of Dena and Carrier descent. Neil and Estella welcome individuals, couples, families, and (through customized arrangements) special interest groups such as caregiver teams suffering burnout.

Address	Comp. 18, Site 23, RR 4, Kelowna, B.C. V1Y 7R3, Canada
Phone	(604) 764-7708. No visits without prior arrangement.
Season	Mid-May through mid-September.
Programs	3-day rejuvenation weekends grounded in Native American medicine ceremonies and teachings.
Lodging	Tepees. BYO warm sleeping bag.

Rates   Program, meals, and tent space $319 plus sales tax.

Meals   3 daily meals, sometimes including buffalo, salmon, or venison. Vegetarian menu also available.

Salt Spring Centre   Salt Spring Island, British Columbia

This center is set among sixty-nine acres of cedar forest and meadows on Salt Spring Island in the Strait of Georgia. The grounds include a school and a large main house. There is swimming in a nearby lake.

The center's most frequent offerings are women's rejuvenation weekends with yoga and meditation classes, aerobics, nature walks, and saunas. Hope Cancer Clinic offers occasional weekend and five-day retreats. Other center programs have included workshops with Angela Farmer and Victor Van Kooten, two of the world's best-known hatha yoga teachers.

The community based at Salt Spring Centre is inspired by their spiritual teacher Baba Hari Dass, the yogi who practices unceasing silence. Baba visits and presides each summer at an intensive Ashtanga yoga retreat followed by a family retreat. The center also offers work-study programs, personal retreat opportunities, and rentals for private groups.

Address   355 Blackburn Road, Salt Spring Island, B.C. V8K 2B8, Canada

Phone   (604) 537-2326. Fax (604) 537-2311.

Season   Year-round. No visits without prior arrangement.

Programs   Women's weekends plus other creative and healing arts programs.

Lodging   Shared rooms for up to 20 people in main house, dorm space for an additional 6, plus summer campsites.

Rates   Weekend program $190–300. 9-day Ashtanga yoga retreat $650.

Meals   3 daily vegetarian meals with homegrown vegetables and fruits during summer months.

Services   Swedan—an Ayurvedic herbal steam and bodywork treatment. Also reflexology and herbal facial during women's weekends.

Serenity by the Sea   Galiano Island, British Columbia

An ocean bluff retreat center on Galiano Island, the forested jewel of the Canadian Gulf Islands between Victoria and Vancouver. The main house and nearby chalet were designed by hostess Shari Street, whose paintings and stained-glass creations adorn every room. Next to the house is a reflecting pond, creekside garden, and steaming "tub on the rocks." The surrounding forests and waters invite hikers and kayakers to venture out among the wildlife of eagles, otters, and seals.

Most Serenity by the Sea self-discovery weekends are facilitated by Shari and/or her husband, Amrit Chidakash, together with artists and healers with talents in painting, mask-making, journal writing, gestalt, reiki, body energy work, yoga, meditation, and life transitions counseling. Other teachers bring skills in psychic counseling; craniosacral balancing; movement; and neuro-linguistic programming (NLP). Serenity by the Sea also welcomes private retreats, with the hosts available to help design or facilitate group or individual programs.

Address	225 Serenity Lane, Galiano Island, B.C. V0N 1P0, Canada
Phone	(604) 539-2655. No visits without prior arrangement.
Season	April through November for group programs.
Programs	2- to 4-day self-discovery workshops.
Lodging	Charming B&B–type single and double rooms with panoramic coastal, ocean, and island vistas.
Rates	Workshop $275–425. Private retreat $70–90 per day.
Meals	3 daily gourmet vegetarian meals. Hot drinks available throughout the day.
Services	Gestalt counseling, massage, and aura and energy work.

Summer Serenity Programs Courtenay, British Columbia

Two hours north of Nanaimo and a mile above sea level, Serenity Farm hosts five-day summer programs at Mount Washington Ski Resort. The major programs are "Mile High Yoga" (levels 1 and 2), "Renew You" health retreat (a holistic approach that includes Ayurvedic health-care tips), and "Deepening Your Love" for couples. Mornings are for sessions. Afternoons are for taking it easy or hiking mountain trails that look out over Strathcona Park and the Straits of Georgia.

All programs are facilitated by Roberta Scotthorne, ME.d., Ph.D., director of the Serenity Farm holistic health center in Nanaimo, British Columbia. Roberta has twenty-five years of experience as a counselor, teacher, and teacher trainer. She is also certified to teach all aspects of yoga in the Sivananda tradition.

Address   Serenity Farm, RR4, S4, C23, Nanaimo, B.C. V9R 5X9, Canada
Phone   (604) 245-2340. Fax (604) 245-7118.
Season   July.
Programs   5-day yoga and wellness programs for individuals and couples.
Lodging   Private and double rooms in ski chalets.
Rates   Individuals $580–625. Couples $650. $225 for meals and accommodations for each person sharing a room who is not enrolled in a program.
Meals   3 daily vegetarian meals.

Summer Yoga Intensive   Victoria, British Columbia

The Victoria Yoga Centre is host each summer to a seven-day intensive for teachers and students with experience in Iyengar yoga. Each day there are morning yoga postures sessions, midafternoon seminars, and late afternoon yogic breathing sessions. Seminar topics include "Patanjali's Yoga Sutras," "Bhagavad Gita," "Symbolism of the Body," and "Musculoskeletal and Back Problems" from a yoga perspective. Classes are held at the Victoria YM-YWCA, centrally located in one of North America's most beautiful cities.

The intensive's head teachers are Shirley and Derek French, longtime students of both B. K. S. Iyengar and Swami Sivananda Radha. Shirley has taught yoga in Victoria for more than twenty years. Derek is a physician who teaches therapeutic yoga. Shirley and Derek are joined at the intensive by two or three other advanced student/teachers of Iyengar and kundalini yoga.

Address   Victoria Yoga Centre, 3918 Olympic View Drive, RR 4, Victoria, B.C. V9B 5T8, Canada
Phone   (604) 478-3775

Season   One week in July.

Programs Iyengar-style, hatha yoga retreat.

Lodging   Single and double rooms for women at the Victoria YM-YWCA. Also single and double rooms at the University of Victoria campus. B&B available with Victoria yoga community members.

Rates   Tuition $375 (includes daily lunch). Lodging: 7 nights at Y $225–337, University of Victoria $37–52 per night, B&B $20 per day.

Meals   Daily cafeteria-style lunch with vegetarian option. Picnic lunch at the Frenchs' residence on the last day.

Thymeways   Galiano Island, British Columbia

Thymeways is the Galiano Island home and studio of Maureen and Bruce Carruthers, students of B. K. S. Iyengar and directors of an Iyengar teacher apprenticeship program. For more than twenty years, Maureen has taught yoga in the Vancouver area and in workshops throughout North America. Bruce is a Vancouver physician whose therapies include health-enhancing practices.

At Thymeways, Bruce and Maureen lead yoga workshops and yoga workshop/retreats tailored to different levels of yoga experience. They also host "Health Focus and Yoga" programs that include yoga postures, silent and music meditation, breath awareness, drumming, haiku composition, mindful work, and nutrition and exercise instruction. Each year, Maureen and a guest teacher lead a weekend workshop for maturing women. Thymeways also hosts weekend yoga workshops taught solely by guest teachers.

Address   790 Devina Drive, RR 2, Galiano Island, B.C. V0N 1P0, Canada

Phone   (604) 539-5071. No visits without prior arrangement.

Season   Late March through early November.

Programs 2- to 7-day workshops and retreats on yoga plus yoga and health.

Lodging   Rooms in house or cottage. Also a studio loft and platform tents, each accommodating 1 or 2 people.

Rates   2- and 3-day programs $180–290. 5- to 7-day programs $500–735.

Meals   3 daily, mostly vegetarian meals. Special diets accommodated.

Services   Massage therapy.

Yasodhara Ashram   Kootenay Bay, British Columbia

Located sixty miles north of the British Columbia/Idaho border, Yasodhara Ashram is a 140-acre yoga retreat center and spiritual community on the shores of Kootenay Lake in the Canadian Rockies. The ashram is distinguished by its longevity (more than thirty years at this spot), a Temple of Divine Light honoring the Light in all religions, and an organic farm that produces much of the ashram's food.

Most ashram programs are on topics such as kundalini yoga, spiritual aspects of hatha yoga, mantra yoga, dream interpretation, and other methods of self-investigation. "Ten Days of Yoga" is an introduction to the ashram's major disciplines. The three-month "Yoga Development Course" is an opportunity for life transformation and a prerequisite for teacher training courses. The ashram also welcomes personal retreat guests, as long as they stay for at least two nights and participate in the ashram's daily schedule of mindful work, meals, and morning and evening worship.

All programs are based on the teachings of Swami Sivananda Radha, one of the first Western women to be initiated into the Swami order. In addition to founding and presiding over the ashram, Swami Radha is founder of the Association for the Development of Human Potential. Emphasizing self-reliance and personal effort as the path to real knowledge, Swami Radha's teachings are noted for their practical applicability to daily life.

Address   Box 9, Kootenay Bay, B.C. V0B 1X0, Canada

Phone   (604) 227-9224. Fax (604) 227-9494.

Season   Year-round except September.

Programs   Workshops and programs ranging from a weekend to 3 months on various aspects of yoga, yoga teacher trainings, plus opportunities to be a guest resident in a spiritual community.

Lodging   Shared accommodations (usually with 1 other person) in spacious, comfortably furnished guest lodge with laundry facilities.

Rates   Programs: weekend $225–325, 5 days $500, 10 days $790–825. 3-month course $6,000. Personal retreats: $75 per day, $490 per week; rates decrease to $25 per night, $140 per week with part-time work; children $10 per day.

Meals   3 daily vegetarian meals with fish, poultry, and\meat dishes served several times each week. Silence observed at most meals.

Services   Private counseling. Summer children's program.

ONTARIO AND QUEBEC, CANADA

In this section, all prices are in Canadian dollars (with one exception). Translated into U.S. dollars, these prices would usually be substantially (20–35 percent) lower.

King View   Aurora, Ontario

This eighty-six-acre Emissary community is located in rolling hill country forty-five minutes north of Toronto. The property includes organic vegetable gardens, maple forests, and marked trails. The forty residents, of varying ages and occupations, come together for Sunday morning spiritual gatherings, which include meditation, ceremony, music, and conversation. All guests are welcome to attend.

The King View community often hosts public programs conducted by visiting teachers. These events include yoga retreats, men's empowerment workshops, interpersonal intensives, and energy awareness trainings. From time to time, the community also hosts retreats of its own—often weekends focusing on an Emissary spiritual healing technique known as an "attunement." King View also welcomes personal retreats and rentals by private groups.

Address	Box 217, Aurora, Ontario L4G 3H3, Canada
Phone	(905) 727-9171. Fax (905) 727-7031.
Season	Year-round.
Programs	2- to 9-day spiritually based workshops and retreats.
Lodging	Single and double rooms plus 4- to 7-person dorms.
Rates	Samples: yoga weekend $325, 8-day men's retreat $600. Daily rates for personal retreat: adults, lodging $45–85, meals $23; children (under 10), free lodging and half-price meals.
Meals	3 daily buffet-style meals with vegetarian options.
Services	Attunements plus spiritual and lifestyle counseling.

Canada—Ontario and Quebec

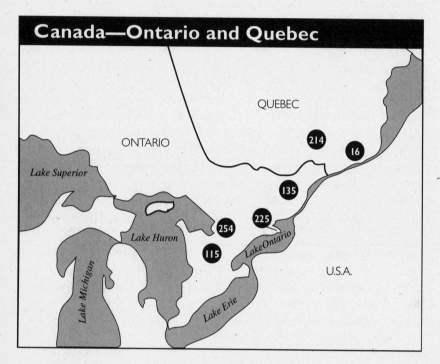

Macrobiotics Canada Summer Conference   Almonte, Ontario

Each summer since 1980, Wayne Diotte and his staff have hosted a six-day macrobiotics conference at Wayne's home/center in the village of Almonte. This farm country hamlet is thirty miles southwest of Ottawa and a five-minute walk from Canada's Mississippi River, whose waters are warm enough for swimming by early June.

Conference activities include daily morning yoga, do-in self-massage, and meditation; macrobiotic cooking classes; lectures by Wayne on macrobiotic lifestyle; videos on the health and healing teachings of Michio Kushi (whose Kushi Institute is profiled earlier in this chapter); a riverside picnic; a party with dancing and guest-provided entertainment; and a farewell brunch.

Address	RR 3, Almonte, Ontario K0A 1A0, Canada
Phone	(613) 256-2665
Season	Conference usually first full week in July.
Programs	Annual 6-day macrobiotic conference plus occasional weekend workshops.
Lodging	Capacity for 30–40 overnight guests in shared rustic rooms at nearby conference center. Single rooms at nearby B&B. Also limited camping.
Rates	Conference $620–1,295. Weekend workshop $225.
Meals	3 daily macrobiotic meals with 100+ dishes served. Vegetables from Wayne's organic garden.
Services	Wayne's macrobiotic consultations, private yoga sessions, shiatsu massage, ginger compress, clay packs, facials.

Still Point Retreat Centre   Picton, Ontario, Canada

A spacious five-acre property on the shores of the Bay of Quinte, Still Point is a combination bed-and-breakfast/yoga retreat seventy-five miles east of Toronto. The center's host is Glenn Mifsud, a Sivananda-certified yoga instructor who leads sessions in a practice studio set right on the water. From time to time, there are also guest yoga teachers.

A typical retreat day begins with early morning tea preceding group meditation. The morning yoga class is followed by karma yoga (i.e., kitchen help), and then brunch. Afternoons vary according to the nature of the group. There may be a sharing time or a dreamwork session on the deck. People also may prefer to go off for a swim, do some canoeing, or just take it easy. The schedule resumes with the late afternoon yoga session followed by karma yoga, dinner, and late evening group meditation.

Address   Village of Newport, RR 2 Picton, Ontario K0K 2T0, Canada
Phone   (613) 476-8061. No visits without prior arrangement.
Season   June through November for retreats.
Programs   2-, 3-, and 7-day hatha yoga retreats.
Lodging   Shared, cottage-style accommodations. Also campsites.
Rates   2 days $140. 3 days $210. 7 days $420.
Meals   Vegetarian at retreats. Nonvegetarian available for B&B guests.

Wyebridge Health Spa   Wyebridge, Ontario

Eighty-five miles north of Toronto is a restored historic lodge on grounds that include an outdoor hot tub and a sandy Georgian Bay beach. In the warmer months of the year, this lodge offers several self-discovery weekends with workshops designed to ease loss, stress, and life transition problems through discovering forgotten memories, strong feelings, unrealized needs, and creative inspirations.

Program facilitators are June and Bronek Zelonka. June is a certified practitioner of Integrative and Holotropic Breathwork. Bronek is a practicing anesthesiologist who has co-led breathwork sessions since 1986. In addition to breathwork, self-discovery weekends include relaxation practices, guided imagery, expressive arts, group process, bodywork, gestalt, and ritual.

Address   Wyebridge Centre in Toronto, 74 Madison Avenue, Toronto, Ontario M5R 2S4, Canada
Phone   (416) 924-9070
Season   May through September.
Programs   Self-discovery weekends grounded in holotropic breathwork.
Lodging   Shared rooms (2 beds in each).

Rates $230 per weekend.
Meals   3 daily vegetarian meals.

Babaji's Kriya Yoga Ashram   St. Etienne de Bolton, Quebec

This forty-acre lakeside retreat center is one hundred miles east of Montreal. It is operated by Marshall Govindan and his wife, Gaetane. Marshall has practiced Kriya yoga intensively since 1970 as a student of yogi S. A. A. Ramaiah, a direct disciple of Babaji Nagaraj. He is also author of the book *Babaji and the Eighteen Siddha Kriya Yoga Tradition.* Gaetane is a holistic therapist trained in polarity, therapeutic touch, Chinese auriculotherapy, energy osteopathy, and Ayurveda.

At their ashram, the Govindans conduct weekend Kriya yoga initiations (and retreats for those already initiated) several times throughout the year. Generally in late August, they also host a weeklong camp cofacilitated by other teachers such as naturopathic doctors and a Vedic astrologer. Upon their departure in late November, the Govindans usually lead a pilgrimage to south India and Sri Lanka, where they visit sacred sites and the ashrams of Indian saints.

Address   Marshall Govindan, 165 De La Gauchetiere West, Apartment 608, Montreal, Quebec H2Z 1X6, Canada
Phone   (514) 284-3551
Season   Open from time to time throughout the year except for one month at year's end.
Programs   Kriya yoga initiation weekends, retreat weekends, and weeklong summer camp. Also annual monthlong trip to India.
Lodging   Shared accommodations (2 beds per room).
Rates   Weekend $195–275. Weeklong camp: adults $445–650, children $140. Monthlong India trip (including airfare from Toronto) $4,200.
Meals   3 daily vegetarian meals.

Sivananda Ashram Yoga Camp   Val Morin, Quebec

Spread across 250 acres of lawns and forest in the heart of the Laurentian Mountains, the Sivananda Ashram Yoga Camp is only a one-hour drive north of Montreal. The environment is one of crisp mountain air, panoramic mountain vistas, waterfalls, forest trails, and tranquil alpine lakes. Summer guests can enjoy hiking, volleyball, and swimming in the lake or large outdoor pool. Winter guests can enjoy ice-skating, cross-country skiing on groomed trails, and a wood-burning Russian-style sauna.

A typical day begins at 6 A.M. with satsang—silent meditation followed by mantra chanting, an inspirational talk or reading, and closing prayers. Next comes a class devoted to hatha yoga postures and breathing techniques. The 10 A.M. brunch is followed by a one-hour work service opportunity. Afternoons are free for recreation, special programs, or workshops. There is a second yoga class at 4 P.M. Dinner is followed by evening satsang. Sivananda Ashram Yoga Camp is headquarters of Sivananda Yoga Vedanta Centers International. During the summer the ashram hosts a number of special Indian cultural programs. It also hosts several monthlong trainings and intensives for yoga teachers. All ashram classes are taught by the large and well-trained resident staff.

Address	8th Avenue, Val Morin, Quebec J0T 2R0, Canada
Phone	(819) 322-3226. Fax (819) 322-5876.
Season	Year-round.
Programs	Hatha yoga camp requiring attendance at all daily classes and meditations. July programs are a teachers' training course (open to all) and a children's yoga camp.
Lodging	2-story wood lodges with private, double, and dorm rooms. Private bath in some rooms. Tent space on the grounds.
Rates	$34–58 per night. Children under 12 pay half rate. Children under 4 free. Teachers' training course $1,295–1,645 (U.S.).
Meals	2 daily buffet-style vegetarian meals.

MULTISITE
GETAWAYS

*T*his chapter profiles twenty-five organizations that offer programs at two or more sites separated by large distances. The profiles are listed in geographical order in three sections: "Caribbean," "North America," and "United States and Abroad."

CARIBBEAN

Feathered Pipe Programs in the Tropics

In late winter/early spring, Feathered Pipe Foundation hosts weeklong programs in the Bahamas and Mexico. The Bahamas site is Riding Rock Inn, a diving resort set beside a white sand beach on quiet San Salvador Island. The Mexico site is Sian Ka'an Oasis (see profile in the previous chapter), a Caribbean coast resort neighboring a Yucatan Peninsula biosphere reserve of tropical rain forests and beaches.

Like Montana's Feathered Pipe Ranch summer programs (see profile in the previous chapter), Feathered Pipe Programs in the Tropics are led by well-known teachers on topics such as natural medicine, Iyengar yoga, and healing through stories and imagery.

Address	Feathered Pipe Foundation, P.O. Box 1682, Helena, MT 59624
Phone	(406) 442-8196. Fax (406) 442-8110.
Season	February and March.
Programs	One-week workshops focusing primarily on yoga, women's wisdom, natural and spiritual healing.
Regions	Bahamas and Mexico.
Rates	Bahamas $1,699 including round-trip charter flight from Fort Lauderdale, Florida. Mexico $950–1,050.

NORTH AMERICA

Eastwest Retreats

Eastwest conducts two annual retreats combining Holotropic Breathwork and Vipassana meditation. One retreat is held on the eastern

Massachusetts campus of New England's oldest boarding school. The other is at a southern California desert facility designed by Frank Lloyd Wright. The daily schedule includes morning lectures and meditation; afternoon breathwork (each person works with a partner) and mandala drawing; evening meditation and small group (sixteen people) discussions. There are up to 160 retreatants at each retreat. Rooms are shared, meals are vegetarian, and silence is observed (except during sessions) throughout the week.

Each retreat is led by Stanislav Grof, Jack Kornfield, and Wes Nisker. Stan is a psychiatrist, scholar, and the inventor of Holotropic Breathwork—a self-healing method for exploring one's own early life, including perinatal and transpersonal memories and images. Jack is a clinical psychologist and Vipassana meditation teacher trained as a monk in Thailand, Burma, and India. Wes is a radio commentator and meditation teacher. And all three are authors. A sampling of their many books are *The Holotropic Mind* (Grof), *A Path with Heart* (Kornfield), and *Crazy Wisdom* (Nisker).

Address   P.O. Box 12, Philo, CA 95466
Phone   (707) 895-2856. Fax (707) 895-2421.
Season   Late summer (East) and fall (West).
Programs   6-day retreats combining instruction and practice of Holotropic Breathwork and insight meditation (Vipassana).
Regions   Central New England and southern California desert.
Rates   Each retreat $820–840.

Hoffman Quadrinity Process

The purpose of the Hoffman Quadrinity Process is to eliminate self-sabotaging emotional and behavior patterns. The process employs a structured combination of techniques including journal writing, guided visualizations, mind revelations, and cathartic work. Although conducted in a group, it is essentially an individual inner-healing journey that is supported by group energy. The groups range in size from fifteen to thirty, with an average of about twenty-two people.

Developed in 1967 by Bob Hoffman and described in his book *No One Is to Blame*, the process is called "Quadrinity" because it involves the balancing of four elements of self: the "emotional child," the "adult intellect," the "spiritual self," and the "physical body." Programs are presented throughout the year—mostly in the San Francisco Bay area but also in other regions. The program's teachers are highly trained, and the process is solidly endorsed by well-known self-help experts Joan Borysenko, Ph.D., and John Bradshaw.

Address	223 San Anselmo Avenue, Suite 4, San Anselmo, CA 94960
Phone	(415) 485-5220 or (415) 485-5539.
Season	June through December.
Programs	7-day program on clearing self-defeating emotional and behavior patterns originating in early child-parent relationships.
Regions	Northern California, northern Virginia, southeastern Wisconsin, and eastern Massachusetts. Also Ontario, Canada.
Rates	Tuition, room, and board $2,850.

Journey into Wholeness

Each year, this organization sponsors a variety of programs designed to foster inner healing by integrating Jungian depth psychology with spiritual and religious themes. Programs are led by Jungian psychoanalysts, healers, ministers, artists, and authors. Some are designed for people in the helping professions, but most are open to all.

Annual five-day spring and fall conferences include lectures, workshops, and special events (e.g., dances, theater, and films). Each is preceded by a two-day "Introduction to Jung" seminar and a two-day couples seminar. Other annual programs include a five-day "Way of the Dream" film series and seminar, a nine-day vision quest program, plus women's and men's weekend retreats.

At their own sixty-two-acre Stillpoint center near Balsam Grove, North Carolina, Journey's directors Jim and Annette Cullipher also host weekend workshops.

Address	P.O. Box 169, Balsam Grove, NC 28708
Phone	(704) 877-4809. Fax (704) 877-3568.
Season	Year-round.

Programs	Conferences, seminars, workshops, and adventures integrating Jungian wisdom with various spiritual perspectives.
Regions	Except for the fall conference (St. Simon's Island, Georgia) and the vision quest (Temagami, Ontario wilderness), most programs are in North Carolina's Blue Ridge Mountains.
Rates	2- and 3-day programs (including tuition, meals, and lodging) $130–345. 4- and 5-day programs: tuition $300–375, food and lodging $250–450.

Men's Wilderness Gatherings

Roughly three times each spring and three times each fall, the Texas Men's Institute hosts men's wilderness gatherings at rustic campsites—mostly in Texas and West Virginia. Each weekend includes discussions, lectures, therapeutic processes, communications exercises, movement, stories, grief, joy, and laughter. The total experience fosters a balanced view of manhood that includes work and play, strength and vulnerability, leadership and following skills, spontaneity, spirituality, and sexuality.

Retreat facilitators are Marvin Allen and Richard (aka "Coyote") Prosapio. Marvin is a psychotherapist, author of *Angry Men, Passive Men*, and the developer of Masculine Relational Therapy. Richard is a psychotherapist, ceremonialist, and author of a book on discovering the power of intuition. Both men have years of experience in facilitating men's retreats.

Address	Texas Men's Institute, P.O. Box 311384, New Braunfels, TX 78131
Phone	(210) 964-4153
Season	Spring and fall.
Programs	Weekend men's workshops designed to help men recreate themselves.
Regions	Nevada, Texas, and West Virginia.
Rates	$175–245 per man.

Metivta Retreats

Metivta is a Los Angeles center dedicated to the renewal of Jewish spirituality. Each year, the center hosts several three-day southern California retreats, plus a weeklong retreat in Santa Fe or a northern California redwoods park. A typical retreat day includes early morning group prayer, a postbreakfast meditation period, late morning and mid-afternoon workshops, an optional late afternoon class, and an evening program. Workshop topics include study of the lives and teachings of Jewish mystics, theater and dance, and arts and crafts.

The primary teachers are Rabbi Jonathan Omer-Man and Rabbi Judith HaLevy. The founder of Metivta, Rabbi Omer-Man appears as a central figure in the best-selling *Jew in the Lotus*. Metivta codirector Rabbi HaLevy has directed programs in theater, the arts, and Jewish education in Israel and Mexico City.

Address 2001 Barrington Avenue, Suite 106, Los Angeles, CA 90025
Phone (310) 477-5370. Fax (310) 477-7501.
Season Usually mid-July.
Programs 3- and 6-day experiential retreats on Jewish spirituality.
Regions California and New Mexico.
Rates 3-day retreat $250–350. 6-day retreat $650–750.

Miracles Retreats

The Miracles Community Network (MCN) hosts at least two annual weeklong retreats designed to inspire spiritual renewal. Each retreat is facilitated by MCN founder Paul Ferrini (also the editor of *Miracles* magazine) along with several guest presenters and musicians. A typical retreat day includes devotional singing and dancing, meditation and prayer, speaker presentations and small group discussions, various experiential exercises, plus free time to explore the area.

All facilitators and most participants are familiar with "A Course in Miracles" (ACIM), so presentations and discussions (on topics like forgiveness and relationships) tend to have an ACIM perspective. However, these are not ACIM study retreats, and no prior ACIM background is required.

Address   P.O. Box 181, South Deerfield, MA 01373
Phone   (413) 665-0555. Fax (413) 665-4565.
Season   Spring and summer.
Programs   7-day retreats designed to facilitate living the principles of "A Course in Miracles."
Regions   Spring retreat on Cape Cod. Late summer retreat in northern New Mexico.
Rates   Tuition $300–350. Room and board $345–580.

Nine Gates Training

Founded in 1985, Nine Gates Training is a two-part, eighteen-day program designed to empower participants by teaching them how to access and utilize the powers of the body's nine energy centers. The trainings address each center in sequence, working up from the feet through the crown of the head, with the first four centers covered in part 1 of the training and the other five centers covered in part 2.

Part 1 of the training, which takes nine days, is offered each year at two locations: in the spring at a private ranch in Sonoma County, California; in the summer at a country retreat in northern Illinois. Part 2, also nine days, unites the two groups from part 1 in mid-September at a spectacular high desert retreat near Joshua Tree, California. Each participant receives two manuals detailing the practices taught in the program. The trainings themselves generally have a high ratio of teachers to participants.

Dr. Gay Luce, the founder of Nine Gates, previously taught at the Mystery School of the well-known author Dr. Jean Houston and is the founder of SAGE, a program for growth and spiritual community among older people. Dr. Luce is recognized as a wise and compassionate teacher who has assembled a staff of Nine Gates teachers skilled in many traditions.

Address   437 Sausalito Street, Corte Madera, CA 94925
Phone   (415) 927-1677 or (800) 995-4459.
Season   Spring, summer, and early fall.

Programs   A 2-part, 18-day self-empowerment training drawing on the secrets of many spiritual traditions.

Regions   Part 1 in northern California and the Midwest. Part 2 in southern California.

Rates   Total tuition is $3,200–3,800, with partial scholarships available as needed. Meals and lodging are $700 for each part.

Omega Winter Programs

Each winter, the Omega Institute for Holistic Studies (see profile in the previous chapter) conducts weekend workshops similar to the programs at its Hudson River Valley summer camp. The three major winter program sites are the Phoenicia Pathwork Center in (see profile in previous chapter) the New York Catskills, Simpsonwood Center twenty-five miles north of Atlanta, Georgia, and Airlie Center estate in the Virginia countryside outside Washington, D.C. Each hosts eight to twelve workshops, often running two or three on the same weekend.

Omega has also offered anywhere from one to four winter workshops in such places as Monterey, California; northern New Mexico; and Clearwater and Saint Augustine, Florida. And as with Omega's huge summer program, most workshops are facilitated by well-known authors and teachers.

Address   Omega Institute for Holistic Studies, Rhinebeck, NY 12572

Phone   (914) 266-4444 or (800) 944-1001 (reservations). Fax (914) 266-4828.

Season   Late December through March.

Programs   Weekend workshops on a variety of personal growth subjects, from health and psychology to multicultural arts and spirituality.

Regions   Primarily the U.S. Northeast, Mid-Atlantic, and Southeast.

Rates   Workshop tuition generally $150–200 but in some cases as high as $495. Weekend lodging and meals $135–210.

Painting from the Source

Painting from the Source is "about painting purely for the joy of explo-ration and expression," explains artist and practicing psychotherapist Aviva Gold. Aviva hosts weekend and four-day workshops and retreats throughout the year at her New York residence—a Berkshires retreat with simple meals and overnight accommodations for eleven to fifteen people. In addition to painting, some weekends offer chi gung with a master instructor.

Primarily during the fall, winter, and spring months, Aviva also hosts four- to seven-day intensives in high desert regions of the Southwest and in the Caribbean. Regular Southwest painting sites are in northern New Mexico (twenty miles south of Santa Fe) and central Arizona (near Sedona). Caribbean sites have included Costa Rica, Puerto Rico, and Belize.

Address   179 Mallory Road, Ghent, NY 12075
Phone   (518) 392-2631 (also accepts fax). Please call before visit-ing.
Season   Throughout the year.
Programs   Weekend and 4- to 7-day workshops, retreats, and inten-sives on "self-evolution through creative expression" in painting and drawing.
Regions   The New York Berkshires, the U.S. Southwest, and the Caribbean.
Rates   Weekend workshop $260–275. 4-day New York retreat $450. 4- to 7-day Southwest intensives $625–905. 7-day Caribbean intensive $1,200. Rates include all art materials, room, and board.

Pilgrim Warrior Training

This physically and emotionally intense women's empowerment pro-gram includes meditation, dance, ritual, psychodrama, high and low ropes courses, communication skills, one-day vision quest, shield mak-ing, and goal setting. A typical day begins at 7 A.M. with a sacred circle meeting. Programs run from 9 A.M. to 9:30 P.M. with two-hour breaks for meals. Except in the case of special dietary needs, meals are vegetarian.

Pilgrim Warrior Training was founded in 1985 as Sandra Boston de Sylvia's vision quest–inspired gift to society. Sandra is a licensed communication skills instructor, social change activist, feminist therapist, and parent of three sons. Each training, limited to ten trainees, is led by Sandra and PWT graduates. The tasks of maintaining community are shared among all participants. The facilities are primitive campsites or rustic cabins in a forest setting.

Address	Full Moon Rising, 15 Abbott Street, Greenfield, MA 01301
Phone	(413) 774-5952
Season	April through September.
Programs	4 annual, 8-day women's empowerment trainings.
Regions	Western Massachusetts (2 trainings), Virginia, and Ohio.
Rates	Determined by each woman within group discussion on "what does economic justice look like in this group?" Individual pledges range from $150 to $2,500. Time payments and barter are possible.

Quantum Shift Retreats

Eight-day retreats designed to enable people to move beyond self-limiting beliefs and behavior into an inner space where self-love and acceptance naturally find expression in loving and accepting others. Each retreat is conducted in a secluded, tranquil, and naturally beautiful place, with afternoons free to explore and enjoy the environment. Workshop sessions are held in the mornings and evenings. There are also daily stretching and meditation periods plus gourmet vegetarian meals.

The retreats are codirected by Joy Nelson and Robert Frey. Joy is a chiropractor; Robert is a therapist. Both are authors, have considerable workshop leadership experience, and are musically gifted (Joy as a dancer and Robert as a singer/songwriter). The "Quantum Shift" process includes guided inner journeys; powerful music, movement, and vocal expression; heartfelt interactive communications; and creative group dynamics.

Address   10 Millay Place, Mill Valley, CA 94941
Phone   (415) 472-4620 or (800) 573-0528
Season   Throughout the year.
Programs   8-day transformative retreats/vacations.
Regions   Maui, Hawaii; Sedona, Arizona; and northern California Redwoods.
Rates $1,000–1,200; in Arizona $800–900 (not including lodging).

Retreats with Doug and Naomi Moseley

Doug and Naomi Moseley host residential workshops at two locations: in the spring and fall at their 5,000-square-foot home at the base of the Taos mountains; in the summer at their lakeside British Columbia retreat center (accommodating up to sixteen overnight guests).

The Moseleys' specialty is bringing dark (and often denied) sides of self into conscious awareness and acceptance. They are the authors of *Dancing in the Dark—The Shadow Side of Personal Relationships*, a book that explores the underbelly of romantic love and how men and women tend to defend against deeper intimacy.

Address   Doug and Naomi Moseley, 425-216M Pueblo Norte, Taos, NM 87571
Phone   (505) 776-1074 or (800) 843-5240. Fax (505) 776-5658. No visits without prior arrangement.
Season   Spring through fall.
Programs   5- and 6-day workshops on discovering and working with denied feelings.
Regions   New Mexico and British Columbia.
Rates   5-day workshop: couples $995. 6-day workshop: singles $795, couples $1,250.

Spirit Journeys

A weekend workshop on "Journey into Wholeness, Facing HIV" is the signature offering of Spirit Journeys, founded by David Frechter to address the spiritual and emotional healing needs of gay men. As with other branches of the men's movement, Spirit Journeys' gatherings include sharing of thoughts, feelings, and celebration in a nonjudgmental environment. Group size ranges from twelve to twenty-six men.

David is often joined by other facilitators appropriate for the program, such as a Navajo guide during a weeklong "Southwest Quest." Other events include frequent "Journey into Ourselves" weekends, an annual trip on the Rio Grande, and an annual summer retreat at Bohdi Mandala Zen Center and hot mineral springs in the mountains of New Mexico.

Address	P.O. Box 5307, Santa Fe, NM 87502
Phone	(505) 351-4004. Fax (505) 351-4999.
Season	Throughout the year.
Programs	Weekend workshops, 4- to 7-day retreats, and 7- to 10-day outdoor adventures fostering self-acceptance among homosexual men.
Regions	Weekend retreats in or near major metro areas around the country. Retreats and outdoor adventures generally in the Southwest.
Rates	Weekend $365–395. 5-day retreat $750. 7- or 8-day adventure $895.

Tai Chi in Paradise

The Pacific School of Tai Chi conducts annual retreats in Costa Rica, Hawaii, and far northern California. The Costa Rica site is a beachside Caribbean lodge bordered by primitive rain forests. The Hawaii site is Kalani Honua, a luxurious oceanside retreat center near black sand beaches and Volcanoes National Park. The northern California site is the rustic Stewart Hot Springs resort near the base of majestic Mount Shasta. At all three sites, accommodations are shared and meals are gourmet vegetarian.

Each retreat includes at least seven hours of daily instruction for all levels (beginner, intermediate, and advanced). Areas covered are tai chi energetics and forms, applied tai chi philosophy, push hands, and chi gung (energy work), to name a few. The lead instructor is Chris Luth, a former American tai chi forms champion and a teacher with a warm style.

Address	P.O. Box 962, Solana Beach, CA 92075
Phone	(619) 259-1396
Season	February, late June, and mid-August.
Programs	6- to 8-day tai chi retreats.
Regions	Costa Rica, Hawaii, and far northern California.
Rates	8-day Costa Rica retreat $1,925, including rain forest and river tours plus round-trip airfare from southwestern U.S. cities. 6-day Hawaii and 6-day Mount Shasta retreats each $650.

3HO Camps

3HO was established in 1969 by Yogi Bhajan "to train teachers, not to collect disciples," in kundalini yoga, meditation, and the yogic lifestyle of India's 500-year-old Sikh tradition. Distinctive in their traditional white dress and turbans, the Sikhs respect every individual's right to choose his or her own spiritual path.

Every year, 3HO (short for "The Healthy, Happy, Holy Organization") hosts weeklong solstice camps. "Summer Solstice Sadhana" is pitched among the pines and piñons of a mountaintop campsite in the northern desert of New Mexico. "Winter Solstice Sadhana" is set in the Lake Wales region of north-central Florida. Both solstice camps include three-day community practice of energy-building Kriya meditations (known as "white tantric yoga"). There is also an annual five-week northern New Mexico "Khalsa Women's Training Camp," which includes sweat lodge purification, herbal mud bath treatments, plus weekend transportation to Santa Fe.

At all camps, there are classes and talks (often given by Yogi Bhajan himself) on yoga, yogic psychology and healing, and Sikh spiritual practice. There are also activities for youths and children (just girls at the women's camp). Campers live simply in their own tents with the basic amenities of hot water, showers, and electrical outlets. The food is spicy vegetarian, and everyone contributes a small amount of seva (service).

Address P.O. Box 351149, Los Angeles, CA 90035
Phone   (310) 553-2972. Fax (310) 557-8414.
Season   Summer and winter.
Programs Weeklong summer and winter solstice camps. 5-week summer women's camp. Focus on yoga, meditation, and conscious living.
Regions Northern New Mexico and Florida.
Rates   1 week $310–375. 5 weeks $1,295–1,480. Substantial discounts for children and teenagers.

Vipassana Meditation Centers

The four major North American Vipassana Meditation Centers (VMCs) are Vipassana Meditation Center (Shelburne Falls, Massachusetts), California Vipassana Center (North Fork, California), Northwest Vipassana Center (Ethel, Washington), and Southwest Vipassana Meditation Center (Dallas, Texas). The Massachusetts and California centers each conduct at least twenty meditation courses each year. Course offerings in Washington and Texas are less frequent.

Virtually all VMC meditation courses are ten days long, and all are taught by instructors trained by S. N. Goenka, a Burmese native (now residing in India) who has taught meditation for more than twenty-five years. Students are asked to adhere to the daily schedule. Each day begins with a wake-up bell at 4 A.M. and ends with lights out at 9:30 P.M. During the day, group and individual sitting meditation periods span at least ten hours. Every evening, students watch a videotape of S. N. Goenka's meditation teachings.

VMC accommodations are generally quite simple. Meals are also simple—vegetarian breakfast and lunch plus an evening tea. New students may take fruit with their tea. All students observe silence except during teacher interviews and evening question-and-answer periods.

Address VMC, P.O. Box 24, Shelburne Falls, MA 01370
California VMC, P.O. Box 1167, North Fork, CA 93643
Northwest VMC, P.O. Box 345, Ethel, WA 98542
Texas VMC c/o Catheryn Lacey, P.O. Box 190248, Dallas, TX 75219
Phone   Massachusetts (413) 625-2160. California (209) 877-4386.

Washington (360) 978-5434. Texas (214) 521-5258. No visits
without prior arrangement.

Season Year-round.
Programs Rigorous, 10-day guided Vipassana meditation retreats.
Regions Northwestern Massachusetts, central California, southwestern Washington, and northeastern Texas.
Rates Instruction, food, and lodging are financed solely by donations from people who have completed at least one 10-day course.

Woman Within

Woman Within conducts two-and-a-half-day self-empowerment workshops for women and committed couples. The workshops' experimential therapies include meditations, visualizations, movement, group and two-person exercises, artistic self-expression, and journal writing. At most workshops, the number of participants is exceeded by the number of staff members, who are workshop graduates with additional training.

Except for "Women Empowering Women" (nonresidential programs conducted at hotels), most Women Within workshops are held at residential (and often quite rustic) country retreats. "Woman Within" initiation weekends are a prerequisite for "Women Empowering Women," "Woman Quest" (mini–vision quest), and "Healing the Wounds of Shame" (also for women) weekends. "Women Healing Incest" and couples weekends are open to all.

Address 7186 Driftwood Drive, Fenton, MI 48430
Phone (810) 750-7227. Fax (810) 750-8386.
Season Year-round.
Programs 2½-day empowerment workshops for women and committed couples.
Regions California, Minnesota, Ontario, Texas, Washington, D.C., Wisconsin. Also in England.
Rates Couples weekend $795 per couple. Women's weekend: residential $395–600, nonresidential $225.

UNITED STATES AND ABROAD

Ammachi Retreats

Born in 1953 in a humble household in southern India, Sudhamani displayed remarkable charity, love, and devotion from her earliest days. During her twenties, she withdrew into a state of bliss after receiving a vision of the Divine Mother. But one day she heard a voice within her say: "It is to give solace to suffering humanity that you have come into this world and not merely for enjoying Divine Bliss. Therefore, worship me by showing mankind the way back to me." Since then, Sudhamani has become known as Mata Amritanandamayi, "Ammachi" for short, "the Divine Mother" in English.

Each summer since 1987, Ammachi has conducted tours of the United States and Europe. The U.S. tour includes weekend retreats in Washington state, northern and southern California, and New England. Each retreat includes devotional singing and meditation, classes on Ammachi's teachings and India's ancient spiritual texts, work periods, darshan (where Ammachi hugs and comforts all who come to her), and Devi Bhava (a darshan where Ammachi dresses as the Divine Mother and showers flowers on all). In the presence of a Great Soul, retreatants usually find that spiritual practice blossoms.

When not on tour or visiting her various Indian service projects, Ammachi lives (along with many other full-time residents and guests) at her ashram on the small tropical island of her birth. All are welcome there, as well as at Ammachi's U.S. ashram in the San Francisco Bay area. The ashrams' daily schedules are similar to the schedule at the weekend retreats.

Address   M.A. Center, P.O. Box 613, San Ramon, CA 94583
Phone   (510) 537-9417. Fax (510) 889-8585.
Season   Regional retreats during the summer. Ashrams open year-round.
Programs   Regional weekend retreats and ashram stays of unlimited duration.

Regions   Retreats on the U.S. West Coast, in New England, and in Europe. Ashrams in southern India and the San Francisco Bay area.

Rates   Weekend retreat $150–200. U.S. ashram visit $20–25 per night or $450 per month. India ashram visits on a donation basis.

Dance of the Deer Foundation

This foundation was created in 1979 by Brant Secunda, who completed a twelve-year apprenticeship in Mexico's Sierra Madre Mountains with the late Huichol shaman don Jose Matsuwa. The Huichols are believed to be the last North American tribe to have maintained their pre-Columbian traditions. The foundation's purpose is to keep those traditions alive.

Dance of the Deer's annual events generally include a summer solstice weekend in the Catskill Mountains, a five-day Mount Shasta pilgrimage, an eight-day event at Montana's Feathered Pipe Ranch (profiled in the preceding chapter), a six-day seminar in the Bavarian Alps, a sixteen-day spring retreat in central Europe, and a ten-day pilgrimage and seminar near Puerto Vallarta on Mexico's Pacific coast. Other programs have included a ten-day Alaska retreat.

Participants experience vision quests, Huichol ceremonies, and the sacred Dance of the Deer. They learn shamanic health and healing practices, including use of dreams for life guidance and empowerment. They also learn how to bring the life-balancing power of sacred places into their hearts.

Address   P.O. Box 699, Soquel, CA 95073

Phone   (408) 475-9560. Fax (408) 475-1860.

Season   May through November.

Programs   Experiential shamanism seminars and pilgrimages to places of great natural beauty and spiritual power.

Regions   Central-western Mexico, the United States (Alaska, California, Montana, and New York), and Europe (southern France, southern Germany, or northern Italy).

Rates   Weekend $225. 5- or 6-day program $350–500. 8-day event

$999. 10-day pilgrimage and seminar $1,199–1,299. 16-day retreat $1,400.

Global Fitness Adventures

These adventures are designed to be "catalysts to an awakening" that are "part stress management, part nutrition, and wholly vacation," says Kristina Hurrell, a former spa-resort physical fitness director, and former top European fashion model, actress, and photographer. Kristina carefully chooses vacation spots with a "fresh, clean, tranquilizing beauty true to the promise of vibrant health and adventure."

A Global Fitness day begins with a yoga/stretch class and meditation before breakfast. The rest of the morning and early afternoon are dedicated to an eight- to eighteen-mile hike, snowshoe, or cross-country skiing outing. After a midafternoon massage, there is free time for such leisure activities as fishing, swimming, Jacuzzi, and siesta. Dinner is preceded by muscle toning and stretch classes. Evening activities include sweat lodge, drumming and dance, visualizations, and holistic health lectures.

A co-leader on many Global Fitness Adventures (particularly those at Aspen) is Rob Krakovitz, M.D., an authority on detoxification techniques, high-energy personal diets, and nutritional supplements. Global Fitness meals are spa cuisine (vegetarian with some fish), with full vegetarian options.

Address   P.O. Box 1390, Aspen, CO 81612
Phone   (303) 927-9593 or (800) 488-8747. Fax (303) 927-4793.
Season   Year-round.
Programs   1-, 2-, and 3-week vacations designed to extend physical limits, de-stress body and mind, and invite greater peace and joy into life.
Regions   Most frequent vacation sites: Aspen, Colorado; Sedona, Arizona; and Santa Barbara, California. Other recent sites: Bali; Bhutan and Nepal; Dominica, Caribbean; Italy; Kenya; Peru.
Rates   7- and 8-day vacations $1,975–2,300. 13- and 15-day vacations $3,475–4,850. 21-day vacation $5,600+. Rates include

all lodging, meals, massage, classes, activities, sightseeing arrangements, fitness evaluation, and home maintenance program. Airfare not included.

International Center for the Dances of Universal Peace

Inspired by the late Samuel Lewis, an American Sufi teacher, the Dances of Universal Peace are a synthesis of folk art and spiritual practice. From "Sufi Sam's" initial body of about fifty dances, the collection has grown over the past twenty years to more than 500 dances drawn from a rich multitude of spiritual traditions. Now performed around the world, the dances are celebrated every month by forty to sixty grassroots groups in the United States alone.

The International Center for the Dances of Universal Peace sponsors four annual weeklong dance camps open to beginners: the late March "Spring Renewal in the Caribbean," the late March "North Pacific Dance Camp" in Washington or Oregon, the early July "Midwest Dance Camp" in Wisconsin or Minnesota, and the mid-August "East Coast Dance Camp" in New England. Meals are vegetarian. And all camp teachers are members of the Dances' Mentor Teacher Guild.

Other annual center-sponsored events include a three-week pilgrimage to Poland or the Middle East plus quarterly weekend dance retreats in Pescadero, California. Annual center-cosponsored events include two weeklong midsummer events: "Mendocino Sufi Camp" and "Sam's Camp" (for teaching the art of leading the dances) at New Mexico's Lama Foundation. All Universal Peace dance camps and retreats are described in the center's annual "Whole Dance Catalog."

Address   International Center for the Dances of Universal Peace, 444 N.E. Ravenna Boulevard, Suite 306, Seattle, WA 98115

Phone   (206) 522-4353

Season   Year-round but primarily spring through fall.

Programs   Dance camps and dance leader trainings. Also pilgrimages.

Regions   Primarily California, the Pacific Northwest, the upper Midwest, the Northeast, and the Caribbean. Also Europe.

Rates   3-week European pilgrimage $1,675–1,875. Weekend $80–100. Weeklong dance camps $410–640.

Person Centered Expressive Arts Therapy

The Person Centered Expressive Therapy Institute (PCETI) is directed by Natalie Rogers, an author, psychotherapist, and daughter of humanistic psychologist Carl Rogers. PCETI offers residential programs in expressive arts therapy. Roughly 60 percent of program attendees come for the professional training. Others attend for the personal therapeutic value of the work.

The level 1 program focuses on the use of the expressive arts—movement, painting, writing, and sound—in a nonjudgmental, person-centered environment. Level 2 extends the experience to include relationship and community. Level 3 leads to a deeper understanding of body and psyche. Level 4 is an internship in facilitating the lower levels. Except for level 4, attendance at the programs is limited to no more than twenty to twenty-five participants, with a participant-to-staff ratio of four to one.

All levels are offered at Isis Oasis, a ten-acre retreat center near hot springs, redwood forests, and the Pacific coast, one and a half hours north of San Francisco. Levels 1, 2, and 4 are also offered at Fawcett Mill Fields, a beautiful converted mill in northern England's scenic Lake District. Programs are also offered in New York State (at Omega Institute for Holistic Studies—see profile in previous chapter), in Moscow (Russia), and sometimes in Guadalajara.

Address	Person Centered Expressive Therapy Institute, P.O. Box 6518, Santa Rosa, CA 95406
Phone	(707) 526-4006 or (800) 477-2384.
Season	No set season; times vary throughout the year.
Programs	6-, 9-, and 10-day level 1, 2, and 3 experiential expressive arts trainings. Levels 1 and 2 are prerequisites for level 3.
Regions	Northern California, southeastern New York State, England's Lake District, Russia, and Mexico.
Rates	United States: level 1 $685–920, level 2 $1,375–1,495, level 3 $1,605. United Kingdom: level 1 £540, level 2 £720, level 3 £900. All prices include tuition, lodging, meals, and materials.

Yoga/Macrobiotic Vacations

For at least a decade, Karin Stephan has been hosting Iyengar yoga vacations. Karin's annual "Cape Experience" offers one-week vacation options over a five-week midsummer period. Her annual September Portugal vacation offers one- and two-week options. Annual one-week vacations are held on Sanibel Island, Florida, in early December and on St. Lucia in the Caribbean in early spring. From time to time, Karin also hosts yoga/ski vacations.

Karin is a student of B. K. S. Iyengar and co-director of B. K. S. Iyengar Yoga Center in Somerville, Massachusetts. She is joined at each yoga vacation by other well-known Iyengar yoga teachers. The usual daily schedule is two hours in the morning and one and a half hours (two hours on weekends) in the late afternoon. This gives vacationers plenty of time to enjoy the area, which offers close access to oceanside beaches (except in the case of yoga/ski vacations).

Other elements of a Yoga/Macrobiotic Vacation include two daily macrobiotic meals plus evening lectures or discussions on topics like "Yoga and Nutrition" and "How to Live a Healthy Lifestyle." At the Cape Cod and Sanibel Island vacations, optional services include private yoga therapy, macrobiotic cooking classes, shiatsu and other massage, ginger compresses, and feng shui consultations.

Address	5 Frost Street, Cambridge, MA 02140
Phone	(617) 497-0218
Season	Year-round.
Programs	Mostly 5-day, 7-day, and weekend yoga vacations.
Regions	Cape Cod, west coast of Florida, Caribbean, and Portugal.
Rates	5-day Cape Cod or 7-day Sanibel Island $850–910, weekend at either place $330–360. 7-day Caribbean $1,150–1,300. Portugal: 1 week $550–650, 2 weeks $1,000–1,200.

Yoga Retreats with Elise Miller

Elise Miller organizes weeklong and weekend Iyengar yoga retreats in Mexico and the western United States. At each retreat, yoga sessions are held in the early morning and late afternoon. This allows vacationers plenty of time to rest or to enjoy such activities as fishing, horseback riding, hiking, and swimming. Packages generally include three meals, or breakfast and a dinner option, with a menu oriented toward fruits, vegetables, and fish.

Weeklong spring and summer retreats are conducted at the Hotel Cabo San Lucas Resort in Baja, Mexico, and Hana-Maui beachside hotel in Maui, Hawaii. Winter and fall weekend retreats are held in northern California at the San Francisco Bay Area's Marianist Retreat Center and Sonoma's Westerbeke Ranch. Elise has also led weeklong yoga retreats in the Rocky Mountains area.

Elise is a certified Iyengar yoga teacher and hypnotherapist with an expertise in treating back problems and other sports-related injuries. Her Maui retreat is co-led by Lolly Font, director of the California Yoga Center. At other retreats, Elise often teams up with other nationally known Iyengar yoga instructors.

Address	Elise B. Miller Associates, 1081 Moreno Avenue, Palo Alto, CA 94303
Phone	(415) 493-1254. Fax (415) 857-0925.
Season	March through November.
Programs	Weeklong and weekend retreats devoted to Iyengar-style hatha yoga.
Regions	Mexico, Hawaii, California, and Rocky Mountains.
Rates	Weeklong retreat $1,190–1,450, weekend $340. Transportation to and from retreat site is not included.

JOURNEYS TO
DISTANT PLACES

$\mathscr{T}$his chapter profiles twenty-eight organizations that lead trips and tours with a significant spiritual, personal growth, or healing orientation. Profiles of organizations specializing in particular regions are arranged in alphabetical order under "Asia," "Europe," "North America," "Ocean Cruises," and "South America." Those that cover more than one continent are listed under "Two or More Continents."

All trip prices include regional ground transportation, accommodations, most meals, and fees for any special cultural or spiritual events. The United States is the point of departure and return for all trips that include international airfare.

In most cases, a participant wishing free time in a foreign country before or after the tour may arrange to pay for only the land portion of a journey. In such cases, a traveler books his or her own flight and joins the group in the city that is the trip's initial destination.

ASIA

Danu Enterprises

Danu Enterprises specializes in tours of Bali. Danu's most frequent offering is "Healing Arts of Bali," which includes meetings with traditional healers, trance purification ceremonies, Balinese music and dance performances, instruction in herbal medicine, massages by Balinese healers, body revitalization experiences, and evening discussions. Danu's "Traditional and Modern Medicine in Bali" explores herbal medicine, the use of trance in psychotherapy, and Bali's successful family planning system.

Danu tours are organized and led by the husband-and-wife team of Made Surya and Judy Slattum, who live in Bali six months each year. The son of a Bali Hindu priest, Made performs and teaches mask dance in California. Judy is author of the book *Masks of Bali: Spirits of an Ancient Drama* and has been leading Bali tours since 1979.

Address   313 McCormick Avenue, Capitola, CA 95010
Phone   (408) 476-0543 (also accepts fax).
Season   January through March, July through September.
Programs   14- to 20-day arts, healing arts, and traditional and modern medicine trips.
Regions   Bali.
Rates   Samples: "Healing Arts" $2,900–3,000. "Traditional and Modern Medicine in Bali," $2,895–3,145. All rates include international airfare.

In the Footsteps of the Buddha

A pilgrimage to India and Nepal "in the footsteps of the Buddha" is usually made twice each year under the leadership of Shantum Seth, who was brought up in India, studied and worked for twelve years in Britain and the United States, and now coordinates a UN Artisan Development Program in south Asia. Shantum organized his first "in the footsteps" pilgrimage in 1988 for his teacher, Vietnamese Zen master Thich Nhat Hanh, who observes that "Shantum's knowledge, insight, and humor bring joy to those journeying with him."

All In the Footsteps pilgrimages follow the same route, taking time along the way to get to know India and its major sacred Buddhist sites. There is no travel on "retreat schedule" days, which are set aside for the practice of mindfulness and meditation, as well as for discussion or just time alone. This is all in keeping with Shantum's stated purpose to "demystify Buddhism—to bring the Buddha alive, as a human being, into people's lives and practice."

Address	Aura Wright, Suite 207, 3439 NE Sandy Boulevard, Portland, OR 97232
Phone	(503) 335-0794. Fax (503) 288-1558.
Season	February and late December.
Programs	16- and 21-day pilgrimages retracing the life journey of Prince Siddhartha Gautama, who later became known as "the Buddha."
Regions	India and Nepal.
Rates	Each trip $3,100–3,600, not including international airfare.

Insight Travel

Based on the ancient view of pilgrimage as a transformative experience, each trip to Asia conducted by Insight Travel includes background lectures, opportunities to meet with Buddhist and Hindu teachers, optional daily group meditation, and free time for individual explorations. Trip leaders are carefully selected for their general knowledge of south-central Asian cultures, their intense interest in Asian religions, and their ability to share knowledge.

In most years, trips are made to Bhutan, "Realm of Padmasambhava"; India and Nepal, "Way of the Buddha"; Dharamsala, "Himalayan Refuge"; Mount Kailas, "Center of the Mandala"; and Ladakh, "Traditional Tibet in India." Group size is usually six to ten participants. Round-trip airfare is not included, so participants often opt to extend their stays—sometimes combining two Insight Travel tours.

Address   602 South High Street, Yellow Springs, OH 45387
Phone   (800) 688-9851 or (513) 767-1102.
Season   January through October.
Programs 2- to 4-week pilgrimages to traditional Buddhist and Hindu sites.
Regions   South-central Asia.
Rates   Samples: 2-week trip $2,600, 3-week trip $3,250–4,850, 1-month trip $5,950. Prices include air transport within Asia.

Kathmandu Valley Tours

These tours are designed to immerse travelers in the Buddhist and Hindu cultures of Nepal, northern India, and Tibet. Trips include visiting temples and other sacred sites, getting to know local families, and enjoying the heroic scale and exuberance of religious festivals, particularly in Tibet. Most trips begin or end in the mystical power spot of Nepal's Kathmandu Valley. Optional tour extensions include a Buddhist meditation course at Kathmandu's Kopan Monastery, Nepal trekking trips, and an eight-day excursion into Tibet.

Tour leaders are Cilla Brady and Namgyel. Cilla is an artist, a former Kathmandu resident, and a longtime Buddhist who feels most at home in settings (such as Kathmandu Valley) where Hindu and Buddhist cultures are intertwined. Known for his sense of humor, Namgyel is a native Australian and former Tibetan Buddhist monk who is now a guide based in Delhi, India. Unique to Kathmandu Valley Tours is a tour of Thailand that includes a ten-day meditation retreat on an island in the Gulf of Siam.

Address   P.O. Box 873, Bolinas, CA 94924
Phone   (415) 868-0285. Fax (415) 868-9766.
Season   Throughout the year.
Programs 14- to 28-day tours focusing on Buddhist and Hindu culture, festivals, and spiritual practice.
Regions   Nepal, India, Tibet, and Thailand.
Rates   Each trip $2,690–4,000, including round-trip airfare from West Coast cities. Sample tour extension: $100–140 for 7- to 10-day meditation course at Kopan Monastery.

Sai Ram

While on pilgrimage to India in 1977, Dr. Wilma Bronkey was taken aside by Sai Baba and told "you will lead tours and you will be very good at it." As director of a residential care facility for older people, Dr. Bronkey had not previously thought of leading trips. But since then she has regularly led pilgrimages to the abode of Sai Baba, India's most widely known and loved living saint.

Since he was a child, Sai Baba has repeatedly performed miraculous healings and object materializations. He has also inspired many books plus hundreds of Indian clinics and schools, where values are learned by studying the lives of the saints of all religions. Worshiped by millions as God incarnate, Sai Baba spends most of the year at his birthplace— now a large south-central ashram known as Prasanthi Nilayam (Abode of Great Peace).

Sometimes while en route to India, Dr. Bronkey's tours stop in the Philippines to visit the "psychic surgeons," whose miraculous physical healing techniques resemble those of Sai Baba. All tours spend at least ten days at Sai Baba's abode. Daily activities include early morning devotional worship, morning and afternoon darshan (viewing of the saint), plus community chanting. After exploring west and central India, each tour group departs from Delhi.

Address	Enchanted Acres, 1151 Summit Loop, Grants Pass, OR 97527
Phone	(503) 479-9066
Season	Summer (between April and August) and winter (December/January).
Programs	Twice yearly, 2½- to 4-week pilgrimage to Sai Baba's ashram. Includes visits to Bangalore, Bombay, Aurangabad, Jaipur, Agra, and Delhi.
Regions	South-central, western, and central India. Stops in Singapore or Taipei and Hong Kong on way to and from U.S. West Coast.
Rates	3-week trip $1,800–1,950, including round-trip airfare from San Francisco.

Yoga in Bali

This vacation and study tour explores a land where art is so much a part of the culture as to be a way of life. Each tour group spends five nights by the ocean at an ashram for orientation to Bali's food, language, and culture. The group then spends one week in Ubud, Bali's cultural center. Ubud accommodations are Balinese bungalows set among tropical gardens, a swimming pool, and an open-air yoga pavilion.

Each trip includes daily yoga classes with trip leader Ann Barros, a certified yoga instructor who has studied in India with B. K. S. Iyengar. Ann also has a strong dance background plus interests in art, music, yoga, and Hindu guidance. She has led Yoga in Bali tours each year since 1985.

Address   Ann Barros, 341 26th Avenue, Santa Cruz, CA 95062
Phone   (408) 475-8738
Season   February and July.
Programs 18-day yoga vacation and study tours.
Regions   Bali.
Rates $2,900, including round-trip airfare from California. Does not include lunch or dinner during week in Ubud.

EUROPE

AnaTours

AnaTours specializes in tours of Asia Minor, focusing on the ancient Great Goddess religion of this region. The tour guide and lecturer is Dr. Resit Ergener, author of *Anatolia, Land of the Mother Goddess*. Dr. Ergener is also a professional tour guide and a professor at Bosporus University in Istanbul, where each tour starts and ends.

Each tour includes visits to famous archaeological sites, holy temples and sacred caves, superb museums, and spectacular natural scenery. Tour participants often choose to create and perform individual and group rituals to honor the spirit within and the ancient focal points of Goddess power. Tours also include opportunities for swimming in the Gulf of Antalya, a Turkish bath, and a hot springs stop.

Address 315 Crestview Drive, Santa Clara, CA 95050
Phone (408) 246-7646 (also accepts fax).
Season Late spring, summer, and winter.
Programs 10- to 17-day "On the Trail of the Great Goddess" tours. Most are open to all, but many are for women only.
Regions Turkey.
Rates Each trip $1,590–2,500, excluding international airfare.

Goddess Pilgrimage Tours

Women's trips to Crete are the specialty of Goddess Pilgrimage Tours, led by Jana Ruble and Carol Christ, Ph.D. Jana is a professional cellist with more than twenty years of experience in women's groups. Carol is a permanent resident of Greece, a retired professor of religious studies (at Harvard Divinity School in Cambridge, Massachusetts, and the California Institute of Integral Studies in San Francisco), and the author of many books (including *Odyssey with the Goddess: A Spiritual Quest in Crete*).

Trip participants explore ancient sacred sites such as Knossos, visit museums, descend into caves, hike in the mountains, and stay in small villages. There are opportunities to meet the villagers, dance to Cretan music, and to dine on freshly caught fish accompanied by locally made wine. Each trip is limited to fifteen women, who should be in condition for rigorous hiking.

Address 1306 Crestview Drive, Blacksburg, VA 24060
Phone (540) 951-3070 (also accepts fax).
Season Spring and fall.
Programs 17-day Goddess pilgrimage tours for women only.
Regions Crete.
Rates $2,950, including round-trip airfare from New York City.

Medugorje Pilgrimages

On June 25, 1981, in the small mountain village of Medugorje, Herzegovina, an apparition identifying herself as "Blessed Virgin Mary, Queen of Peace," appeared and spoke to six children. She has continued to appear to these young people, now in their twenties, with the message that "God exists. He is the fullness of life, and to enjoy this fullness and obtain peace, you must return to God" through prayer, fasting, and penance.

Since the apparition's first appearance, millions of pilgrims have gone to Medugorje. Some villagers and pilgrims notice rays of light when Mary appears daily to the original visionaries. Most pilgrims feel a deeply peaceful, healing presence. Many have reported spiritual, emotional, psychological, or even physical healings.

Halted for a time by the civil war in the former Yugoslavia, the pilgrimages to Medugorje conducted by the Center for Peace have now resumed. The Center for Peace was founded by American lay Catholics to serve as a conduit to the United States for the messages given to the visionaries by the apparition. The center's Medugorje pilgrims (including many non-Catholics) stay as guests with local families who provide breakfast and dinner. They also meet with the visionaries and Father Jozo Zorko, a Medugorje parish priest recognized by "Blessed Mary, Queen of Peace," as "a living saint."

Address   Center for Peace, P.O. Box 1425, Concord, MA 01742

Phone   (508) 371-1235. Fax (508) 369-4472.

Season   Throughout the year, with special trips for June anniversary of first appearance and early December Feast of Immaculate Conception.

Programs   9-day pilgrimages to site of ongoing Marian apparitions.

Regions   A small village in a primitive mountainous region of Herzegovina, one of the nations liberated by the Yugoslavian civil war.

Rates   Pilgrimage $1,090–1,390. Includes food, lodging, ground transportation, and round-trip airfare from Boston or New York.

NORTH AMERICA

Discovery Passages

Since 1981, Discovery Passages has offered tours led by David Brandstein, a professor of folklore, anthropology, and Native American studies. Annual passages include explorations of the lifeways, history and traditions, arts and crafts, and current concerns of the Hopi, Navajo, Apache, Pueblo, and other Native American peoples. Often co-led by Native Americans, most trips include visits with Native American families and participation in tribal ceremonies.

While no previous outdoor experience is necessary, the tours include hiking, rafting, and packing and riding horses to experience the land more fully. Accommodations are generally at national, state, or private campsites, with Discovery Passages providing all equipment except sleeping bags. Most meals are prepared outdoors in chuckwagon style with an emphasis on local cuisine. Long-distance land travel is usually by van, though some trips include river or sea excursions.

Address	P.O. Box 630, 1161 Elk Trail, Prescott, AZ 86303
Phone	(520) 717-0519
Season	April through September.
Programs	3- to 14-day journeys that explore the "spirit of place" by living simply on the land among Native American peoples.
Regions	U.S. Southwest and northern plains.
Rates	Samples: 3-day "White Mountain Apache Connection" $250, 6-day "Hopi Land" $400, 14-day "Rio Grande Pueblos" $1,350.

OCEAN CRUISES

Dreamtime Cruises

The specialty of Dreamtime Cruises is intuition, personal growth, and holistic health seminars and workshops at sea—on world-class cruise ships with beautiful staterooms, abundant shipboard service, and large windows opening onto breathtaking ocean vistas. The relaxed shipboard atmosphere is a wonderful environment for making new friends, and roommates are intuitively matched by Dreamtime owner Dianne Billings.

The Intuition Cruise is an integrated and comprehensive program of intuition development techniques such as dolphin communication, dreamwork, breathwork and stress reduction, divination tools, free trials of inner guidance systems, and intuitive stock market and career choices. It is also a chance to socialize with dozens of leaders in the field of conscious living. Shipboard experts include well-known authors, magazine editors, dream researchers, intuitive counselors, and parapsychologists. "Go with the flow" is the attitude of Intuition Cruise director Peter Einstein, a former advertising creative director now living his vision.

Holistic health cruises include seminars and workshops with leading innovators on natural health and alternative medicine, usually with a focus on reiki, free massages, aromatherapy, hypnotherapy, and low-fat and vegetarian cuisine. All Dreamtime cruises offer daily yoga and meditation plus such standard cruise features as a health club and nightly entertainment. Usually booked to capacity, each cruise accommodates up to 200 guests.

Address   3312 Buffam Place, Casselberry, FL 32707
Phone   (407) 695-1467 or (800) 787-8785. Fax (407) 695-8265.
Season   Throughout the year.
Programs   7- to 10-day intuition, personal growth, and holistic health cruises.

Regions   Caribbean, Bermuda, Hawaii, Europe, and south coastal Alaska.

Rates   Prices begin at $1,000 and go up from there, depending on the cruise, the ship, and the type of cabin.

SOUTH AMERICA

Earth Dream Alliance

This nonprofit organization is dedicated to conserving forests and to preserving ancient shamanic healing traditions. Earth Dream Alliance (EDA) currently owns more than 600 acres of virgin cloud forest in the Andes of northwestern Ecuador, where it intends to establish shamanic learning centers. In the meantime, contact with shamans is facilitated by experienced trip leaders.

During EDA's three or four annual trips to Ecuador, tour members stay at a bed-and-breakfast while in the Andes and with indigenous families while in the Amazon. The Andes cloud forest visits focus primarily on the remarkable biodiversity of that region. The itinerary also includes a hot springs stop and time spent with native shamans. Rain forest visits are a total immersion experience in the healing, hunting, permaculture, and leisure ways of indigenous peoples.

Address   P.O. Box 2219, Jupiter, FL 33468
Phone   (407) 744-7600
Season   Throughout the year.
Programs   7- to 10-day shamanic/environmental discovery trips.
Regions   The cloud and rain forests of Ecuador.
Rates   7- or 8-day cloud forest $1,490. 9- or 10-day cloud and rain forest $2,290. All trips include round-trip airfare from Miami.

Journey to Shamans

Author John Perkins first lived among the Amazon's Shuar Indians as a Peace Corps Volunteer in the late 1960s. Revisiting that region in 1991, John was shocked to discover this virgin jungle region being torn up by business interests. Determined to stop the destruction, he was told by the Shuar to "bring in those who seek knowledge. Show them the magnificence of our land. Let us help them change the way they dream."

So today, John leads trips to the land of the jaguar, the giant anaconda, and sacred waterfalls. Each trip includes hiking and canoeing with the indigenous peoples of this region and working with shamans to attune to the consciousness of plants, animals, rivers, and rocks. Most trips have ten to fifteen participants.

Address   Dream Change Coalition, P.O. Box 31357, Palm Beach Gardens, FL 33420
Phone   (407) 622-6064 or (800) 245-7330.
Season   Usually early spring and late summer.
Programs   9-day trips.
Regions   Ecuador's Andes and Amazon regions.
Rates $2,290, not including international airfare.

Magical Journey to Peru

Magical Journey leads five annual journeys to Peru. Each trip visits and explores the ancient Andean city of Cusco, the Sacred Valley of the Incas, the medicinal hot springs of Aguas Calientes, the Amazon jungle, and the ruins of Machu Picchu, once the Incas' great City of Light. Trip participants spend two days on a Quechua farm below Machu Picchu Peak. (The Quechua people are descendants of the Incas.) They also usually have the option of a two-day trek along the Inca Trail.

The trip leaders are Carol Cumes and Romulo Lizarraga Valencia, coauthors of a book on the traditions and spirituality of the Quechua people. All trips include meditations at sacred sites plus participation in shamanic healing ceremonies.

Address   P.O. Box 3239, Santa Barbara, CA 93130
Phone   (805) 569-1393. Fax (805) 682-8440.

Season   June through December.
Programs 16-day transformative journeys and wilderness treks.
Regions   Peru.
Rates $3,050–3,350, including airfare from Los Angeles; or $2,550–2,700, excluding airfare for groups leaving from Miami. Inca Trail option $300.

Master Plan Adventures

Master Plan Adventures offers tours to Peru and Bolivia that are led by Oscar Miro-Quesada. This warm and energetic man was born and raised in Peru, educated in the United States, and has advanced degrees in transpersonal psychology and ethnopsychology. An expert on the wisdom teachings and healing practices of his native region, Oscar gives workshops and talks throughout the southeastern United States.

Since 1985, Oscar has led trips to the lands of the Incas. An annual June trip coincides with the celebration of the return of the sun upon Pachamama. An annual October trip explores Quechua and Aymara spiritual traditions, ceremonial shamanism, and Inca prophecy. All trips include optional participation in Inca power place ceremonies; pre-Columbian initiation rituals; native earth offerings, healing sessions, and divination rituals.

Address   2006 NW 3rd Avenue, Delray Beach, FL 33444
Phone   (407) 265-1445. Fax (407) 272-4642.
Season   June and October.
Programs 14- and 15-day trips to Peru and Bolivia.
Regions   Peru and Bolivia.
Rates $2,950—3,150, including round-trip airfare from Miami.

VJ Enterprises

In 1988, Brazilian Vera Lopez traveled to Peru with Luiz Gasparetto, a friend, psychologist, psychic, and channel (profiled in Shirley MacLaine's book *Going Within*) with whom Vera had studied for fourteen years. While at Machu Picchu, Gasparetto introduced Vera to a light being named Chuma, who explained that Machu Picchu had been a spiritual university where special young students studied spiritual science. Soon thereafter, Vera received the message to lead groups to Peru.

Since 1989, Vera has been leading trips for Brazilians and now (after marrying an American) Americans as well. Vera assists travelers in meditations, rituals, and other spiritual awakening processes. Native American medicine wheel teachings are included in occasional trips to the U.S. Four Corners Southwest region. Vera is also planning trips to Brazil, to learn from the African religions and psychic healers of that region.

Address	Vera Lopez Shapiro, 9324 Home Court, Des Plaines, IL 60016
Phone	(708) 699-9701 (also accepts fax).
Season	May through September.
Programs	2-week spiritual adventures in the sacred places of the Native American "ancient ones."
Regions	Peru, Brazil, and the American Southwest.
Rates	Peru $2,999–3,199, including round-trip airfare from Miami. The American Southwest $2,375 from Phoenix.

TWO OR MORE CONTINENTS

A.R.E. Adventure Tours

Since 1962, the Association for Research and Enlightenment has been leading A.R.E. Adventure Tours. (A.R.E.'s Camp, Conferences, and Medical Clinic are profiled in prior chapters.) The multiple purposes of these trips are to visit places frequently mentioned in the Edgar Cayce materials, to enjoy fellowship and community with other seekers, to grow into a greater sense of oneness with other peoples by direct experience of other cultures, and to come to "know ourselves" and our past through the insights of spiritually focused educational travel.

Of the ten or so trips led each year by A.R.E. Adventure Tours, the most frequent and popular destinations are Egypt ("Awakening the Initiate Within"), Bimini ("In Search of Lost Atlantis"), and Sedona, Arizona. All tours are led by A.R.E. resource experts, who facilitate spiritual growth through meditation, prayer, dreamwork, and group discussions. Each tour also includes a guide who is intimately familiar with the place and culture that is being explored.

Address   P.O. Box 595, Virginia Beach, VA 23451
Phone   (804) 428-3588
Season   Throughout the year.
Programs 7- to 18-day spiritual adventure trips.
Regions   Egypt, Greece and Turkey, Italy, Switzerland, Bimini, Sedona, Peru, and China.
Rates   Samples: 7-day Bimini $1,225, 12-day Egypt $3,150, 18-day Switzerland $4,190. European trip rate includes round-trip airfare.

Deja Vu Tours

Deja Vu Tours hosts about a dozen spiritual adventure trips a year, each led by an intuitive tour leader trained at the Berkeley Psychic Institute. Leaders offer insights on the power places and sacred sites visited on every trip. They also lead daily meditations. Tours include ample leisure time and meetings with lamas, shamans, and other spiritual healers.

Annual Deja Vu offerings include a Hawaii retreat for working women, trips to Nepal and Egypt, "Dolphins and Atlantis" cruises in the Bahamas, Brazil/Amazon spiritual healing trips, plus visits with Philippine "psychic surgeons" (who employ miraculous psychical healing techniques). In northern California, Deja Vu also has hosted weekend and weeklong "Women's Intuitive Training" retreats along with one-day San Francisco Bay area "Spiritual Field Trips."

Address   2210 Harold Way, Berkeley, CA 94704
Phone   (510) 644-1600 or (800) 204-8687. Fax (510) 644-1686.
Season   Throughout the year.
Programs 7- to 21-day spiritual adventures to sacred and magic sites.
Regions   Australia, Philippines, India and Nepal, the Middle East, Europe and the British Isles, Bahamas, Hawaii, South and North America.

Rates   Samples: 9-day Bahamas $2,255, 2-week Philippines $3,395, 3-week Egypt or Nepal $4,795–5,395. All trips include round-trip airfare from San Francisco.

Goddess Tours

In 1993, a dream became a reality with the creation of Goddess Tours by Julie Felix and Lydia Rule. Julie is a singer/songwriter who was a leading voice of the cultural revolution in England during the 1960s and is now a healer/singer of the Goddess. Lydia is a visual arts professor and artist whose work explores inherited images and myths of women from many cultures. Julie and Lydia met on a tour called "Magical Britain."

Goddess Tours offers a variety of trips. One explores the legends and sites of France's Black Madonnas. Another uncovers the natural world and sacred neolithic landscapes of England, Wales, and Cornwall. Others go to native sacred sites in Hawaii and the American Southwest to learn from rock art, ruins, and storytellers of the mythical women in those ancient cultures. All trips allow time for group celebration and individual expression of musical and artistic creativity.

Address   2101 24th Street, Greeley, CO 80631
Phone   (303) 352-1643
Season   Throughout the year.
Programs   10- to 17-day women's tours of sacred sites.
Regions   France, Great Britain, the U.S. Southwest, and Hawaii.
Rates   Samples: 10-day Southwest $1,995, 17-day Great Britain $2,500. Prices do not include airfare.

Institute of Noetic Sciences Travel Program

Each year, the Institute of Noetic Sciences leads at least a dozen trips designed to encourage personal growth and to explore the traditional values and beliefs underlying various cultures. Most trips are led by well-known experts in the host culture. All trips encourage experiential learning through meetings with both average and remarkable people plus participation in healing, spiritual, and other activities.

Typical IONS trips include "Art and Consciousness" in Italy, "Healing with Tone and Chant" in France, "Hill Tribes and River Cruises" in Thailand, "American Indian Reservation Experience" in Montana, "Drawing from the Creative Right Brain" in Mexico, and "Studying with Shamans in the Andes and Amazon." The number of participants in each trip is usually about fifteen and never more than twenty.

Address	475 Gate Five Road, Suite 300, Sausalito, CA 94965
Phone	(414) 332-4366
Season	Throughout the year.
Programs	8- to 16-day personal growth and cultural exploration journeys.
Regions	South, Central, and North America. Also Europe and Asia.
Rates	Samples: 8-day Belize $2,500, 9-day Italy $2,950, 13-day Grand Canyon $3,250, 14-day Bali $3,350, 16-day Tibet/Nepal $4,990. Overseas trip fees include round-trip international airfare.

Myths and Mountains

A powerhouse in educational adventure travel, Myths and Mountains sponsors more than seventy trips each year. "Religion and Holy Sites" journeys are for people who want to "invite their soul" and experience other religions. Most of these trips go to India and Nepal, but some also go to strongholds of native culture in the Americas. "Folk Medicine and Traditional Healing" trips allow participants to learn firsthand about healing practices from doctors, shamans, and traditional healers in Central and South America.

Myths and Mountains is directed by the multilingual Antonia Neubauer, Ph.D. An energetic and well-connected consultant and former educator, Toni is able to attract interesting and well-qualified trip leaders. She limits each trip to ten participants, with five to eight being the average.

Address   976 Tee Court, Incline Village, NV 89451
Phone   (800) 670-6984. Fax (702) 832-4454.
Season   Throughout the year.
Programs   5- to 28-day educational adventure trips, including trips focusing on religion/holy sites and folk medicine/traditional healing.
Regions   South-central Asia and the Americas.
Rates   Samples: 10-day Costa Rica $2,350–2,625, 22-day India $2,550–3,390. Rates do not include international airfare.

Noah's Travel Adventures

Noah Linda Gale is an experienced international guide who personally escorts each one of her tours. She also conducts group discussions to explore the mysteries, legends, out-of-place artifacts, and alternative historical accounts of each unusual archaeological site. Whenever possible, she also invites shamans and guides to share their knowledge of local myths and traditions.

Out of her experiences with shamans, mystics, and masters from around the world, Noah has created "The Lion Path Way"—a series of lectures and workshops designed to encourage spiritual growth and healing. Those who travel with Noah to Machu Picchu, the Great Pyramid of Egypt, or other sacred and mysterious places are introduced, through "The Lion Path Way," to personal and transformative initiations.

Address   3029 231st Lane SE, #301, Issaquah, WA 98027
Phone   (206) 313-0268 (also accepts fax).
Season   Throughout the year.
Programs   7- to 10-day metaphysical and spiritual trips to the world's most mysterious places.
Regions   Bahamas, Mexico, Belize, Guatemala, Peru, Egypt, Greece, England.
Rates   Samples: 8-day Mexico $1,097, excluding airfare; 8-day England $2,222, including airfare from Seattle; 9-day Egypt $2,199, including round-trip airfare from New York; 10-day Peru $1,949, including airfare from Miami.

Omega Journeys

Omega Journeys sponsors trips that combine outer and inner explorations. Regular offerings include late spring and early fall "Rites of Passages for Women" in New Mexico, spring and summer Utah Canyonlands vision quest retreats, spring and summer "Tracking and Hiking" in New Mexico, and trips to foreign lands such as Bali and Tibet.

Each journey is limited to twenty participants and led by experienced guides or well-known authorities on the host region. For example, vision quests are led by the experienced guides of Colorado's Animas Valley Institute (see profile in the following chapter). And Bali trips are led by Southeast Asia specialist Doungjun Yana and Ken Ballard, whose ten-year journey around the Pacific rim was documented on PBS and in a subsequent book entitled *Ring of Fire*.

Address   Omega Institute for Holistic Studies, RD 2, Box 377, Rhinebeck, NY 12572

Phone   (914) 266-4444 or (800) 944-1001.

Season   April through December.

Programs   5- to 20-day adventure travel trips combining inner and outer exploration.

Regions   Primarily the U.S. Southwest and Asia.

Rates   Samples: 5-day "Rites of Passage for Women" $715, 11-day vision quest $930, 15-day Bali trip $3,150, 19-day Tibet trip $4,550. Asia trips include round-trip airfare from Los Angeles.

Power Places Tours & Conferences

Power Places conducts conferences at, and leads tours to, some of the world's most magnificent and spiritually powerful places. There are usually at least twelve conferences each year plus three or four tours. All programs are selected by Power Places owner Toby Weiss, a multilingual expert in transformative travel and holder of a Ph.D. in the history of consciousness.

Annual events include February and November conferences in Egypt (e.g., "Life, Death, and Beyond"), a June Earth conference at Machu Picchu, plus an August "Crop Circles, Stonehenge, and UFOs" conference in Salisbury, England. Other annual conferences (e.g., "Mystery School of the Angels") are held in different places each year. Each conference has about fifty to sixty participants and features presentations by up to a dozen experts in the field, along with workshops, rituals, ceremonies, music, dance, and community building. Most conferences offer an optional one-week tour of the surrounding area.

Power Places tours include an annual trip to Tibet and at least one trip each year to Peru. Most tours have about twenty participants. All tours are led by guides chosen for their sensitivity to the spirituality of the region.

Address   285 Boat Canyon Drive, Laguna Beach, CA 92651
Phone   (714) 497-5138 or (800) 234-8687. Fax (714) 494-7448.
Season   Throughout the year.
Programs   1- to 3-week conferences and tours at sacred and mystical sites.
Regions   Bali, Egypt, continental Europe, British Isles, New Mexico, the Amazon and Brazil, India, Tibet, and Nepal.
Rates   Sample conference rates: 1-week Caribbean "Angel Energy" $1,899 from Miami, 1-week England $1,999 from New York, 9-day Egypt $2,199 from New York, 10-day Machu Picchu $2,299 from Miami. All prices include round-trip airfare from various U.S. cities.

Purple Mountain

Purple Mountain Tours leads trips to power places. Annual journeys include a pilgrimage to Egypt and Mount Sinai, a mystical journey to the ancient God and Goddess centers of Greece and Turkey, and an Earth mysteries initiation journey to the British Isles. Each journey includes rituals and attunements to align with the power of these sacred places.

All tours are led by Helene Shik—a scholar, metaphysical teacher, psychic healer, and spiritual midwife. At her healing center in southern Vermont, Helene also hosts occasional gatherings where people are encouraged to challenge limiting fears and belief systems, to awaken to the voice of their soul, and to become living vehicles of Light.

Address   RD 2, Box 1314, Putney, VT 05346
Phone   (802) 387-4753 (also accepts fax). Call before visiting.
Season   March through November.
Programs   12- to 15-day sacred journeys and Earth mysteries initiations.
Regions   France, British Isles, Greece and Turkey, Egypt and Mount Sinai, Italy and Malta, Bolivia and Peru. Also a healing center in Vermont.
Rates   Samples: British Isles $2,699–2,799, Greece and Turkey $2,995, Egypt $3,320, Bolivia and Peru $2,795. Except for British Isles trips, prices include round-trip airfare from New York or Miami.

Quest Tours

Traveling around the world to sites where the "Goddess of Many Names" is still honored today, Quest Tours is no stranger to France, Sicily, Crete, Greece, Turkey, or Nepal. Tours leaders (two on each trip) have included classical archaeologist, Anneli Rufus and Kristan Lawson, authors of *Goddess Sites in Europe*; renowned storyteller Laura Simms; and Miranda Shaw, author of *Passionate Enlightenment: Women in Tantric Buddhism.*

All Quest Tours have a day-by-day itinerary with enough built-in flexibility to allow events to develop in response to serendipity and as an expression of the group's own energy, evoked and amplified by group-created ritual and circles of sharing. Ritual creator Carol Wilken, owner of Quest Tours, welcomes men on some tours. Others are for women only.

Address   1630 Brandywine Drive, Charlottesville, VA 22901
Phone   (804) 977-7344 (also accepts fax).
Season   March through October.
Programs   15-day trips to sites that honor the "Goddess of Many Names."
Regions   Europe and Asia.
Rates   Each trip $3,250–3,950, including round-trip airfare from New York or Los Angeles.

Visions Travel

Visions Travel organizes deluxe metaphysical tours to all areas of our planet. Each tour is led by a well-known author or teacher plus a guide familiar with the region. The purpose of each tour is to bring together people in the spirit of the New Age for an interactive experience with the energies of power places and sacred sites. For example, a recent "Starlink" trip to Machu Picchu was led by channel Lyssa Royal (author of *Preparing for Contact*) to initiate extraterrestrial contact.

Directed by Abbas Nadim, Visions Travel provides an escort for each group to ensure that all promised services are provided. (Group size generally ranges from twenty to forty people.) The agency also ensures that all rituals and ceremonies are conducted in private. For example, Visions Travel arranged exclusive private entry to the King's Chamber in the Great Pyramid of Giza at the time of a significant astrological event.

Address	9841 Airport Boulevard, Suite 520, Los Angeles, CA 90045
Phone	(310) 568-0138 or (800) 888-5509. Fax (310) 568-0246.
Season	Throughout the year.
Programs	8- to 13-day metaphysical adventure tours to mysterious and sacred places.
Regions	Egypt, Greece, British Isles, Peru, Bali, North America.
Rates	Samples: 10-day Greece $2,424, 12-day Peru $2,592, 13-day Egypt $2,783. Includes round-trip airfare from major U.S. cities.

Well Within

Each year since 1982, Well Within has led tours to mysterious, sacred, and healing places. In recent years, annual trips have included "Mystical Ireland," "Enchanting Scotland," "Mysterious England/Wales," plus tours to Egypt and to Greece. Each tour is enhanced by home-study courses both before and after the trip, as well as by experiential workshops while the trip is under way.

Reflecting the background of Well Within's director, Sheri Nakken, R.N., most trips include visits to healing centers or classes on homeopathy, Bach Flower remedies, or women as healers. Well Within also conducts occasional weekend retreats, in both northern and southern California, on alternative approaches to health and wellness.

Address	P.O. Box 1563, Nevada City, CA 95959
Phone	(916) 478-1242. Fax (510) 799-5871.
Season	Throughout the year.
Programs	10- to 18-day trips to healing, mysterious, and sacred sites.
Regions	Egypt, Greece, British Isles, central Europe, California, Hawaii.
Rates	Samples: 14-day Egypt $2,195, 17-day Greece $1,895, 18-day Ireland $1,895. Rates do not include international airfare.

WILDERNESS AND
OCEAN PROGRAMS

*T*his chapter profiles twenty-three organizations that run programs (e.g., vision quests and dolphin swims) wherein the wilderness or ocean experience is a major component. The profiles are arranged in alphabetical order under "North America," "Oceans," and "United States and Abroad."

NORTH AMERICA

Animas Valley Institute

The Animas Valley Institute (AVI) specializes in vision quest trips to the semi-alpine desert canyonlands of southeastern Utah. Most trips begin at River House bed-and-breakfast in Durango, Colorado, or Faraway Ranch in Telluride, Colorado.

The institute's director is Bill Plotkin, a psychologist who has led quests since 1980. AVI's two other senior guides are Steve and Jessica Zeller. Steve is an addictions counselor, Jessica a psychotherapist.

Address   54 Ute Pass Trail, Durango, CO 81301
Phone   (303) 259-0585
Season   April through October.
Programs   10- to 13-day vision quest programs.
Regions   The Utah Canyonlands.
Rates $850 program fee includes all meals. Generally an additional $20–100 for pre- and postwilderness lodging.

Antelope Retreat Center

Located just north of the Colorado border and a few miles west of Medicine Bow National Forest, Antelope Retreat Center is a family-oriented ranch and wilderness retreat. Scheduled summer programs include a Native American teachings week led by Native American elders, a women's healing week with a two-day desert solo fast, one-week wilderness quests, and a weekend with a one-day solo fast. Guests and their children are invited to help out with ranch chores or to enjoy swimming, hiking, cross-country skiing, and trips to the nearby desert and mountains.

The retreat center is run by John and Liz Boyer, Tom Barnes, and Gina Lyman. John and Tom facilitate Wyoming wilderness quests plus weekend and weeklong quests in western Massachusetts during the spring and summer. Gina facilitates the women's week in the summer. The ranch can also arrange private weekend quests as well as weekend or weeklong programs in survival/nature awareness and crafts/primitive skills. As a courtesy to guests, transportation is provided to and from the Steamboat Springs, Colorado, airport and the Rawlins, Wyoming, train station.

Address P.O. Box 166, Savery, WY 82332
Phone (307) 383-2625
Season Year-round with scheduled programs in the spring and summer.
Programs Vision quests, Native American teachings, and women's week.
Regions Far south-central Wyoming, near the Sierra Madre Range.
Rates Weeklong program $500-650. Weekend program $225-275. Guest stay: adults $36-58 per day, $235-375 per week; also family rates.

Breaking Through Adventures

These adventures explore the intimate relationship between wilderness experience and personal growth. Each trip includes backpacking, rock climbing, mountaineering, and/or white-water rafting. A deep sense of community is fostered by the teamwork involved with these risky physical activities and by communal ceremony and sharing. Each adventure also offers centering/attuning experiences such as solo vision quest, wilderness navigation, stalking, yoga and tai chi, and journal writing.

All "Breaking Through Adventures" are led by a staff of therapists and wilderness skills experts directed by Rick Medrick, a pioneer in the field of transformative outdoor learning. Rick's organization, Outdoor Leadership Training Seminars (OLTS), offers courses throughout the Rocky Mountain West in mountaineering, rafting, ski touring, and desert/canyon travel. OLTS also sponsors paddle rafting trips for families, individuals, and groups.

Address P.O. Box 20281, Denver, CO 80220
Phone (303) 333-7831 or (800) 331-7238.

Season   Mid-March through mid-September.
Programs 7- to 9-day wilderness adventures designed to expose and
              transform self-limiting behaviors and beliefs.
Regions   The mountains and high deserts of southern Colorado,
              southeastern Utah, and central Arizona.
Rates $550–725, including meals. BYO tent, sleeping bag, and trail
              snacks.

Choices Along the Path

Ten-day vision quests, four-day vision quests, and nature weekends are
just a few of the trips offered by this organization. The long quests also
entail two days of preparation and four days of wilderness solo time.
The short quests include one day of training and two days of solo time.
Nature weekends involve medicine wheel teachings, purification ceremonies, drumming circles, and shamanic journeywork.

All programs are led by Sheryl Peterson, who has trained with vision
quest elders John Milton, Tom Brown, and the School of Lost Borders.
Sheryl has also trained in psychotherapy, hypnotherapy, and breathwork. She approaches her quest work with great enthusiasm and deep
appreciation, while respecting the concerns of each participant. For example, Sheryl's solo questers need not travel more than a few hundred
yards from base camp, need not fast, and need not be ashamed if they
come back early.

Address   1249 Hoover, Suite 2, Menlo Park, CA 94025
Phone   (415) 323-5755
Season   March through September.
Programs 10- and 4-day vision quest programs. Also nature weekends.
Regions   California and Nevada mountain and desert regions.
Rates   10-day quest $550. 4-day quest $350. Nature weekend $285.

Circles of Air and Stone

The vision quest programs conducted by Circles of Air and Stone help
individuals learn to live from their strengths rather than from their

wounds. Each program is an eleven-day experience in the traditional three-step vision quest format of four days of preparation, four days of solo fasting in the wilderness, and three days of reentry. Each quest is limited to six people.

All programs are led by Sparrow Hart, who in 1971 undertook his first wilderness rite of passage, a five-month solo pilgrimage in the Cascades and Canadian Rockies. Since then, Sparrow has logged thousands of hours alone in U.S. and Mexican wilderness areas. He has also apprenticed with Native American and non–Native American "medicine teachers" including Steven Foster and Meredith Little, whose School of Lost Borders (Box 55, Big Pine, CA 93513) trains and certifies vision quest teachers. Foster and Little recognize Hart as "perhaps the best who ever enrolled in the program."

Address   P.O. Box 48, Putney, VT 05346
Phone   (802) 387-6624
Season   March through September.
Programs   11-day vision quest programs.
Regions   Primarily New Mexico and Vermont.
Rates $400–600 per program.

Desert Star

Desert Star quests are led by Ted Gies, Ph.D., an environmentalist, geologist, botanist, and certified counselor with training in CPR, first aid, and (from the School of Lost Borders) vision quest leadership. Each of Ted's weeklong vision quests consists of three phases: a two-day "severance" period, with ceremony and instruction in fasting and wilderness safety; a three-day solo "threshold" period; and a two-day "reincorporation" period.

For those with limited time or who want a "taste" of the vision quest experience, Ted also leads weekend "solitude quests" with one day of preparation and one day of wilderness solitude. Wholesome vegetarian food is provided at all Desert Star quests, with shared responsibilities for cooking and cleaning. There is carpooling from the meeting site to the quest area. Participants provide their own camping and backpacking equipment.

Address   2320 North Sierra Highway, #4, Bishop, CA 93514
Phone   (616) 872-3011
Season   April through August.
Programs   7-day vision quest programs. Also weekend "solitude quests."
Regions   The Eastern Sierras region of California.
Rates   7-day vision quest $390. Weekend "solo quest": singles $100, couples $160.

Earth Rites

Since 1979, Earth Rites has guided nine-day rites of passage in the high desert wilderness of southeastern Utah. All trips are backpacking journeys that include group ritual, music, and dance; three days of solitary fasting ending with an all-night vigil; and story sharing to celebrate new beginnings. Most trips are open to both men and women.

Each trip is led by Leav Bolender and Jed Swift. Leav is an artist, clinical social worker, and psychotherapist specializing in women's issues and the use of art to heal the soul. She is also an Outward Bound instructor and a certified emergency medical technician. Jed is director of the Colorado Sacred Earth Institute. He also teaches ecopsychology and "transpersonal psychology in the wilderness" at Arizona's Prescott College.

Address   1550 South Pearl Street, #203, Denver, CO 80210
Phone   (303) 733-7465. Fax (303) 744-7747.
Season   Spring, summer, and fall.
Programs   9-day wilderness rites of passage.
Regions   Southern Colorado and Utah Canyonlands.
Rates $650 per program. Participants carpool from Denver.

Esalen Wilderness Programs

While the Esalen Institute is known primarily for its workshops on human potential (see profile in the "Single-Site Getaways" chapter), it also hosts wilderness hiking and camping excursions. Participants work with Native California Indian traditions and contemporary awareness practices to enhance consciousness of both self and nature. Some trips include a one- or two-day solo vision quest. Most journeys include an introduction to the natural history, ecology, geography, and cultural history of the Ventana Wilderness. All trips are led by experienced guides.

Address	Esalen Institute, Highway 1, Big Sur, CA 93920
Phone	(408) 667-3000 (general information) or (408) 667-3005 (reservations).
Season	April through October.
Programs	7- to 9-day nature and self-awareness camping trips.
Regions	California's Ventana Wilderness and Santa Lucia Mountains.
Rates	$740–790 per wilderness trip.

Four Seasons Healing

Four Seasons Healing facilitates wilderness experiences to empower men and women with greater vision and purpose. Programs include "Wilderness Awakenings" (with two- or three-day solo quests), men's weekend gatherings, plus daylong workshops on topics such as "Caring Couples," "Past Lives, Present Stories," and "Meeting Your Inner Shaman." The weekend programs are at a private campground a short drive from Hanover, New Hampshire. The grounds include a campfire circle, a sweat lodge, and a creekside swimming hole.

Four Seasons' quest and weekend leaders include B. Israel Helfand, Ari Kopolow, Cathie Helfand, and Eve Greenberg. Israel is a certified marriage and family therapist. Ari is a psychiatrist. Both Israel and Ari were trained in vision quest leadership at Colorado's Animas Valley Institute (profiled earlier in this chapter). Cathie is a psychotherapist with vision quest training from the School of Lost Borders. Eve has been trained in psychodrama and past-life therapy.

Address	961 New Boston Road, Norwich, VT 05055
Phone	(802) 649-5104
Season	Mostly late spring through fall.
Programs	7- and 8-day vision quest programs, men's weekend gatherings, plus single-day weekend workshops.

Regions   Vermont's Green Mountains and Connecticut River valley.
Rates   Vision quest program $525–825. Men's weekend gathering
               $85. Single-day workshop $85.

Golden Eagle Vision Quests

In the Montana wilderness in 1988, a golden eagle and its mate guided
Michael Young to a power spot where he entered into a "sacred place."
This experience—inviting Michael to live in heartfelt connection with
all forms of life—also inspired him in 1990 to begin leading vision
quests. In this regard, Michael's reliance on spirit for guidance has made
his training personal and internal. For more formal training, Michael has
studied spiritual healing and holistic counseling at the Barbara Brennan
School of Healing and the New England School of Acupuncture.

The Golden Eagle quest format follows traditional lines: several days
in ceremony, community building, and spiritual practices; four days of
fasting on water in wilderness solitude; and the final two days in sharing and celebration back at camp. Regions in which Michael often leads
quests include Montana's Bull Mountains, Vermont's Green Mountains,
North Carolina's Blue Ridge Mountains, and Central America (e.g., Belize).

Address   P.O. Box 1496, Asheville, NC 28802
Phone   (704) 254-7747
Season   July through September, plus one quest in winter.
Programs   10-day vision quest programs.
Regions   Montana, Vermont, North Carolina, Central America.
Rates   U.S. quest $1,000. Central America quest $1,200.

Her Wild Song

Anne Dellenbaugh invites women to join Her Wild Song on wilderness
journeys grounded in the development of outdoors competence and involving a community of women living simply and in harmony. Some
trips offer a particular practice (e.g., meditation, mindfulness, or ritual)
to open awareness and deepen this intimacy. Others are more loosely

structured, developing in accordance with the mood and rhythms of the women in attendance. Participants bring their own sleeping bag and backpack. All meals are gourmet vegetarian.

Anne is a registered Maine guide trained in outdoor leadership and certified in emergency medicine and canoeing instruction. She also holds a master's in theological and women's studies from Harvard Divinity School. Assisted by ten or so co-leaders and apprentices, Anne leads wilderness trips that include hiking, backpacking, cross-country skiing, sea kayaking, and canoeing. While most trips are conducted in Maine, annual trips are made to the Florida Everglades and the Arizona desert.

Address	P.O. Box 515, Brunswick, ME 04011
Phone	(207) 721-9005
Season	Throughout the year except late November and December.
Programs	3- to 10-day wilderness journeys for women.
Regions	Mostly Maine. Also Florida, Arizona, California, Utah, and Texas.
Rates	Samples: 3-day Maine $215–375, 5- or 6-day Maine $595–650, 8- or 9-day Arizona or California $795–850.

Holos Institute

Every year, the Holos Institute conducts three "Quest for Wholeness" trips and three "Medicine Time" trips. Each "Quest" trip takes seven days, four of which are spent fasting alone in the wilderness. It also includes four weekly meetings before the trip and a one-day reunion after the trip. "Medicine Time" trips are daylong guided group wilderness excursions with time alone for healing in nature.

The institute's director is Alan Levin, a licensed marriage, family, and child counselor. Alan has more than twenty years of experience in teaching a wide range of approaches (e.g., meditation, yoga, shamanism, and Western psychotherapy) to personal change and transformation.

Address	5515 Taft Avenue, Oakland, CA 94618
Phone	(510) 287-8816 or (415) 750-0478.
Season	Spring, summer, and fall.

Programs	7-day "Quest for Wholeness" and 1-day "Medicine Time" programs.
Regions	Southern California desert for "Quests." San Francisco Bay area wilderness sites for "Medicine Times."
Rates	"Quest for Wholeness" $400, including 4 pretrip meetings and a 1-day post-trip meeting. "Medicine Time" $50.

Mind-Body River Adventures

These river raft trips are designed to create a relaxed, intuitive relationship among the participants and also between the participants and their environment—the desert sandstone canyons of the U.S. Southwest. All trips offer Iyengar yoga and massage sessions. Some also include meditation, journal writing, tai chi, biokinetic movement, or ceremony. Trip leaders are experienced river guides, psychotherapists, massage therapists, and yoga teachers.

Most trips include one layover day—a full day of free time and relaxing camp-based activities. On nonlayover days, participants practice a mind/body discipline for up to two hours in the morning; float down the river for seven to fourteen miles during midday; then spend one to three hours in group activity, hiking, meditation, or rest. Evening is a time for group sharing. Meals are vegetarian unless otherwise requested.

Address	P.O. Box 863, Hotchkiss, CO 81419
Phone	(303) 921-3455
Season	Spring and early fall.
Programs	4- to 6-day river raft trips focusing on ecology plus various creative and mind/body disciplines.
Regions	Portions of the Colorado, Dolores, and Green Rivers in southwestern Colorado and Utah.
Rates	$360–590.

Northwaters Wilderness Programs

Operating from two camps in northern Ontario's vast and ruggedly beautiful Temagami Wilderness, this organization offers a number of summer wilderness programs: a father-and-son canoe trip; women's, men's, and mixed-gender canoe trips; a vision quest program; and the "Temagami Experience."

Most programs combine exhilarating outdoor adventure with group process work and Native American ritual. For example, the "Temagami Experience" includes outdoor initiatives, supportive feedback, group discussions, sweat lodge, long dance, and a forty-hour solo vision quest. Some programs also include dreamwork.

For well over twenty years, the Northwaters programs have been run by highly trained experts in canoeing, wilderness survival, Native American rituals, Jungian psychology, leadership, and team building.

Address	September to mid-June: P.O. Box 478, Saint Peters, PA 19470
Phone	September to mid-June: (610) 469-4662. Fax (610) 469-6522.
Season	July through August.
Programs	Canoe trips and wilderness island camps integrating adventure with personal and spiritual growth opportunities.
Regions	Canadian wilderness areas, including the Temagami region of northern Ontario and the Dumoine River area of northwestern Quebec.
Rates	Samples: 1-week vision quest $1,150, 10-day "Temagami Experience" $1,650.

Peaceways

Peaceways programs in Earth-based spirituality include six- to eight-day vision quests, sacred journeys, weekend seminars on topics such as "Native Earth Connections" and "Couples Commitment," and daylong workshops on topics such as "Women's Wellness" and "Pathways to the Creative Self." The vision quests and sacred journeys are generally conducted in the Four Corners region of New Mexico, Arizona, Utah, and Colorado. The weekend seminars and single-day workshops are held in or near Boulder, Colorado.

All Peaceways programs are facilitated by Lynne Ihlstrom, sometimes with the help of others. Lynne is a holistic psychotherapist, herbalist, and master gardener specializing in diet, meditation, yoga, inner-child work and vision quests. A massage therapist is available (for an additional fee) at the weekend seminars, which are held in a rustic mountain retreat.

Address   P.O. Box 388, Nederland, CO 80466
Phone   (303) 258-7904
Season   Year-round.
Programs   6- to 8-day solo vision quests and weeklong sacred journeys, weekend seminars, and single-day workshops.
Regions   Colorado, Utah, Arizona, and New Mexico.
Rates   6- to 8-day solo vision quest $250, weeklong sacred journey $500–550, weekend seminar $150, and daylong workshop $55. Rates include meals (usually vegetarian) and (for quests and journeys) camping fees.

Reevis Mountain School

Reevis Mountain School is a wilderness learning center at a creekside homestead in Tonto National Forest. School offerings include vision quests, fasting meditation retreats, land navigation workshops, and "vision quest treks" in the nearby Superstition Mountains. The school also welcomes work-study guests. All visitors camp out or rent a "yurpi." The two daily meals are provided primarily from the school's organic gardens.

Reevis Mountain's resident directors are Peter Bigfoot Busnack and Angelique Zelle, experts in herbology, natural and touch healing, meditation, and natural foods preparation. Peter has tested his self-reliance skills by walking eighty-five miles in fifteen days through the Sonoran Desert (temperatures up to 135 degrees F) with no food or water (foraging for his needs). Angelique has completed five forty-day fasts.

Address   HCO2 Box 1534, Roosevelt, AZ 85545
Phone   (602) 467-2675. No visits without prior arrangement.
Season   Year-round.
Programs   1- to 3-month work-study and 3- to 7-day wilderness programs focusing on self-discovery and self-reliance.
Regions   South-central Arizona.
Rates   Work-study $350, 3- to 7-day programs $175–680. Personal retreat daily rates: adult $20–30, discounts for children.

Rites of Passage

Rites of Passage runs vision quest programs for adults in any stage of life transition. All programs begin with a series of pretrip meetings in the northern San Francisco Bay area. Questers living outside the area receive the meetings' contents by mail and phone. The one-week trip includes a three-day quest of fasting (or light meals) alone in the wilderness. Two weeks after the quest, the group holds a reunion where participants share stories to increase their understanding of the gifts of this experience.

Founded in 1977 by Steven Foster and Meredith Little, Rites of Passage is now directed by Michael Bodkin, a licensed family therapist, resident of an intentional community, and vision quest guide since 1983. Michael leads the quest programs with the assistance of several other experienced guides. In most years, Rites of Passage conducts three to five quests.

Address   P.O. Box 148, Sonoma, CA 95476
Phone   (707) 537-1927
Season   Throughout the year.
Programs   7-day vision quest programs plus father-and-son weekends.
Regions   Southern California desert: high desert (often over 8,000 feet) in summer and low desert (often under 2,500 feet) in winter.
Rates $495, not including food en route or potluck food in the field.

Vision Quest Wilderness Passage

This organization conducts seven-day vision quests in remote California desert and mountain regions such as Joshua Tree National Monument, Mount Shasta, and the White Mountains. One week before each trip, a daylong preparation meeting (including a sweat lodge purification ceremony) is held in the San Francisco Bay area. On the trip, each participant spends three days in the wilderness alone and without food (unless he or she is unable to fast for medical reasons).

All trips are led by two licensed psychotherapists, Brian Winkler and Chayim Barton. Brian has more than fifteen years of wilderness experience, including vision quest leadership training at the School of Lost Borders. Chayim contributes expertise in dreamwork, meditation, and Jungian psychology. Both are also available to lead ad hoc quests for couples, families, groups, or businesses.

Address 139 Forest View Road, Woodside, CA 94062
Phone   (415) 851-1715 or (408) 479-1564.
Season   Late April through mid-September.
Programs 7-day vision quest programs.
Regions California desert and mountain regions; also north-central Arizona.
Rates $510, including pretrip meeting, handbook, and 2 meals.

Wilderness Transitions

"A simple, yet extraordinary experience" is one participant's summary of a Wilderness Transitions vision quest. Each quest includes three or four days of solitude (fasting optional) in a California mountain or high desert area, chosen shortly before departure on the basis of weather forecasts. The eight-day program is preceded by four evening meetings in the northern San Francisco Bay area. Participants living in other areas are prepared through phone calls, letters, and written materials that include a sixty-four-page handbook.

Wilderness Transitions conducts six trips each year led by Marilyn Riley and Betty Warren. Marilyn is a life transition counselor who was on the original (1979) staff of Rites of Passage (profiled earlier in this section). Betty is a naturalist, student of meditation, and experienced wilderness guide. Trips do not require prior backpacking experience. All are designed to create a profound group experience as well as a time of individual self-discovery.

Address 70 Rodeo Avenue, Sausalito, CA 94965
Phone   (415) 332-9558, (415) 456-4370
Season   Throughout the year.
Programs 8-day vision quest programs, each with preparation and reunion.
Regions Central and southern California mountain and desert wilderness areas east of the Sierra Nevada range.

Rates   Each trip $475, including pretrip meetings and materials, some equipment, vegetarian meals and snacks at base camp. Does not include carpool transportation and meals en route.

OCEANS

Dolphinswim

While studying psychotherapy at Santa Fe's Southwestern College, Rebecca Fitzgerald suddenly began having vivid dreams about a pod of spotted dolphins. At the library, she discovered that spotted dolphins are a coastal species, which gibed with the calm, shallow, turquoise waters and white sands of her dreams. Eventually these energetic dolphin images became so compelling as to surface in her mind even during waking hours.

Several years later, after repressing the dolphin images to complete her studies, Rebecca was working in a hospital when she read a Jungian journal article on how dolphins were being used in therapy for autistic children. She was soon on a flight to Miami, became acquainted with a pod of spotted dolphins in 1983, and has been leading Bahamas dolphin swims continuously since 1988. On these trips, Rebecca is sometimes accompanied by specialists in interspecies telepathy or shared dreaming.

While at sea, guests live on a first-class dive vessel with opportunities to snorkel, scuba dive, water ski, or just relax in the sun. But the healing spontaneity and joy of swimming with wild dolphins is the high point of these trips. Scuba divers cavort with the dolphins on rented underwater scooters. Weak swimmers too, kept afloat by snorkel vests, are approached by these heart-opening "messengers from the inner kingdom."

Address   P.O. Box 8653, Santa Fe, NM 87504
Phone   (505) 466-0579
Season   Mostly from late April through mid-September.
Programs   6-day dolphin swim expeditions and 10-day dive certification/dolphin swims.

Regions   The Grand Bahama and Bimini ocean areas of the Bahamas.

Rates   6- to 10-day dolphin swim $1,545–2,000 (including Bahamian tax). Half-day scuba course $75.

UNITED STATES AND ABROAD

Great Round

The Great Round leads ten-day vision quests in California, Nevada, and southern Australia. Each quest incorporates shamanic traditions to encourage in participants a more expanded and confident sense of self. Programs range in size from four to fourteen participants plus two to five staff members. All are led by trained psychologists Sedonia Cahill and Barton Stone. Sedonia is a counselor and coauthor of *The Ceremonial Circle*. Barton is a sculptor, dreamwork teacher, and longtime Zen practitioner.

U.S. quest programs begin an hour north of San Francisco with a day of orientation, instruction, and ceremony in a private home. On the second day, staff and questers carpool to the desert. Base camp is established on Sunday, and each participant finds a quest spot on Monday. Tuesday through Thursday is solo time (fasting optional), ending with an all-night vigil. Friday and Saturday are for telling one's story, celebrating, and beginning the integration process. Highlighting the final Sunday is a stop at a hot springs on the way home.

Southern Australia quests are usually scheduled for October and November. These quests are frequently held in the Grampians (departing from Balharring, Victoria) or the Flinders Range (leaving from Stirling, South Australia).

Address   P.O. Box 1772, Sebastopol, CA 95473
Phone   (707) 829-6681. Fax (707) 829-6691.
Season   May through November.
Programs   10-day vision quest programs.

Regions   California and Nevada desert: low desert in spring, high desert in summer. Also Southern Australia mountains in October and November.

Rates   U.S. quest $500, including transportation and all meals (ample and delicious vegetarian food). Australian quest about $900.

Inward Journeys

Each winter and summer in the United States, and each spring and fall in Europe, Inward Journeys conducts five- to fourteen-day intensives imparting the essence of shamanism: healing, service, teaching, prophecy, ritual and ceremony, and the ability to bring peace into any situation. Most participants have previously taken weekend workshops on subjects like "Intimacy and Opening," "Shamanic Wisdom," and "Mastery of the Elements." All intensives are held at wilderness campsites (with an available house nearby in winters), and some include solo quests and foraging. Otherwise, there are two vegan meals each day.

Inward Journeys was founded by Laeh Maggie Garfield, who has taught and practiced shamanism for more than twenty-five years. Her work derives a great deal of its power from the teachings of her Native American mentor (Pomo shaman Essie Parrish) as well as from the wisdom of Kabalism and Tibetan Buddhism. Laeh has written three books and is joined in her workshop presentations by Edwin Knight, a yoga and holistic health teacher who completed a six-year apprenticeship with Laeh in 1993.

Address   P.O. Box 10204, Eugene, OR 97440

Phone   (503) 344-4957

Season   Throughout the year.

Programs   Weekend workshops plus 5- to 14-day intensives leading toward healing, personal growth, and shamanic wisdom.

Regions   Western North America, the British Isles, Scandinavia, Switzerland, and Germany.

Rates   Weekend workshop $300. Two-week intensive $1,800–2,000.

Sacred Passage

This organization conducts guided wilderness experiences designed to help participants realize the oneness of their inner nature with the outer world. Most "Sacred Passages" are eleven days long, with seven days (six nights) of solo wilderness time. Pretrip training covers camping and safety skills, discovering one's natural totem, healing movement, awareness skills, meditation, and opening the heart. Participants bring their own camping equipment and food.

Sacred Passage also leads pilgrimages to sacred natural places around the world. These trips include ceremony, meditation, and whatever environmental projects are inspired by communion with the land. In addition, Sacred Passages leads weekend trainings. All "Sacred Passages," pilgrimages, and weekend workshops are guided by John Milton, a teacher of deep ecology, meditation, and tai chi with more than twenty years of wilderness retreat leadership experience.

Address   P.O. Drawer CZ, Bisbee, AZ 85603
Phone   (520) 432-7353
Season   Throughout the year.
Programs 11-day "Sacred Passage" wilderness quests, 10- to 25-day pilgrimages to sacred natural places, and weekend workshops.
Regions   Most "Sacred Passages" in the mountains of Arizona, Colorado, and Baja California. Pilgrimages have gone to the U.S. Southwest, Mexico, Bali, Cambodia, Nepal, and Ireland.
Rates   "Sacred Passage" $780–990. Pilgrimage $1,325–3,590, not including international airfare for non-U.S. destinations.

Profile Criteria

*W*ith only a few exceptions, organizations profiled in this directory have four common characteristics:

- They are open to people of all races, cultures, religions, and nations.

- They are committed to enhancing well-being in a context broader than the physical body alone.

- They provide programs/services/activities that emphasize experiential learning/healing.

- They offer a total immersion experience with accommodations plus meals (generally vegetarian) or cooking facilities. Exceptions include a few centers that do not yet (but that eventually plan to) provide lodging and/or all meals with their programs.

Other criteria were established by the format of the book's four profile chapters.

The "Single-Site Getaways" and "Multisite Getaways" chapters profile organizations that offer either at least four weekend programs each year or at least one annual program of at least five days in length. "Single-Site Getaways" organizations conduct programs at single sites (i.e., one site per organization), while "Multisite Getaways" organizations conduct programs at multiple sites (i.e., at least two sites per organization).

The "Journeys to Distant Places" chapter profiles organizations that conduct at least two trips per year, each of at least one month in length.

The "Wilderness and Ocean Programs" chapter profiles organizations that offer at least two scheduled programs per year, each of at least five days in length.

Other Organizations

$\mathcal{T}$he following is an alphabetical list of sixty-two additional host organizations that were not profiled either because they were not discovered until the late stages of the editing process, because they were then new or going through significant changes, or because they did not meet this edition's profile criteria (see pages 285–86).

Abunda Life Health Hotel   (908) 775-4141
208 Third Avenue, Asbury Park, NJ 07712
Naturopathic stress relief, detoxification, weight loss, and rejuvenation clinic, including massage and acupuncture services, on the Jersey shore.

Akala Point Retreat   (902) 823-2160
Box 1626, RR 1, Tantallon, N.S. B0J 3J0, Canada
Coastal, hostel-style retreat with weekend workshops on topics such as organic gardening, vegetarian cooking, and the healing process in aging.

Annapurna Inn   (360) 385-2909
538 Adams, Port Townsend, WA 98368
Seaport Victorian bed-and-breakfast (vegan meals) offering retreat packages with yoga, foot and craniosacral massage, plus steam bath/sauna.

ATP Annual Conference   (415) 327-2066
Association for Transpersonal Psychology, P.O. Box 3049, Stanford, CA 94309
Four-day early August conference, with a significant experiential component, in Monterey, California.

Ayurveda at Spirit Rest   (970) 264-2573
P.O. Box 3537, Pagosa Springs, CO 81147
Weeklong program of pancha karma therapy, hatha yoga, meditation, and counseling at a southwestern Colorado retreat center.

Camp Ronora   (616) 463-6315
9325 Dwight Boyer Road, Box 823, Watervliet, MI 49098
Three-day holistic health and re-creation retreats with meditation, movement, cooking classes, massage, and play.

Cancer Support Intensives   (415) 327-6166
Cancer Support & Education Center, 1035 Pine Street, Menlo Park, CA 94025
Two-week San Francisco Bay area self-empowerment residential programs for people with cancer.

Cedarhill   (541) 345-1619
92201 West Fork Road, Deadwood, OR 97430
Thirty-acre Coastal Mountains retreat offering spring and summer weekend workshops on topics such as men's and women's spirituality, tai chi, crafts, herbalism, astrology, and tarot.

Center for Spiritual Growth   (612) 689-5502
35197 Wakenen Drive, NE, Cambridge, MN 55008
Nonsectarian weekend retreats (often for specific gender or sexual preference groups) facilitated by a couple trained in Lutheran ministry.

Centerpoint Retreats   (206) 622-8070
1326 Fifth Ave., 658 Skinner Building, Seattle, WA 98101
Occasional four-day retreats in western Washington with individual and small-group counseling on life and career-change options.

Common Boundary Annual Conference   (301) 652-9495
5272 River Road, Ste. 650, Bethesda, MD 20816
Washington, D.C.–area three-day November weekend of workshops led by well-known authors and teachers on subjects relating to psychology, spirituality, and creativity.

Crestone Mountain Zen Center   (719) 256-4692
P.O. Box 130, Crestone, CO 81131
Residential training in Buddhist meditation and practice in the high
foothills of the Sangre de Cristo Mountains.

Dolphin Connection   (808) 323-9605
P.O. Box 2016, Kealakekua, HI 96750
Six- to eight-day dolphin and whale swim seminars led by psycholo-
gist/dolphin communicator Joan Ocean and her associates off the
Hawaiian coast.

DolphINsight   (619) 792-0919
Ilizabeth Fortune, 1155 Camino Del Mar, Suite 4500-449, Del Mar, CA
92014
Dolphin and whale-swim cruises in the Caribbean and Pacific Ocean
structured around themes such as "Helios and Our Ascension into
Light."

Embodiment Trainings   (604) 743-5971
RR 2, Cobble Hill, B.C. V0R 1L0, Canada
One-, three-, five-, and twelve-day private residential body-awareness
trainings, each including bodywork and movement sessions plus meditation.

Foundation for Shamanic Studies   (415) 380-8282
P.O. Box 1939, Mill Valley, CA 94942
Weekend (nonresidential) "Way of the Shaman" workshops plus five-
day (residential) "Soul Retrieval" trainings conducted by Michael
Harner, Sandra Ingerman, and other FSS staff at various North Ameri-
can sites.

Foxhollow   (502) 241-8621
8909 Highway 329, Crestwood, KY 40014
Manor house weekend programs on health and well-being (e.g., men's
and women's health issues, compulsive eating, "Journey to Wholeness
after Divorce"), all including massage and either yoga or chi gung sessions.

A Gathering   (513) 677-1710
P.O. Box 4685, Maineville, OH 45039
Large three-day spring gathering near Cincinnati with ceremonies and
healing practices based largely on Native American and Taoist wisdom.

HeartQuest   (808) 573-1076
P.O. Box 1143, Kula, Maui, HI 96790
Three- to six-day rites-of-passage workshops in Hawaii and Colorado
for teens and their parents.

Holotropics   (415) 721-9891
38 Miller Ave., Suite 158, Mill Valley, CA 94941
Weekend Holotropic Breathwork workshops facilitated by Tav Sparks
or Stanislav Grof, usually at hotels in or near major cities.

Inner Harmony Retreat Center   (801) 590-2009
P.O. Box 7366, Phoenix, AZ 85011
Weeklong workshops and retreats held at a scenic southern Utah mountain site and led by well-known teachers of yoga, wellness, and personal-growth skills.

Inspiration University   (540) 886-4413
P.O. Box 1026, Staunton, VA 24402
Leonard Orr and his staff conduct weekly five-day trainings in spiritual
purification and intuitive energy breathing, or "rebirthing."

Institute of Mentalphysics   (619) 365-8371
P.O. Box 1000, Joshua Tree, CA 92252
Four-hundred-acre high-desert retreat with weekend workshops and
nine- and fourteen-day August and October conferences on spiritual
self-awareness and healing.

Interface   (617) 876-1168
55 Wheeler Street, Cambridge, MA 02138
Evening, day, and weekend holistic education classes with occasional weekend and four-day residential programs in the New England
region.

**International Transpersonal Association Annual
Conference**   (415) 383-8819
ITA, 20 Sunnyside, Suite A257, Mill Valley, CA 94941
Six-day event (each year in a new city) promoting psychological and
spiritual healing through presentations and experiential sessions.

La Casa de Maria   (805) 969-5031
800 El Bosque Road, Santa Barbara, CA 93108
Two- to six-day personal- and spiritual-growth retreats sponsored by
the Immaculate Heart Community at an ecumenical Christian center.

La Casa de Vida Natural   (212) 673-2272
41 East 20th Street, New York, NY 10003
Beachside "natural living" vacations in Puerto Rico, including individualized body/mind workshops and spa treatments.

Lakota Teachings   (308) 432-4652
Richard Sparrow Eagle, 342 Chadron Avenue, Chadron, NE 69337
Native American spiritual teaching camps led by a Lakota elder in Cali-
fornia, Oregon, South Dakota, and Utah.

Living Waters   (954) 476-7466
11450 SW 16th Street, Davie, FL 33325
Three-day weekend retreats, each at a different resort setting, with
yoga, Kabala, ancient ceremonies, and new rituals.

Men Are from Mars, Women Are from Venus   (800) 821-3033
4730 E. Warner Road, Suite 4-100, Phoenix, AZ 85044
Seven-day luxury cruises, romantic weekends and vacations at worldwide destinations exclusively designed for couples to improve communication, deepen passion, and enhance intimacy. Based on the work of
John Gray, Ph.D.

Mercy Center at Madison   (203) 245-0401
167 Neck Road, P.O. Box 191, Madison, CT 06443
Long Island Sound retreat center where the Sisters of Mercy host private, directed, and occasional guided theme retreats.

Mid-Life Directions   (201) 373-6118
45 Poe Avenue, Vailsburg, NJ 07106
Three- to five-day midlife and late-life workshops and retreats, conducted mostly in the Northeast and Midwest, to facilitate personal and
spiritual growth.

Naropa Institute   (303) 546-3468
2130 Arapohoe Avenue, Boulder, CO 80302
Summer and continuing-education programs in contemplative disciplines, dance, music, psychology, theater, writing, and visual arts.

New Millennium Institute   (808) 593-2297
1170 Waimanu Street, Honolulu, HI 96814
Weeklong and scholar-in-residence retreats with eminent visionaries of
planetary, cultural, social, and spiritual transformation.

New Vrindaban, City of God   (304) 845-7539
RD 1, Box 319, Moundsville, WV 26041
Retreats and festivals at a large, picturesque, and self-sufficient Hindu
community of Vishnu and Krishna devotees and their children.

New York Open Center   (212) 219-2527
83 Spring Street, New York, NY 10012
Classes and workshops on holistic culture, plus concerts, performances, celebrations, and gatherings.

Oasis Center   (312) 274-6777
7463 North Sheridan Road, Chicago, IL 60626
Classes, workshops, and trainings on personal growth and pro-
fessional-development skills.

Ojai Foundation   (805) 646-8343
P.O. Box 1620, Ojai, CA 93024
Rustic camp offering weekend workshops designed to deepen the rela-
tionship with self, others, and the Earth.

Opening Doors   (520) 282-2125
Jyotika Schiavone, P.O. Box 10941, Sedona, AZ 86339
Yoga and hiking journeys in Sedona and the Grand Canyon region.

Options Unlimited (512) 328-0288
1515 Capital of Texas Highway South, Suite 220A, Austin, TX 78746
Eleven-day codependency treatment program in a "new family" setting.

Osage Monastery Forest of Peace (918) 245-2734
18701 W. Monastery Road, Sand Springs, OK 74063
A Christian monastic ashram that honors Western, Eastern, and Native American mystical traditions in an atmosphere of contemplative prayer.

Other Dimensions Training Center (604) 832-8483
Box 2269, Salmon Arm, B.C. V1E 4R3, Canada
Five-day transformational healing retreats, sacred circle dance trainings, and monthly group meditations in a wooded setting near Shuswap Lake.

Passages to Recovery (704) 682-4844
New Hope Counseling, 525 West Main Street, Burnsville, NC 28714
Blue Ridge Mountains retreats applying group counseling and creative self-expression to twelve-step recovery issues.

Peace Valley (501) 356-2908
HC 65, Box 73B, Caddo Gap, AR 71935
New center hosting spiritual and personal-growth workshops near Hot Springs National Park.

PeerSpirit (360) 321-8404
P.O. Box 550, Langley, WA 98260
Empowerment retreats, trips, workshops, and circles given around the country for women and men.

Penuel Ridge Retreat Center (615) 792-3734
Rte. 4, Box 304-2, Ashland City, TN 37015
Weekend spiritual-theme retreats, often with a contemplative or meditative focus, at an ecumenical Judeo-Christian retreat center in the wooded hills of central Tennessee.

Pictured Rocks Retreat   (520) 744-3400
P.O. Box 569, Cortaro, AZ 85652
Ecumenical center (run by the Redemptive Fathers) offering weekend
and weeklong programs on topics ranging from tai chi to energy healing
to male spirituality to contemplative prayer.

Quest Haven   (619) 744-1500
20560 Questhaven Road, Escondido, CA 92029
Nondenominational, metaphysical Christian center hosting three-day
holiday retreats, weekend theme workshops, and guided journeys to
foreign places.

Resources for Ecumenical Spirituality   (507) 387-4276
P.O. Box 6, Mankato, MN 56002
Two- to nine-day retreats integrating Eastern and Western spiritual
practices (particularly Buddhist Vipassana meditation and Christian
Eucharist) at Forest Monastery in Springfield, Missouri, and other U.S.
sites.

Retreats of the Divine Feminine   (206) 696-1645
Mary Achor, 7419 NE 13th Avenue, Vancouver, WA 98665
Weekend women's retreats facilitated by artist/musician/storyteller Mary
Achor at comfortable Oregon coast and mountain-view retreat houses.

RIGPA Retreats   (510) 644-1858
816 Bancroft Way, Berkeley, CA 94707
Guided retreats, in California and other North American regions, based
on the Tibetan Buddhist teachings and meditation practices of Sogyal
Rinpoche, author of *The Tibetan Book of Living and Dying*.

Rites of Passage Retreats   (704) 682-4684
Barbara Lange, P.O. Box 1312, Burnsville, NC 28714
Personal growth/social retreats (some for women only) in the North
Carolina mountains (in the fall) and the Florida islands (in the spring).

The Sacred Circle (406) 542-2383
400 Cote Lane # 1, Missoula, MT 59802
Dr. Susan Rangitsch conducts workshops of personal empowerment through group energy and the healing and shamanic arts in Montana and elsewhere.

San Diego Health Classic (805) 969-0444
P.O. Box 5087, Montecito, CA 93150
Annual fall four-day event with classes, workshops, and well-known teachers of macrobiotic and natural-health lifestyles.

Sawan Kirpal Meditation Centers (804) 633-7410
Route 1, Box 24, Bowling Green, VA 22427
Centers in northeastern Virginia, northwestern Washington, and Connecticut offer meditation retreats based on the science of inner sound and light taught by India's Masters of Sant Mat.

Self-Realization Fellowship (213) 225-2471
3880 San Rafael Avenue, Los Angeles, CA 90065
Weekend and work retreats at Los Angeles– and San Diego–area retreat centers, based on the SRF teachings and meditation techniques of the late Paramahansa Yogananda (author of the classic *Autobiography of a Yogi*).

Shared Heart Foundation (408) 684-2299
P.O. Box 2140, Aptos, CA 95001
Joyce and Barry Vissell, a nurse and medical doctor, host workshops at their home center and around the country on enhancing relationships.

Soulwork Retreats (510) 524-0833
P.O. Box 11604, Berkeley, CA 94712
Therapist Anna Billings leads soul-opening/spirit-of-nature retreats in areas of natural beauty such as Mount Shasta, Sedona, and Pacific Mexico.

Spiritual Life Center   (316) 744-0167
100 E. 45th Street, North Wichita, KS 67226
Frequent weekend retreats (e.g., couples programs, rest-and-renewal weekends, directed and thematic spiritual-practice weekends) arranged under the auspices of the Catholic Diocese of Wichita.

Temagami Canoe Trips   (610) 891-0182
Michael Madden, Box 261, Wallingford, PA 19086
Weeklong men's and father-and-son canoe trips in northern Ontario for spiritual and personal growth.

Transformational Studies Institute   (407) 697-5953
321 Northlake Boulevard, Suite 207, North Palm Beach, FL 33408
Occasional spiritual retreats and dolphin-swim weekends.

True North   (907) 455-6499
Alaska Places, P.O. Box 81914, Fairbanks, AK 99708
Alaska retreats (some for women only) with outdoor exercise (e.g., snowshoeing and canoeing) and inner-focus work (e.g., yoga and meditation).

White Lotus Foundation   (815) 964-1944
2500 San Marcos Pass, Santa Barbara, CA 93105
Sixteen-day yoga trainings and occasional weekend workshops on San Marcos Pass overlooking the Pacific Ocean.

Wilderness Rites   (415) 927-4405
20 Spring Grove Ave., San Rafael, CA 94901
Transpersonal psychotherapist Anne Stine leads occasional ten-day vision quests for women.

Womongathering   (609) 694-2037
RR5, Box 185, Franklinville, NJ 08322
Four-day festival of women's spirituality, usually held the third week of June in the Pocono Mountains.

Other Directories

*H*ere are twelve books that include information on spiritual communities and retreats, holistic educational resources, residential health spas, and tour leaders. The listing is in order of publication date, beginning with the most recent book.

Specialty Travel Index is published twice each year in magazine format by Alpine Hansen Publishers. Each issue includes more than 500 advertiser-paid profiles of tours, expeditions, and charters addressing virtually all travel interests.

Directory of Intentional Communities. Second edition published in 1995 by *Communities* magazine. Profiles more than 400 North American and more than 50 overseas intentional communities of all types. It also contains over 200 resource listings.

Healthy Escapes by Bernard Burt. Third edition published in 1995 by Fodor's. Profiles 240 fitness and beauty resorts (plus seventeen luxury fitness cruises) in the United States, Canada, Mexico, and the Caribbean.

Paradise Found: The Beautiful Retreats & Sanctuaries of California & the Southwest by Melba Levick. Published in 1995 by Chronicle Books. Descriptions and lovely photos of twenty-three retreat centers in California, Arizona, New Mexico, and Colorado.

Spas: The International Spa Guide by Joseph Bain and Eli Dror. Published in 1995 by Bain Dror International Travel. Profiles more than

300 fitness and beauty spas in the United States and thirty-five other countries around the world.

Common Boundary Graduate Education Guide. Published in 1994 by Common Boundary. A comprehensive guide to North American holistic programs and resources integrating spirituality and psychology.

Transformative Adventures, Vacations & Retreats: An International Directory of 300+ Host Organizations by John Benson. Published in 1994 by New Millennium Publishing. A guide to self-transformative residential programs in North America, Mexico and the Caribbean, Continental Europe and the British Isles, India, and Australia and New Zealand.

Sanctuaries: The West Coast and Southwest: A Guide to Lodging in Monasteries, Abbeys, and Retreats of the United States by Marcia and Jack Kelly. Published in 1993 by Bell Tower. Profiles more than ninety places in British Columbia and six western U.S. states that accommodate individual retreatants.

The Spiritual Seeker's Guide: The Complete Source for Religions and Spiritual Groups of the World by Steven Sadleir. Published in 1992 by Allwon Publishing. Describes the histories, ideologies, and practices of over 120 current religious and spiritual traditions and movements.

A Guide to Monastic Guest Houses by Robert J. Regalbuto. Published in 1992 by Morehouse Publishing. Profiles eighty monasteries in Canada and the United States that allow visitors on an overnight or short-stay basis.

Silence, Simplicity, and Solitude: A Guide for Spiritual Retreat by David Cooper. Published in 1992 by Bell Tower. Describes how to prepare for, and what to expect from, a spiritual retreat.

Sanctuaries: A Guide to Lodging in Monasteries, Abbeys, and Retreats of the United States: The Northeast by Jack and Marcia Kelly. Published in 1991 by Bell Tower. Profiles more than ninety places in nine eastern states that accommodate individual retreatants.

About the Author

John Benson has written for *Yoga Journal, Body Mind Spirit, Backpacker* magazine, and many regional publications. He is also the author of a self-published international directory that was the predecessor to this book.

Originally a native of Illinois, Benson is an ardent traveler and freelance writer who now makes his home in the Pacific Northwest.